RAF Harrier
Ground Attack –
Falklands

To Dad

Warrant Officer Sydney James Pook
RN 1923–46 and Reserve Fleet Devonport 1951–55

RAF Harrier Ground Attack – Falklands

Jerry Pook

Pen & Sword
AVIATION

First published in Great Britain in 2007
and reprinted in 2011 & 2014 by
PEN & SWORD AVIATION
An imprint of
Pen & Sword Books Ltd
47 Church Street
Barnsley, South Yorkshire
S70 2AS

ISBN 978 1 84884 556 5

A CIP catalogue record for this book is
available from the British Library

Typeset by Concept, Huddersfield, West Yorkshire

Printed and bound in Great Britain
by CPI Group (UK) Ltd, Croydon, CR0 4YY

Pen & Sword Books Ltd incorporates the Imprints of Aviation, Atlas,
Family History, Fiction, Maritime, Military, Discovery, Politics, History,
Archaeology, Select, Wharncliffe Local History, Wharncliffe True Crime,
Military Classics, Wharncliffe Transport, Leo Cooper, The Praetorian Press,
Remember When, Seaforth Publishing and Frontline Publishing

For a complete list of Pen & Sword titles please contact
PEN & SWORD BOOKS LIMITED
47 Church Street, Barnsley, South Yorkshire, S70 2AS, England
E-mail: enquiries@pen-and-sword.co.uk
Website: www.pen-and-sword.co.uk

Contents

Author's Preface

B lack Death – *Muerta Negra* – was the name given by Argentine troops to the Fighter Ground Attack Harriers that brought death and destruction from the air during the Falklands war. Most of these missions were flown by a small group of eight[1] RAF pilots of No. 1 Fighter Squadron, flying RAF GR3 Harriers from HMS *Hermes* – though the Royal Navy was not keen to admit as much at the time. Until now there has been no adequate coverage of these difficult and dangerous missions.

This is their story, a belated tribute to their courage, skill and determination in the most daunting circumstances.

This personal account of the war was put together shortly after my return from the South Atlantic, my memory of events still fresh. The opinions and views expressed are those of the author alone and do not necessarily represent those of Her Majesty's Government, the MoD or the RAF. At the time, my overriding emotion was seething anger at the way we had been misused and abused by RN Senior Officers, in spite of our carrying out the vast majority of the most dangerous missions in theatre. As professional Ground Attack pilots we were glad to do our part and sought no advertisement; however, in the childish PR frenzy that followed the war the Navy continued to attempt to play down the RAF's contribution. As a result I became determined to write my own account of the operations we were involved in so that there would be at least some record of the shabby treatment 1(F) Squadron pilots had received at the hands of RN Senior Officers. My comments on the manner in which those Senior Officers directed our Ground Attack and Recce operations are uncompromising and, I believe, still representative of the views of my RAF colleagues who took part in the shooting war.

The war made huge demands on our experience of European Cold War preparation and training. All of us in the RAF Harrier Force had trained hard in the extremely demanding Low Level Ground Attack and Recce roles. At the same time we also carried out a lot of Air

Combat training, including Air Interception using ground radar direction and the Mk 1 eyeball to find targets – just as the Sea Harrier pilots were to do in the Great South Atlantic Turkey Shoot to come. In the European theatre we came under the operational control of the (usually) professional and competent NATO Air Tasking and Intelligence organisations.

Down south, things were different. Because RN Senior Officers were incapable of controlling and directing Ground Attack and Recce operations effectively and because intelligence backup was non-existent for most missions (once again largely due to RN deficiencies in Intelligence Management), individual 1(F) Squadron pilots had to improvise and take considerable risks in the air in order to achieve any worthwhile results in support of our hard-pressed troops. At the same time we struggled with potentially disastrous aircraft unserviceabilities (some the result of enemy action), being forced to accept aircraft with defects we would not dream of flying with in peacetime, because of a lack of spare parts.

We had been sent south initially to fly Air Combat missions as Attrition Replacements for Sea Harriers lost in action. However, once the Navy realised how difficult and dangerous the essential Low Level Ground Attack and Recce task would be they left us to carry out those missions, keeping the much less-hazardous (and infinitely more glamorous) Air Combat work for themselves. Once that decision had been made we 1(F) Squadron pilots hid our disappointment and got stuck in to do the job we knew best, although we would have loved to fly some nice relaxing Combat Air Patrol missions with Sidewinders and get stuck into the Argy air raids. We expected – and received – little recognition for doing most of the dirty work. We were treated with ill-disguised contempt by our Naval masters, our professional opinions ignored despite the fact that they knew next to nothing about Ground Attack and Recce operations. Very soon after starting operations from HMS *Hermes* we realised that we were considered as more or less Expendable Ordnance, to be kicked into the air on a whim of the Navy hierarchy, with only the most rudimentary preparation and briefing. Where the Navy did interfere directly with our operations, the result was often to reduce or even nullify their effectiveness.

As we sailed south to the War Zone, we realised that in order to carry out Ground Attack we would have to rely on the familiar European theatre Low Level tactics we knew so well. *There was no other option.* Lacking all navigation aids and in the absence of Smart weapons, the only way we could achieve results was to get low down and close in to our targets and, if necessary, carry out re-attacks to destroy high-value targets. We expected to take a lot of hits on the way.

As anticipated in any European war, our survival prospects would be no better than those of a bomber crew of the Second World War – measured in weeks rather than months. It was a sobering prospect. And how would our vulnerable old Harriers cope with battle damage? We had no armour of any kind and lacked the most elementary self-protection gear, carrying only a very basic RHWR, which had its own severe limitations. (It interfered badly with our already appalling radio communications.)

During the Falklands war 1(F) Squadron pilots flew Air Interdiction, Armed Recce, Close Air Support and Airfield Attack as well as pure photo recce missions, using free-fall and retard bombs, cluster bombs, rockets and 30-mm cannon fire, plus Paveway Mk 2 Laser Guided Bombs (LGBs). Most of these weapons were delivered from extreme Low Level attacks, although some high-level attack profiles were used. Of these weapons only the free-fall bomb, 30-mm cannon and rockets had previously been used in action by the RAF. Additionally, no British pilot had used a recce camera pod in action before. All our navigation was *map-and-stopwatch*, without the assistance of any modern navigation aids. Our GR3 Harriers lacked the most basic self-protection aids, up to the last few days of the war. Over the islands we were up against 10,000 well-armed troops who put up an impressive weight of fire whenever we attacked them. (Our own forces also fired away enthusiastically whenever we overflew them!) The Argentines were equipped with modern SAMs (surface-to-air missiles) and radar-directed AAA (Anti-aircraft Artillery) guns, which they used to great effect, one of their gun batteries at Goose Green shooting down three aircraft during the war, as well as coming close to shooting me down on two separate occasions. Eventually, I was able to put this battery out of action with a rocket attack at dusk. After ten days of war operations 50 per cent of our aircraft had been shot down and two more seriously damaged in action. Three of our pilots were shot down and they were lucky to survive. One pilot became a POW.

Eventually – against the odds as it seemed to us at the time – British forces prevailed and we 1(F) Squadron pilots eventually returned home to peacetime operations. We were not to know that in 1982 British forces had fought the last truly honourable war, without foreign assistance, against a worthy and brave foe who had given us a good run for our money and had almost defeated us.

After the war I found that the experience had left me disillusioned and weary of conflict of any kind. For some time I suffered intense nightmares, waking sweating in the night to the chilling sound of HMS *Hermes'* alert Klaxon and hearing the whine of Harrier engines starting up, ready to scramble. Although I immersed myself in work, I was nervous and on edge for many months. At the time I was ashamed of myself for my perceived weakness. In time the nightmares died out, but the anger remained.

Having written my story, I then bottled out of attempting to get it published. I was still in the RAF and was fully aware of the furore that would follow its publication – not least among my immediate superiors, many of whom were interested mainly in their own career advancement. Encouraging inter-service acrimony would not be the best way for them to maintain their career progression – regardless of the truth. I took the easy way out and kept my head down, taking comfort from the fact that I had written it all down and could attempt to get it published in the future. Then in 2006 I read Hugh Bicheno's *Razor's Edge* – a stunning and venomous account of the war and its background of dubious behaviour from our own politicians and civil servants. During the war we Ground Attack pilots were starved of any information before or after our missions; intelligence backup was non-existent and there was little feedback about the results we achieved. Hugh's book was an eye-opener. At last I discovered the effect on the enemy of many missions we had flown. Reading *Razor's Edge* made me determined to attempt the publication of my story. Both Hugh and Alfred Price kindly read it for me and made helpful suggestions, for which I am most grateful.

In 1982 I had been OC A Flight of No. 1 Fighter Squadron for two years, following a Hunter Day Fighter/Ground Attack tour, two previous Harrier Ground Attack/Recce tours and a Fighter Recce tour flying the RF104G Starfighter with the Dutch Air Force. I was married, with two small children, and lived in Stamford. I had been flying in the single-seat Fighter Ground Attack/Recce role since 1970, when I completed my first RAF flying tour as a Flying Instructor.

No. 1(F) Squadron was assigned to NATO's Allied Command Europe Mobile Force, with many wartime deployment options all over Western Europe, from the Mediterranean to the Arctic. Some of these we practised regularly in peacetime, but we had no planned option to operate from a Navy carrier. Apart from brief carrier trials carried out many years previously (without the benefit of the ski-jump) there had been no RAF Harriers deployed at sea.

No doubt there will be some errors and omissions in this story. I apologise in advance to anyone who may be offended by this. I will be most grateful for corrections of facts and will incorporate them in later editions.

Acknowledgements

I would like to thank the following for their advice and kind assistance in the preparation of this book: the Royal Air Force Air Historical Branch, the MoD Directorate of Intellectual Property Rights, Hugh Bicheno, Alfred Price, Bob Iveson, Tony Harper, David Morgan, Ian Mortimer, Jeff Glover, Syd Morris, Fred Trowern.

Jerry Pook
October 2006

Foreword

by Alfred Price

Jerry Pook flew Harrier GR3s throughout the 26 day period that No. 1 Squadron Royal Air Force was committed to the Falklands conflict in 1982. The story he tells, from first hand experience, is primarily one of frustration. Frustration at operating an aircraft tailored to fight a quite different type of battle, which had been hastily and not very effectively modified for carrier based operations. Frustration with the weather, which was distinctly unpleasant on occasions. And most of all, frustration at being sent into action, ineffectively, by senior Royal Navy officers who did not understand the Harrier GR3's offensive air support role, refused to speak to people who did, and whose word on all matters was final. Compared with those factors, the Argentine air defences were a minor inconvenience.

Consummate professional that he is, Jerry Pook took these frustrations to heart. Had it been properly directed and targeted, his message is implicit, the Harrier GR3 force could have performed so much more effectively that it did. Yet as things turned out the Harrier GR3 force had only one opportunity to exert a decisive influence on the land battle. That occurred during the critical phase of the battle of Goose Green on the afternoon of 28 May, and the unit responded in spades. Just as the issue was in doubt three Harrier GR3s – one flown by Jerry Pook – suddenly appeared over the battle area and darted in at low altitude to drop cluster bombs and launch rockets against the Argentine artillery position. Those guns had caused severe problems for the advancing British paratroops, but now fell silent. The attack gave a powerful boost to the attacking paratroops' morale, and shattered that of the defenders. The threat of a further such attack led to the Argentine forces at the settlement to surrender the following morning.

Arguably No. 1 Squadron's main influence on the Falklands campaign is revealed not by what did happen, but by what did not.

Argentine troops never made a serious attempt to concentrate forces for a counter-attack on the advancing British troops. Had they done so, their commanders knew, they would have been savagely mauled from the air. Instead, the Argentine troops remained hunkered down in their various positions. That presented the initiative to the British para-troops and commandos, who were able to seize these points one at a time.

Field Marshal Lord Wavell once wrote 'When things are going badly in battle, the best tonic is to take one's mind off one's own troubles by considering what a rotten time one's opponent must be having.' The Argentine troops did indeed have a rotten time. The sight of Harriers frequently passing low over their heads, and the continual risk of sudden air attack, had a draining effect on morale. By itself that was not a war winner, but in combination with everything else it was. It should be remembered that when Argentine resistance collapsed it was due not to the defeat of a major part of the defending force in action, nor to lack of supplies or ammunition. It was due to the collapse of morale. The vast majority of Argentine troops never saw a British soldier, until one marched up to escort them into captivity.

Jerry Pook has written an excellent 'warts and all' account on the realities of the Falklands campaign. It deserves to be required reading for current and future ground attack pilots, those likely to direct them into action, and anyone else seriously interested in the business of modern air warfare.

Dr. Alfred Price
2006

CHAPTER ONE

In at the Deep End

T
he first time that most of No. 1(F) Squadron pilots became directly involved in the Falklands War was on 13 April 1982. On that day we had ferried eight Harriers across the Atlantic to Goose Bay in Labrador, for use in exercise *Maple Flag.* It was a Tuesday after a long Bank Holiday weekend and before we had stacked for the weekend I already knew that a lot of our Victor tanker force were tied up with air movements down to Ascension Island. Before the weekend none of us except the Boss had any inkling that we were going to get involved in operations in the South Atlantic. I had laughed like a drain when my brother Robin rang me up on the day of the Argy invasion, singing, 'Don't cry for me, Argentina!' Robin was an infantry Major and his gallows humour always gelled with mine. On that Tuesday the whole cross-Atlantic ferry operation was in doubt for us right up to 0800 hours, which was keeping me pretty annoyed as I had been responsible for our planning. Eventually, 38 Group gave us the go ahead and we set off on the tedious seven-hour flog across 'The Pond'.

At Goose Bay that night we had a great barbecue party with the Canadians (in the open air, with the air temperature below zero). We fell into conversation with the crew of the Maritime Patrol Nimrod, which had provided Search and Rescue coverage for us across The Pond. They said that they might not be able to take us back to Wittering next day as they were on standby to fly direct to Ascension. Obviously, things were hotting up. We already knew that the Navy was recalling all the Sea Harrier pilots it could lay hands on, to be trained up at Yeovilton to form a reserve squadron as reinforcement for the two squadrons already sailing south aboard *Hermes* and *Invincible*. The Navy was also taking on more RAF Harrier GR3 pilots (it already had a few) direct from squadrons, to be given a hasty cross-training on the Sea Harrier, such was its shortage of experienced pilots.

In the morning the weather at Goose Bay was appalling, with heavy snow falling all day. We climbed aboard and taxied out once in the Nimrod, but had to taxy back again as the pilots were only able to see a

1

few feet in the blizzard conditions. Much later, the weather cleared sufficiently for us to take off and, much to our relief, we arrived back at Wittering after midnight. We were met by Pat King, the Station Commander, who immediately cornered the Boss for a private briefing. The Boss said that he couldn't tell me what was up, but we would all find out the next morning at a briefing in the squadron. Bob Iveson, my fellow flight commander, had been taken off the ferry programme at the last moment and sent off on a secret mission to Liverpool to assess the suitability of a certain container ship for Harrier operations. Later, we discovered the name of the ship – *Atlantic Conveyor*.

At the briefing at 0900 hours we learned that the plan was for us to embark on the *Atlantic Conveyor* at Plymouth, with an as yet unspecified number of aircraft and pilots, and sail to the war zone. The Boss described the ship to us: there was obviously going to be a shortage of accommodation as she would be packed full of various stores and weapons for the operation. The immediate task was to start modifying our aircraft to make them suitable for operations at sea, and also to start work-up training for the pilots. The Boss started allocating jobs to various people and it was clear that we were now into a full wartime training mode, the balloon having gone up as far as we were concerned. From now on our destinies were being driven by events in the South Atlantic. As Training Flight Commander I was given responsibility for all the necessary work-up training, which had already begun. The first priority was ski-jump training at Royal Naval Air Station Yeovilton, where the training ramp was located. Two of our pilots had been sent there that morning to try out the ramp. (RAF clearance for this was not given until later in the day.) We were also told that our task in the South Atlantic was to serve as Attrition Replacements for Sea Harriers shot down on operations – a sobering thought. When Sea Harriers were lost from either carrier we would be called forward from the *Atlantic Conveyor* to operate in the Air Defence role. Although our primary role within the RAF was as a Ground Attack squadron, we included a lot of Air Combat and Low Level Intercept training in our regular squadron routine. We all knew that lookout was only kept at the highest standard if there was a 'Bounce' lurking somewhere along the route. The Bounce consisted of one or two fighters (Phantoms, Lightnings etc.), or – if none was available – some of our own squadron aircraft flown by designated Aggressor pilots. As Air Combat Training was my responsibility, it fell to me to train up suitable experienced pilots in this very demanding role (see Appendix 8 – Air Combat). Although we had no air-to-air missile fit, we had always considered missile as well as gun 'kill' parameters during our Air Combat training sorties. About a third of our pilots were qualified Aggressors, which meant that they had regular practice at intercepting formations at High and Low Level, in most cases using only the 'Mk 1 Eyeball' to achieve a successful interception. Ironically, this was to be by far the most common type of interception carried out by Sea Harrier pilots during the air engagements that began in early May. Because of problems with the Sea Jets' radar and poor radar coverage over the Falklands, there was to be precious little of the traditional type of radar-assisted fighter interception in the Great South Atlantic Turkey Shoot to come.

I devised a training programme that would sharpen up our skills in all areas of Air Combat as number one priority. With hindsight, most of this effort was to be wasted because of the major change of role allocated to us by the Navy once it was realised how difficult and dangerous the Low Level Ground Attack task would be for its precious few Sea Harriers.

I rang up some contacts at RAF Brawdy and Binbrook, to set up a Dissimilar Air Combat Training (DACT) programme in order to re-familiarise our pilots with the characteristics of Low Wing loading (Hunter), and Supersonic (Lightning) opposition. By now we had been told the secret code name Operation *Corporate* to be used for the operation. Although I could not mention it by name, it seemed as if everyone I rang knew what was up and, more important, was prepared to give us unlimited co-operation. Later in the day some more pilots flew down to Yeovilton to continue the ski-jump training into the early evening, after which I went home exhausted with the tension and excitement of our first full day of war preparation.

The next day I took a formation of our aircraft up to Binbrook to fly DACT sorties against the Lightning. I briefed up with Squadron Leader Dave Carden, an old Lightning 'hairy' of great experience. I felt very out of touch and regretted that I had usually considered the Lightning to be fairly easy meat in combat, especially after a Harrier tour in Germany fighting them at Low Level on exercises. Dave was an ace exponent of the vertical fight: he gave me a very hard time throughout. I landed feeling like a wet rag, the violent physical exertion while severely overdressed in a tiny, overheated cockpit having taken its usual toll. Later I wrote a note in my diary, 'Must sharpen up!' After returning to Wittering, I rang Squadron Leader Dave Jackson, our tame Staff Officer at 38 Group, to ask for some live cluster bombs to drop somewhere. I already had some nagging doubts about what we were going to end up doing in the Falklands, and I had a shrewd suspicion that we would end up doing some Ground Attack – whatever the Navy was saying at present. If so, we had to get some realistic practice in with what was our primary Ground Attack weapon: our squadron armourers were also in need of practice at preparing and loading the real thing.

'How many do you want?' asked Dave.

'About thirty – to start with,' I said, hopefully.

'You can have them on Monday,' replied Dave, 'I'll fix up a Splash Target[2] for you in the North Sea.' What a player.

After a rather subdued 'happy hour' in the bar, we stacked for the weekend in anticipation of much hard work to come. Our planned embarkation date was now 24 April, leaving precious little time for the engineers to complete the aircraft modifications. They would be working through the weekends from now on.

On the following Monday for our first mission of the day I led a four-ship cluster bomb attack on a Splash Target in the North Sea. We each carried three cluster bombs and I managed to get three hits with mine. Like all bombing in the Harrier, it was very much a 'seaman's eye' exercise, and even with the large area of coverage of the bomblet pattern, it was still possible to miss. Over water it was particularly difficult to estimate the 'Pass Distance' over the target (see Appendix 8). By making a sharp turn during the pullout off target, it was possible to see your fall of shot: I was to use this tactic later in operations in the Falklands. Our clearance to carry out the cluster bomb attacks came in the form of a written signal from MoD: this was the normal peacetime method of conveying orders. I had launched for this mission even though the signal had not arrived; it was waiting for us on landing. This was to become a running joke for the next couple of weeks as pressure built up on signal traffic, delaying communications more and more. I just carried on doing what I thought was necessary, expecting the relevant clearances to turn up in the fullness of time. Anything really urgent was cleared by phone – if not, we just went ahead and did it anyway. Naturally enough the Boss was heavily engaged on other essential tasks and I tried to disturb him as little as possible.

Next we flew Air Combat training sorties against Hunters from RAF Brawdy. The pilot I flew against was an overconfident lad who thought it all a bit of a waste of time, as the combination of him plus the Hunter was bound to be more than a match for any mere Harrier pilot. As a birthday treat for me I pulled out all the stops and managed to duff him up him quite comprehensively, bringing back lots of gun camera film of his aircraft, and leaving him to slink back to base with his tail between his legs. He had made the elementary mistake of trying to outfight the Harrier in the vertical, and kept on falling out of the fight out of control, with me behind him. At the end of the day I rang the long-suffering Dave Jackson at Group to ask for some more 'realistic' training opposition for our Air Combat training, i.e. Super Etendards and Mirage 5s, the principal Argy fighters.

'Any ideas where I can get them?' asked Dave.

'Uuuh, how about the French – they use Mirage 5s and their Navy use the Super E.'

'OK, I'll see what I can fix up, but I can't promise anything.'

Our hard-working squadron engineers had been given instructions to prepare sixteen aircraft with the shipborne operating modifications. By now, the plans for our operations were changing daily. At the end of each day the Boss would brief the Flight Commanders on the latest update on who was going south to the war zone, who would be staying at Ascension etc. Fairly early on in this business I had decided to get blown with the breeze, following my usual reluctance to volunteer for anything. (This was a bit of superstition on my part – my usual experience was that anything I actually volunteered for turned out to be a bit of a shambles!) Naturally, all of these changes of plan were very frustrating for the Boss, as the powers that be could not decide how many of us were going to be sent down south, and how they were going to get there.

In parallel with the engineers' work, the personnel strength of the squadron was building up day by day as the postings department at RAF Barnwood played a blinder, sending back to us various old hands who had recently been on the squadron. Characters such as Ross Boyens, Tim Smith, Clive Loader and Pete Harris turned up with or without smiles on their faces, depending on their enthusiasm at the prospect of going to war. This presented a bit of a training problem for me as I had little idea of exactly who was going to be on the squadron on any particular day. By this time (much to his disgust) our new Flight Commander, the excellent Pete Moules, had been posted to 18 Maritime Group HQ as their Harrier adviser (and source of sanity) for the duration. This was an essential move as no one else there had the remotest idea of what the Harrier could or could not do. The RAF Maritime Operations people lived in a different world. Operating the large, multi-crewed Nimrod primarily in the Anti-Submarine role, their type of flying bore as much resemblance to ours as Formula One racing does to driving a bus.

On the morning of 22 April six of our pilots travelled to RAF Coningsby, an Air Defence base, to be briefed on the Air Combats with the Mirages and Super Etendards, which, true to form, the ever-resourceful Dave Jackson had fixed up. The previous evening we had been told that it was 'on', that the French would provide the oppo-sition, and that the whole thing was terribly secret. We weren't even allowed to discuss it. To preserve secrecy, we were to go to Coningsby and be briefed there by their Station Commander. Total ballsache really, but our commanders were concerned about the political implications of what we were planning. That night some Air Attaché's lackey rang me up at home from Paris and proceeded to blab about the whole business on the phone! I had to shut him up quickly and ring off. Most of the day at Coningsby was a waste because of poor weather, although two of us did get in one mission of two versus two combat against a couple of Mirage 5s in the afternoon. We were not even allowed to write what we were doing in the Authorisation Sheets.[3] The Mirage pilots weren't much good at close-in fighting and kept reversing in front of us to give some easy shots. Next day we got in some missions against Super Etendards of the French Navy. These guys were quite sharp and we had some good combats with several 'kills' claimed by each side. Their machine seemed to perform like a very fast Hunter, with a good turning performance. That afternoon we all trooped across to Coningsby again – maximum security as usual – to debrief with the French, who had been flown across for the occasion. After a very interesting debrief via an interpreter (during which we were joined by some Navy Sea Harrier pilots who were listening in), we were flown back in style to Wittering aboard the Navy Heron transport. As usual – unlike the RAF – the Navy was prepared to use its communications aircraft as 'hacks' to save pilots' time as and when required. After an exhausting week ,we stacked late in the day for what was to be our last free weekend. For me, the time was spent sorting out the garden and trying to get odd jobs done that I knew would cause problems for my wife while I was away. Today our embarkation date was postponed yet again ...

Later in the morning I flew down to the English Channel with Jeff Glover in the two-seat Harrier in company with Mark Hare, our Electronic Warfare Officer, as wingman to carry out some practice attacks against a Type 42 destroyer. Although I thought it extremely unlikely that the Navy would task us to attack the Argentine Type 42s, I wanted to have a good look at the Radar Warning Receiver indications we would get from them as I suspected that a major hazard in the combat zone would be our own defences. As usual the Navy claimed to have shot us both down with their Sea Dart system before we got anywhere near the ship: *typical Navy Bullshit*, we thought. In our opinion all these SAM operators were the same: they made outrageous claims for the effectiveness of their particular system, with little thought for the problems they would face in a realistic wartime engagement. Subsequent events were to justify fully our scepticism concerning SAM effectiveness.

Weapon training continued in parallel with these other activities. We had managed to get hold of some Navy 2-inch rocket pods, and one of our Weapon Instructors fired them on Holbeach range. His opinion was: 'Same sort of firing technique as SNEB rockets (our usual rocket armament), but much more of a shotgun spread.'

Level rocket-firing from 100 feet above ground with level break out had been part of our regular squadron training for over twelve months, and I thought that this would be a very useful means of attacking ships. Hence I got permission to fire some SNEB rockets at the ship target on Holbeach range.[4]

On 27 April I took off for Holbeach range to try out some level rocket attacks on the ship target. The technique was easy, as the rockets had a natural tendency to level off just above the water, slamming right through the ship and out the other side like a mini-Exocet, to bounce away into the distance. I felt that we had a winner here if we had to do it in anger: it was a pity we couldn't take the heavier-calibre SNEB with us on the carrier. By the end of the day we heard that our earliest date of movement had by now been set in concrete for 3 May. By now *Atlantic Conveyor* had already left UK for Ascension, so this meant that we were in for a marathon nine-hour ferry flight over 4,000 miles direct to the island to meet up with her. This was to be the longest ferry flight yet attempted in the Harrier, and was bound to present a few problems. As this was going to be my pigeon to organise from our end, I set about planning the route in conjunction with the Tanker Force Air-to-Air Refuelling experts. Late in the day an RAF Air-to-Air missile expert arrived to give us a briefing on how to use the Sidewinder missile: several aircraft had already completed the modification programme by now, and the next priority was for us to fire some missiles to prove the system. Ross Boyens was about to fly back from Dunsfold, where the first Launcher/Missile system had just been fitted. As usual, we had no clearance to do this, so I rang him up and told him to get on with it: the clearance signal arrived while he was airborne.

One of the certainties was that most operational Ground Attack flying in the Falklands would be at Extreme Low Level, i.e. 'nap of the earth' flying (see Appendix 2 – Low Flying). Because of the obvious risks involved, this type of flying had been progressively restricted over the years since I had joined my first fighter squadron in Bahrain in 1970. At that time we were allowed to fly at 100 feet above ground as a matter of course, and towards the end of my tour I was lucky to be selected for a mini Fighter Recce course during which I was authorised to fly at an eye-watering 50 feet above ground over the deserts and mountains of Oman and the Trucial States. The old hands told me,

'50 feet flying is dead easy – you just try to fly *as low as you possibly can* and after a couple of sorties you'll be down around the right height!'

They were right, but it never felt easy. Flying at 7 miles per minute (700 feet per second) puts a lot of pressure on the pilot. Time available for map reading was minimal, and all cockpit tasks had to be done instinctively, with the absolute minimum of time spent looking in. Every second with your head in the office was another moment closer to eternity, you and your machine smeared across the landscape in an obscene orange streak of burning fuel and disintegrating wreckage. The proximity of sudden death concentrated the mind wonderfully; even so, there was no opportunity to look around and cover other members of a formation – the phenomenon of 'tunnel vision' was well known during that type of flying. Like a computer close to overload, the brain was unable to take on the simplest extra task; calculating how long your fuel was going to last became almost impossible.

By coincidence most 1(F) Squadron pilots had just completed an intense work-up programme for exercise *Maple Flag* in the weeks preceding the invasion. This practice had been flown in the Falklands-like terrain of the north of Scotland, and with a liberal interpretation of the low-flying rules – we had got in some excellent training. To train up our newly arrived pilots I asked for some OLF training slots. We were allocated two slots to check out just two of the half dozen or so pilots who needed the training. This was all we were to be allowed initially by HQ Strike Command, on the direct orders of Air Vice-Marshal L.A. Harris, whose response on hearing our request was, 'No, they're not having any more – they're only trying it on!' Fortunately, the C-in-C overruled this order later on.

We heard about this incident from Squadron Leader Dave Binnie, a Harrier Staff Officer who worked at HQ Strike Command. Dave was doing his best to help our case and was enraged beyond reason because this Senior Officer had assumed that we were going in for some kind of 'jolly'.

By now the frantic aircraft modification programme was running into some serious problems. The sixteen aircraft involved were being virtually torn apart and rebuilt in order to fit them for seaborne operations. Apart from basic changes such as making them waterproof and proof against sea water corrosion, many time-consuming wiring modifications had to be carried out to fit the various extra bits of radar and Electronic Counter Measures (ECM) gear we needed, on top of the basic Sidewinder wiring. With the relentless approach of our departure date, we bitterly cursed the RAF's parsimony, which had denied us the Sidewinder wiring as a normal peacetime fit, just to save a few thousand pounds. Our main concern now was how the aircraft were going to perform, having been so extensively modified. There was going to be precious little time to prove that all the new bits of kit worked. While work-up training continued apace, I flew an Air Combat sortie against a Sidewinder-armed Phantom in order to update our tactics and find out some more about our infrared signature.

The Deployment Plan was constantly being revised. Now, because of the ferry distance to Ascension, we were going to have to start from RAF St Mawgan in Cornwall, or else we would be critically short of fuel. As it was, the tankers were going to have to take off 6,000 lb over their normal maximum weight, and go 5,000 lb below their normal minimum peacetime fuel reserves to get us to Ascension. Another slightly chilling piece of news was that the tankers were going to have to abandon us over 1,100 miles short of our destination. This would leave us with only our unreliable Inertial Navigation and useless on-board radio navigation aids to find the tiny volcanic outcrop in the vast wastes of the South Atlantic. At that time, because of their commitments the Nimrods were not able to offer Search and Rescue coverage for us. The Boss promised to look into this.

Later in the day Tim Allen, an ex-Harrier Test Pilot, rang from Boscombe Down with details of yet another wiring modification, which would give us a Sidewinder aiming diamond in the Head up Display. Up to now there had been no provision for this, and we assumed that we were going to have to use a suitable part of one of the Head up Display test pictures to achieve acquisition with the missile. This was not as silly as it sounded; the field of view of the missile was quite large and no great aiming accuracy was required. There was an historical precedent for this as we older hands had all used the Head up Display test pictures for such precision-aiming exercises as Air-to-Ground Rocket and 30-mm cannon firing in the early days of the Harrier. This drastic expedient was forced upon us for the simple reason that for years the Ferranti company was unable to sort out accurate weapon aiming displays for these weapons. Tim assured me that this final modification was 'a simple wiring job', which should not delay the programme. I took a hard line and told him that we would make do with what we had: with our existing problems we needed another wiring modification like a hole in the head.

That night the Boss was woken at 2300 hours and told to have all his ground crew ready to embark on Hercules transports by 0700 hours in the morning, to be flown direct to Ascension. This was all because someone at MoD had decided that there was an immediate Air Threat to the island! The Boss sprang into frantic activity in conjunction with our engineer officer trying to organise this: however, within an hour a phone call from HQ Strike Command told him that it was all a false alarm and to stand everyone down. The Boss was not pleased.

On Friday 30 April six of us flew across to RAF Valley in a Dominie to join Tim Allen, who had been running the firing trials with the first two of our modified aircraft. Unfortunately, they had only managed to carry out one test firing, when MoD had insisted on three. I couldn't see why the hell they had to do all these trials, apart from proving the wiring, as the United States Marine Corps had been firing Sidewinders off Harriers for decades. I said as much to Tim, who apologised but insisted that the next two firings had to be done by Test Pilots. My sense of humour having been sorely tried by now, I bluntly told Tim that this was not good enough: this was our last chance to fire as the deployment to RAF St Mawgan in Cornwall started tomorrow. Tim then played a blinder and agreed to a plan, hastily concocted between us, that the Boss and I should be designated as official Test Pilots by MoD for our sorties. Tim sorted it all out on the phone direct to MoD, and we got on with it.

On the first sortie, with the Boss and I due to fire, the Jindivik tug was U/S and we had to come back and refuel for another try. On the second sortie the first flare didn't light, so I went home straight away as there were only two flares. The second flare lit, but the Boss got no 'growl' from the missile and had to bring it home. On the third attempt, with the Boss and I in the same aircraft as before, the Boss said I should fire first as he thought it might have been a problem with his aircraft. By now, I was determined that I was going to get rid of the damn missile whatever happened. I had a frustrating problem on taxying out, as I was unable to get the parking brake fully off. A loose cable was fouling the brake lever and every time I closed the throttle, the parking brake was put on, bringing me to a halt. Determined to get airborne at all costs, I blasted my way out of dispersal using too much power against brake. All the way out to the runway I was wrestling with this wretched piece of cable, and I prayed that I would be able to get airborne before the brakes burned out. The stupid things you do when there's a war on.

At last I was airborne on the range in Cardigan Bay with a fully serviceable aircraft. As briefed, I was flying at about 1,000 feet above the sea as the Range Controller directed me towards the pilotless Jindivik tug. As I closed to firing range the Range Controller ignited the powerful flare behind the Jindivik, and my sense of relief was overwhelming as I heard the change of tone in my headphones, the Sidewinder locking on within a second of my pressing the rockets button on the stick. The 'growl' changed to a steady tone; I called 'Contact Flare!' and pressed the *Fire* button. As expected, there was a one-second delay as the missile's internal power pack wound up in preparation for launch. After what seemed like an eternity the Sidewinder was off with the roar of an express train, trailing a brilliant yellow flame. I watched all the way to impact with the flare, an unspectacular puff of smoke from the training warhead. Still, it was nice to know that they worked, confirming my view that this was truly an 'idiot's weapon', capable of being used successfully by even Low Average pilots. Considering the far better low-level performance of the AIM9L model, which we were due to use in anger, it promised to be like shooting rats in a barrel. We had already had some interesting intelligence briefings about the capabilities of the Argentine Air Force and Navy pilots. We knew that they had been trained originally by Americans, and that their tactics were very outdated. Also, the simple facts of geography showed that they were going to be tight on fuel on all sorties over the Falklands from their mainland bases over 300 miles away at Rio Grande, Rio Gallegos and Commodoro Rivadavia. For them, this was the fighter pilot's nightmare: not having enough fuel to do anything but run when attacked by enemy fighters. However, when it came to the Argies' Surface Attack capabilities, our naval forces were about to receive a series of bloody noses, as the unsophisticated Argy pilots used near-kamikaze tactics to cause mayhem among the 'grey boats' in and around Falklands Sound. A potent combination of Latin élan, aggression and sheer courage would more than compensate for their lack of tactical skills.

The remainder of the day's firings were equally successful. The only good laugh was at Bob Iveson's expense as he somehow managed to miss, being the only one of us who had fired a 'Winder' before, during his exchange tour with the US Marine Corps. Wearily, we returned to base to complete last-minute preparations for our final departure. Later in the evening we all had to report to Admin Wing for an interminable briefing on the administrative details of our as yet unspecified period of absence. This had been the main source of concern for us over the past fortnight: we had only the vaguest idea of how long the operation might last and estimates of how long we would be away varied from three to nine months. Not least of interest to us were the arrangements for looking after our families while we were away. One of the many forms we had to fill in was a Will Form, bringing home the fact that some of us might not be coming back. As I collapsed in bed I was assailed by doubts about the coming adventure. I couldn't believe that we were going to be so fortunate as to remain aboard ship doing the easy job of Air Defence, and the prospect of doing Ground Attack flying from a Harrier deployed site ashore filled me with misgivings. That kind of thing was OK in peacetime in good weather, but I knew that dry terrain and suitable cover were hard to come by on the islands. We would need to lay down the world's known reserves of aluminium planking (much-used on peacetime deployments in wet weather), and our site would then become one of the most valuable – and vulnerable – targets on the islands, with little chance of effective concealment. At last I fell into a disturbed sleep. Later, I woke up sweating after a vividly realistic dream in which I had been giving a speech at our first Squadron Dinner Night after the war: of the four Squadron Executives, I was the only one left alive.

Saturday, 1 May 1982

After a breakneck deployment to the South Atlantic, the RN Task Force was now deployed in the waters of the Falkland Islands, over 8,000 nautical miles from our once sleepy hollow at Wittering. In true 'blitz-krieg' fashion the RAF had launched a long-range Vulcan bombing mission, co-ordinated with a dawn strike by Sea Harriers on Port Stanley Airport. I was fascinated by the news of the Vulcan raid. I hadn't imagined that we would be able to mount the Herculean Air Refuelling operation necessary to carry out such an attack. Bearing in mind the limited range of the Vulcan and our tankers, I couldn't see this kind of thing being done regularly; however, it was bound to have a major effect on the morale of the Argies, serving notice that even their mainland bases were not immune to air attack. With more interest, I read of the air engagements between Sea Harriers and Mirages, three of the latter having been shot down for no loss on our side. I noted that two out of the three kills were scored by RAF pilots serving on loan to the Navy, a trend that was to cause increasing discomfort among RN Senior Officers as the air battles continued. Already a quarter of the Sea Harrier pilots in theatre were RAF, the Navy being unable to fill their cockpits with sufficient dark blue candidates. Even so, they had had to strip their Sea Harrier training unit of all its instructors, recall ex-RN Sea Harrier pilots who had recently left the service, and even send partly trained youngsters direct to the war zone without completing their operational training. This latter action seemed particularly crazy to us, as there were plenty more experienced RAF Harrier pilots available who could have been cross-trained to fly the Sea Harrier in just a few sorties. The requirement to be able to use the Sea Harrier's radar to a high standard was not a major factor at the time because, like most newly developed British fighter radars, it was a fairly unreliable piece of kit and had no significant Look-Down capability. Later on I was in a position to speak to most of *Hermes'* Sea Harrier pilots shortly after each successful Air-to-Air Kill: I cannot remember any occasion on which the pilot claimed to have used his radar to achieve a kill. The situation was a little different aboard *Invincible*, where pilots had more confidence in their more serviceable radars.

I was spending a much-needed day off at home and later in the day I checked in with our operations desk to see how the day's flying programme had progressed. The news was not good. Hardly anything had been achieved because of aircraft unserviceabilities and crosswind problems. One of the major tasks was to 'flow check' and 'cold soak' each aircraft with its 330-gallon ferry tanks at high altitude. We knew from bitter experience that this was an essential prerequisite of any ferry operation, to show up any fuel feed and hydraulic leak problems. If encountered on a ferry flight, such problems would usually entail an en-route diversion to the nearest suitable airfield. We couldn't afford too much of that on the long route to Ascension. We were committed to our departure for St Mawgan in the morning. The washed-out flying programme meant that the remaining Air Test requirements would have to be completed during the first leg of our deployment – not an ideal solution with the lack of Harrier engineering support en route. I spent my last night at home trying not to worry about the technical state of our aircraft. I feared a major technical disaster, with U/S aircraft scattered the length and breadth of the Atlantic coastline. The Harrier GR3 was not the most serviceable aircraft at the best of times and the last thing we wanted was to take a load of technical problems with us at the start of our long trek south.

During this hectic period of work-up training there had been a thousand and one tasks to prepare us for our trip to the combat zone. Not least was the problem of what personal kit to take with us, bearing in mind the large variations in climate we were likely to encounter. We knew that a lot of our time would be spent in the deep South Atlantic winter, and so we were all issued with cold weather clothing. However, we had to be prepared for the traditional mudbath of a deployed site on land in wet weather, and so wet weather clothing was also necessary. Finally, there was no guarantee that any of us would not remain on the tropical island of Ascension for some time, and so some tropical kit was also required. Along with our extensive wardrobe of bulky flying clothing there was far too much kit, and we agonised for days over what was really necessary, anticipating that we would be living in cramped conditions aboard ship for at least a fortnight.

While all this work went on each day had become busier and busier, with us starting work earlier and finishing later at night. I remember a conversation with a supply squadron NCO who wanted me to come to stores and draw my tropical kit.

'When will you be able to get down here, Sir?'

'About 10 o'clock tonight.'

They were still open.

On Sunday morning I said my goodbyes to my wife and children, who were a bit too young to understand what was going on. I had no idea how long we would be away. At the squadron there was a low-key send-off with just a few station 'wheels' present. After an uneventful trip I was relieved to discover only minor snags on my aircraft, landing safely in an increasing crosswind. Unfortunately, the crosswind limit for landing with 330-gallon tanks was very low, and shortly after landing I received an uncompromising message from Pat King, our Station Commander, to say that on no account was anyone to exceed the crosswind limits, and we should divert aircraft if necessary. We had the highest respect for Pat, but with all our other problems this was one restriction we did not need; the instruction was quietly ignored and the rest of the pilots landed without incident. (We had always considered the limit to be unrealistically low.) We were next ushered into a briefing at which we discovered that the Nimrods would, after all, be able to provide us with Search and Rescue cover all the way to Ascension.

Apart from the wind the weather was fine, and that afternoon I took a stroll on my own through the country lanes around the base. I realised that there was a very real possibility that this would be my last ever look at the English countryside. I tried to analyse my feelings but soon gave up as my brain was in turmoil with the details of the ferry plan and the problems we might encounter. Self-analysis had never been my strong point, and my overwhelming emotion was to get to the combat zone as soon as possible. By now I knew that I was to go all the way south, so there was no going back; I was going to find out one way or another exactly how I would stand up to being in action with the squadron. Later, we spent an interesting evening in the bar of the Officers' Mess as John Knott, the Secretary of State for Defence, dropped in while passing through. He seemed to be pretty confident about the state of affairs in the war so far. He hinted that we were due for some morale-boosting news about a Navy success in the TEZ (Total Exclusion Zone), which had recently been established around the islands. Soon we heard of the sinking of the *General Belgrano* – next to the carrier *25th of May*, the Argentine Navy's most important capital ship. 'Pity it wasn't the carrier!' was our unspoken thought.

Very early next morning, five 1(F) Squadron pilots sat in a briefing in the main operations room of RAF St Mawgan. The briefing was to be given by some 'Kipper Fleet' character and the room was full of Co-pilots, Navigators, Air Electronic Officers and all the other cooks and bottle-washers who made up the very large crews of the Nimrod.

Straight away we noted their propensity for 'milling' – hanging about in groups waiting for something to happen. This kind of thing was strictly frowned on in RAF Harrier squadrons, as it showed obvious inefficiency in that everyone's time was being wasted. A briefing either started on time, or the senior man present would want to know the reason why. RAF Harrier squadrons were very much under strength in peacetime and every squadron pilot had to pull his weight all day long in order to get the task completed, hence our irritation at having to wait around before and after briefings. Fortunately, Group Captain Wood-forde, the St Mawgan Station Commander, recognised our impatience and started to crack the whip to get the important parts of the brief covered.

The plan for that day was for the Boss to lead five Harriers to meet up with no fewer than six Victor tankers overhead the airfield. Three tankers would top up the other three tankers, and then the three full tankers would proceed to Ascension in company with three of the Harriers, leaving the two remaining Harriers to return to St Mawgan. We had to launch five Harriers to get three on their way because of the high probability that our aircraft would go U/S. We had to guarantee three serviceable Harriers at the start of the route to make the best use of the critically overstretched tanker force. Of course, this meant that the two spare pilots had to pack all of their kit into the aircraft and be as completely prepared as the others to go all the way en route. This was a bit of a pain, as the whole formation sat for an hour on the ground before take-off, in order to guarantee enough time to fix any last-minute snags. The departure time was set in concrete once we heard that the Victors had taken off from Marham. John Rochfort and I were the spares for this sortie, and we accompanied the formation as far as we could out into the Atlantic before breaking off to return to base. I remember watching with some concern as some of our pilots had difficulties on their first plug into the heavy centreline hose of the Victor, most peacetime training having been done on the wing hoses. I also felt that the formation was cruising at an uncomfortably high Mach number for the altitude we were flying. Next day I resolved to tell the Victor leader to fly slower to avoid us all running short of fuel, which is what was to happen to the Boss's formation that day. Although John and I felt a sense of anticlimax, the long drawn-out procedure of waiting on the ground followed by the join up with the tankers was a useful practice for our turn on the following day.

Much later that day we heard that the Boss's formation, comprising himself, Tony Harper and Mark Hare, had run critically short of fuel, causing the Boss to divert with a tanker to Banjul on the West African coast. Tony and Mark had continued alone and had not been met by a

Nimrod, due to a cock-up on the part of the Maritime Ops people. As expected, neither on-board radio beacon worked during this unescorted part of the flight: however, very fortunately one of their Inertial Navigators was giving good enough information to find the island. They had had to do a certain amount of weaving to thread their way between the storms on the infamous Intertropical Convergence Zone (ITCZ), which lay between them and Ascension on their unaccompanied leg. As Tony described it later: 'It wasn't a very comfortable feeling!' The Harrier Inertial Navigator was a most untrustworthy piece of kit at the best of times. Even when given a perfect alignment on land, it seemed to have some kind of sixth sense, which recognised those rare occasions when you were forced to trust it completely. Invariably, at that moment it would choose to start misbehaving, giving duff navigational information without any obvious signs of equipment failure. In clear weather you could check exactly where you were at any time, the equipment would work perfectly for sortie after sortie. However, just get yourself a little bit lost or stuck above cloud with radio failure, and it would let you down. On board ship we were supposed to use the much-heralded FINRAE shipborne alignment system for our Inertial Navigators, especially built by Ferranti for Operation *Corporate*. My opinion on Ferranti's ability to produce the goods was conditioned by nearly a decade of Harrier experience, and was shared by my fellow pilots. We did not expect much from FINRAE. At the same time we could never rely on the Harrier's radio installation; the system was still scandalously unreliable, in spite of years of complaints from pilots.

After refuelling at Banjul, the Boss set out for a night transit to Ascension, in company with a Victor, which had diverted with him. The Boss had to make some plugs at night, which for me was ample justification for my much-reviled peacetime training programme of Night Formation and Air Refuelling. I had introduced this after my arrival on the squadron in 1980, when I had been made the Training Flight Commander. Shortly before my arrival, 38 Group had suddenly tasked the squadron with an overnight flight-refuelled deployment to Cyprus. Although none of the squadron pilots had done any night refuelling (or night formation, for that matter), the squadron had been forced to take on the task, selecting one of our most experienced Flight Lieutenants for the job. Anticipating more of that kind of thing, I introduced a programme of regular Night Formation and Air Refuelling training. This was not popular with the squadron pilots, needless to say. 'But night flying's dangerous, and anyway, it keeps us out of the bar!' was a typical reaction.

The next day the Nimrod guys expressed profound embarrassment about their failure to meet up with Tony and Mark the previous day, and promised that everything would work as briefed today. Bob was to lead our flight and we agreed to take this promise with a pinch of salt. After the brief we began the long preparation for the nine-hour ferry flight. In an extremely cramped single-seat cockpit, this kind of trip can generate all sorts of problems unless you make some sensible preparations. The flight refuelling part of the sortie (we had to make at least a dozen plugs) would be pretty routine – as long as we didn't run into bad weather. The forecast was pretty good, except for the usual unknown factor of the ITCZ. However, anticipating technical snags, we had to be prepared for possible unaccompanied diversion into any one of a dozen airports on the coasts of Europe and Africa. In flight, the main enemy was going to be boredom and each pilot had his own little pack-up of tapes and books to keep himself amused. Like other electronic systems in the aircraft, the Harrier's cockpit tape recorder gave atrocious sound reproduction, so I never bothered to take music tapes. My preference was for old Goon Show and Hancock recordings, but I also carried a Clive James book to read between plugs. (The Harrier GR3 had no autopilot but it was quite possible to trim the aircraft out well enough to be able to read in flight.) Our main efforts of preparation went towards in-flight catering. Being a 'heavy' base, St Mawgan found no difficulty in producing extremely high quality lunch boxes for us. (The situation was very different at Wittering, and all other single-seat bases I knew, where the provision of decent grub for aircrew was very low down on the list of priorities: a corned beef sandwich and an apple were about as much as you could expect.) Although we were provided with 'pee-bags', they were almost impossible to use. My technique was to drink a lot but stop drinking about three hours before take-off; I then had to pee as much as possible in those remaining three hours. In flight, I would drink nothing at all until I started to feel the effects of dehydration. In this way I was able to complete the flight without too much bladder agony.

John Rochfort was the third member of our formation due to go all the way and, after an interminable wait on the ground, we launched to join up with the tankers. Our tiny cockpits were crammed full of en route essentials such as maps, tapes, books, food and drink cartons. Typically for an RAF fighter there was no useful stowage space available for anything – what you couldn't cram into your flying suit pockets had to be distributed carefully around the cockpit, covering up various switches, instruments and levers that you hoped you wouldn't need to use in a hurry.

The weather was glorious for most of the route, as we flew over vast fields of puffy cumulus clouds stretching to the horizon in all directions. For long periods there were no clouds at all and our eyes ached for relief from the endless blue dazzle of sea and sky. At 30,000 feet our formation was a gaggle of individual dots hanging motionless in the blue, each pilot lost in his own thoughts as we trailed far behind the graceful curve of the tankers' wings. Time passed excruciatingly slowly at first, and I forced myself into the tedium routine. This involved sitting passively for as long as possible until you were almost prepared to eject to relieve the boredom, and then doing something with your in-flight entertainment. To eat a sandwich was a major event, to be planned and looked forward to for an hour or more. Each 'plug' offered some excitement at first; there was the ever-present risk of a ham-fisted 'spokes' contact (in which the pilot managed to break the refuelling basket).

Not far from Madeira John Rochfort called up with the laconic statement that he had a fuel transfer failure, with no fuel feeding from one ferry tank. The decision was made to send him to Porto Santo, the nearest diversion, and our Nimrod escort (who was flying some way ahead of us) turned back to pick him up on radar. Naturally, John had no map of the islands and nearly landed at Funchal (far too short!) by mistake. Eventually the Nimrod guided him to Porto Santo, where he landed safely with one ferry tank still full of fuel. 'That's the last we'll see of him for a while,' we thought. As we approached the Equator the tankers departed and we were joined by the relief Nimrod, which had taken off from Ascension. We crossed the line in close formation on this second Nimrod while our previous escort took some 'happy snaps' for the squadron album. I felt a bit punch-drunk for the last three hours, and we were all pleased to pass through the ITCZ in one of its quieter moods. It was a daunting view as we approached, a line of huge thunderstorms stretching up to 40,000 to 50,000 feet in the stratosphere, with only narrow gaps between each cell.

To my surprise, at 120 miles I got a lock on to the Ascension radio beacon. As we approached within 20 miles, there was still no sign of the island in a sea of large cumulus clouds. Eventually, when we were already in radio contact, the island appeared from behind a cloud; we were amazed to see how small it looked in the vastness of the ocean. The single main runway stretched across the south of the island between volcanic outcrops and we were grateful for the lack of crosswind on approach. After a long ferry flight the final landing was a risky exercise, and you had to summon up all your reserves of concentration to get down safely, even in ideal conditions. The USAF issued their ferry pilots with benzedrine tablets to pep them up for landing, but our aviation medics were still not geared up for the real problems of air-crew fatigue in wartime.

Landing the Harrier with the big 330-gallon tanks was not easy. The tanks always looked far too big for the tiny airframe and you had to be very careful about how much power you used on finals. Basically, the tanks put the centre of gravity of the aircraft too far aft, and if you used too much power on finals with the nozzles down, you rapidly ran out of nose-down pitch control. This would lead to the aircraft pitching up out of control, the only remedy being an immediate selection of a lesser nozzle angle. This was also a bit tricky, as you could run yourself out of lift if you pushed the lever too far forward. I had already encountered this problem once before, during a night landing at Boca Chica Air Base in the Florida Keys, after an eventful Hurricane Evacuation from Belize in 1980, but that's another story.

CHAPTER TWO

Ascension

We taxied wearily into the huge parking area, to be met by our pilots and enthusiastic ground crew. As we climbed stiffly from our cockpits the tropical-scented air greeted us like a warm bath in the evening sun. Gratefully, we each sank a can of beer presented by Bruce Sobey, our Senior Engineering Officer. Most of us met the challenge of downing the beer before peeing – the first relief for over ten hours. After unloading our baggage I looked around the squadron ops set-up, comprising two tents just off the Aircraft Servicing Platform (ASP). We were then taken to our 'accommodation' at the small hamlet of Two Boats in the centre of the island, about 5 miles away. Darkness fell rapidly, and we unrolled our sleeping bags to bed down in what seemed to be a large disused cattle shed in company with a horde of other characters from all three services. This was our introduction to life at Ascension, which over the last couple of weeks had metamorphosed from a sleepy communications station into one of the busiest military bases in the world.

I fell into conversation with a pilot lying on a camp bed next to mine. He was an Air-to-Air Refuelling Instructor Pilot from Marham, and had taken part in the first of the Vulcan raids. None of the Vulcan pilots had done any Flight Refuelling and so this guy had been dragged out of Marham and sent to Ascension after a short familiarisation sortie in the Vulcan simulator at Scampton. (He had never flown the Vulcan before.) Within a few hours of arrival at Ascension, he found himself airborne in a Vulcan heading for Port Stanley. In the middle of the night when the first 'plug' was due, he was called up into the cockpit and told: 'Keep an eye on us while we plug into that tanker.' (The original plan was for him to fly all the plugs.)

His job completed, he was sent below to wait for the next 'plug'. A rather elderly Flight Lieutenant, he took a somewhat jaundiced view of the whole business, and was not particularly looking forward to his next bombing raid.

The next morning, while hitching a lift to Wideawake airfield, we had a good look at the island for the first time in daylight. It was a weird place, the dark soil and conical hills of volcanic rock giving the impression of a municipal rubbish dump, the odd satellite communications dish decorating a hilltop here and there. The only greenery was to be found at the centre of the island on top of the highest mountain just next to Two Boats camp. The thousands of transient service personnel were scattered in various shanty towns and tented camps all over the island. There seemed to be no organised MT (Military Transport) system, but it was easy to hitch a lift. In the bar at Two Boats camp the previous night we had observed all shapes and sizes of service personnel, most of whom carried personal weapons even in civilian clothes. Some reticent, tough-looking characters stood quietly drinking in smart suits at the end of the bar. They carried squat, vicious-looking sub-machine-guns and we assumed them to be SAS or SBS. We didn't ask questions. As for the rest of the island, there seemed to be no formal discipline anywhere, no one appeared to give orders to anyone else, and security was totally absent. Anyone, carrying any weapon, could go anywhere he pleased on the island. There was no routine peacetime system of accounting for personnel and, thankfully, there were no Service Police or any other security arrangements to interfere with our activities. This was the secret of success at Ascension in those early frantic days, as any sort of routine bureaucratic control would have stifled the highly charged atmosphere of 'Can Do' that prevailed. Everyone seemed to realise that only by unstinting super-human effort could be guaranteed the success of those going 4,000 miles onward to the combat zone. Outwardly all seemed chaos, but throughout the island in every field of activity there was an electric spirit of preparation for war.

Apart from launching the various long-range Vulcan, Victor and Nimrod sorties, the current task at Ascension was to tranship huge quantities of weapons, stores and personnel on to the main south-bound convoy, which was already assembling offshore. Supplies were airlifted in and dumped in rows a hundred yards long at the edge of the ASP. I wandered around this area and saw racks of live Sidewinder missiles standing next to bombs, crates of fresh vegetables, toilet rolls and the thousand and one other requirements of ships and armies going to war. The helicopter lift out to the waiting ships went on twenty-four hours a day, using both RN and RAF helicopters, the whole operation being controlled by a very sunburnt Army sergeant who tramped the ASP with a back-pack UHF radio. The main operations room looked a shambles, with RN and RAF Ops people trying to keep tabs on what was going on. An RN Captain was in overall charge and he appeared to spend most of his time complaining and trying to score points off the RAF, accusing them of being the cause of most of his problems.

During the day our ground crew had sweated to remove the guns and ferry tanks from our aircraft in preparation for our flying them on to *Atlantic Conveyor* next day. Because of the extreme heat, VSTOL (Vertical/Short Take-Off and Landing) performance was going to be very limited. The Boss left me to organise the operation and I had spent a lot of time anxiously working out the VSTOL performance for each individual aircraft. It was going to be tight, and there was no room for error on the tiny vertical landing pad at the bows of the ship. Later that day Tim Smith, Pete Harris and Jeff Glover turned up, having set out from UK as a four-ship. Ross Boyens (BOY) had diverted to Banjul with fuel transfer failure. By now we had also met up again with the pilots of the newly formed 809 Naval Air Squadron, who had ferried their Sea Harriers out without ferry tanks, stopping off at Gibraltar en route. (In conversation later with Flight Lieutenant John Leeming, an ex-GR3 pilot, he told me that he flew his Sea Jet the whole way without LOX (liquid oxygen for breathing). Cruising at about 10,000 feet cabin altitude to avoid hypoxia, he would take a deep breath and zip up to the tanker operating altitude for each 'plug' and then descend rapidly when he started to feel faint. The crazy things people do in wartime. The pilots of 809 Naval Air Squadron were also due to load their eight Sea Harriers on to the *Atlantic Conveyor*, which arrived late in the afternoon. They were a good bunch and we had already met most of them before. We were to develop a close friendship, as we shared the same doubts and adventures en route to the combat zone. That night we all met up in the bar of the Exiles Club in Georgetown, the tiny capital of the island. We arrived a bit late in the evening, to find a monster piss-up going on. The Navy were commiserating the loss of HMS *Sheffield*, which had just been sunk by the Argies. This was a typical Service TCIA (Thank Christ I'm Alive) party. No disrespect was intended to those killed in action: the idea was that they would have done the same thing if the positions had been reversed.

I briefed six of our pilots carefully on the problems of landing aboard *Atlantic Conveyor*, which rode at anchor a couple of miles offshore. At high temperatures the Harrier needed almost full power just to hover. Overuse of the reaction controls bled large amounts of hot air from the engine, further reducing the limited thrust available. For the precision vertical landing exercise due to be carried out that day, it was essential that the pilots flew as smoothly as possible, keeping control movements to a minimum at all times. Any over-controlling caused by the stress of a first-ever ship landing could lead to disaster in the confined space available. There was always the option of 'going through the limiters' – pushing the throttle through the gate to override all the built-in protective circuits – but this would be an absolute last resort to prevent a crash, and could result in irreparable engine damage.

The landing on of our GR3 Harriers had to be carefully synchronised with the arrival of the Sea Harriers of 809 Naval Air Squadron. The deck of *Atlantic Conveyor* was going to be packed solid and there was precious little room for the deck-handling parties to manoeuvre aircraft along the deck to their parking slots. There was to be a total of fourteen Harriers and Sea Harriers, four Chinook heavy-lift and eight Wessex troop-carrying helicopters parked between the containers stacked along the sides of the deck as rudimentary protection against the elements. Because of the location of the single take-off and landing pad at the bows, all these aircraft had to be parked in the correct sequence, as only the nearest aircraft to the pad had enough space to taxy once the deck was loaded. For reasons that became apparent later, the nearest aircraft to the pad had to be a Sea Harrier. The operation proceeded smoothly with only minor hitches, except for the performance of Mark, who made a rather unsteady arrival on deck. Ross Boyens turned up with his aircraft at lunchtime, and later on John Rochfort arrived on a Hercules, after various adventures in Madeira.

These new arrivals threw yet another spanner into the constantly revised personnel plan. I had to see the Boss to discuss this. He was now settled aboard the *Atlantic Conveyor,* and this posed some difficulties as there were no ship-to-shore radio communications available for non-RN personnel. In the end, I had to hitch a lift on a helicopter to see the Boss. We had written off Ross Boyens as one of the team of eight because we didn't expect him to get to Ascension in time for the sailing of the convoy the next day. Pete Harris had by now taken his place, and was fully geared-up to come with us. My view was that either Pete or Ross would be excellent value, but that Pete's position as a Weapons Instructor and his greater overall flying experience tended to tip the scales in his favour. The Boss decided in favour of Pete Harris. Pete was delighted; Ross was disconsolate. I felt for him but there was too much to do to worry about the justice of this decision.

That night I handed over command of the remaining 1(F) Squadron element on Ascension to Tim Smith, who was to operate the three remaining aircraft in the Air Defence role for the time being. Just before I handed over, I received a phone call on the secure link to Northolt (with the Boss and Bob aboard *Atlantic Conveyor* I was Acting Squadron Commander). It was Pete Moules asking a lot of questions about the land-on and whether we had enough kit, etc. At the end he said, 'By the way, Jerry, we haven't yet decided to release you to the Navy for this operation!'

This was a laugh: if they thought that the Navy was solemnly going to disentangle our jets from the jigsaw puzzle aboard *Atlantic Conveyor* at this late stage, then they were dreaming. I said as much to Pete Moules, who seemed a bit taken aback that our aircraft were already irrevocably under the control of the Navy. I said that there was no way of stopping *Atlantic Conveyor* from sailing the next day with our aircraft, and as far as I was concerned, eight of our pilots would be sailing with them. Pete Moules went on to talk about Air Defence, and I reassured him that Tim Smith would have enough Sidewinders and cannon ammunition to do the job for the time being. The Senior Naval Officer was listening to this conversation from the other side of the room and he shouted across to me, 'Are they talking about Air Defence of Ascension?' I confirmed this, and without moving from his seat he roared back, 'Tell them to fuck off! There is no air threat to this island. If I think there is then *I* shall decide how to deal with it. Tell them to *piss off!*' I laughed and passed on the gist of these comments to Pete, who rang off in disgust. For those of us with any doubts left as to the RN attitude toward the RAF, this was a good lesson for the coming weeks.

On 7 May we were ready to embark and the six remaining 1(F) Squadron pilots arrived at the airfield. We were told that the promised helicopter lift was not on and we were to report to Georgetown quay to be ferried aboard by lighter. I hastily arranged transport for the 5-mile journey and we set off. Realising that we had a couple of hours to kill, we decided to drop in at the Exiles Club for a final drink in civilisation before departure. We strolled down to the jetty where our baggage lay to join a motley crew of paras, sailors, SAS, RN helicopter pilots and several other unidentified characters who could have been Argy agents for all we knew. About 100 of us stood idly around, watching the crystal-clear waves breaking hard on the dazzling coral-white beach. (Ascension is notorious for its dangerously unpredictable ocean rollers.) A Navy Lieutenant was supposedly in charge of the move, and to our horror we discovered that the 'lighters' were no more than large steel pontoons with a single outboard motor. Floating just a few inches out of the water when loaded, there was no rail and nowhere to sit apart from the baggage, which was piled in the middle. This Naval Herbert had not the faintest idea how to get the ball rolling, so we took over the organisation of loading the pontoons and getting a suitable number of people aboard each time. Fortunately there was only a light swell, or the whole operation would have been fraught with danger. (No one had a life jacket). Even so, the pontoons pitched and rolled alarmingly during the 2-mile trip out to *Norland*. Alongside the ship the swell was more significant, and we spent an anxious few minutes throwing baggage through the loading hatchway in the ship's side as our pontoon rose and fell with the waves. Once aboard, we discovered that all of the lifts were U/S and in the midday heat we sweated blood carting our gear up seven decks to our allocated accommodation.

CHAPTER THREE

A South Atlantic Cruise

Our home for the next ten days, MV *Norland* was a North Sea car ferry taken over for the duration of the operation. She was packed full of personnel: nearly 1,000 members of 2 Para; 18 Squadron (Chinook) aircrew; 848 Naval Air Squadron (Wessex) aircrew and just six 1(F) Squadron pilots plus Squadron Leader Syd Morris, who was to be our Ops Officer and, later on, the 'Airport Manager' of the famous Port San Carlos forward airfield. The seven of us were living in two first-class cabins on the upper deck. This was more comfortable than we had expected; each cabin had a shower and toilet, and the food was pretty good. Most important of all, we had a very comfortable Wardroom where the officers could mingle and relax over a pint of beer, while we talked about all aspects of the coming operation.

That night we sailed from Ascension in convoy with several other STUFT ships (Ships Taken Up From Trade). These were merchant marine ships of all types, some passenger-carrying like *Norland*, plus many cargo ships. Each ship was manned by its full peacetime crew, who had volunteered to remain on board for Operation *Corporate*. Each ship also carried a small RN complement who had suitable communications to keep in touch with CTG (Commander Task Group) and other RN formations. Aboard *Norland*, the senior RN officer was a Lieutenant Commander helicopter pilot, while *Atlantic Conveyor* – with its vital cargo of war materials – had an RN Captain in charge of the Naval Party. The aim of the Naval Parties (NPs) was to relay instructions to the civilian captains of their respective ships and keep them informed as to likely military hazards. At this stage the NPs operated in a purely advisory capacity, but as we approached the TEZ (Total Exclusion Zone), their role became dominant. I was amazed to discover that every man and woman in the crew was a volunteer, for what was an extremely open-ended engagement. They were being paid extra for their service, but at this stage no one seemed to be sure exactly how close to the action they would be expected to sail. Only much later in the voyage did the crews realise that their ships were to be sent in-shore, to become prime targets for enemy attack.

After a couple of days' sailing we were joined by the assault ships HMS *Fearless* (the Command Ship for the landings), HMS *Intrepid* and the frigates *Ardent* and *Argonaut* as escort. Later on *Ardent* would be sunk and *Argonaut* severely damaged by air attack. We were also joined by SS *Canberra*, carrying nearly 3,000 troops of 5 Brigade. For us RAF pilots it was surreal to be sailing to war in a convoy through the beautiful ultramarine waters of the tropical South Atlantic. I remembered tales of wartime convoys from my father, who had served in the RN throughout the Second World War, escorting nine Russian convoys. I could not quite reconcile the tales of his grim experiences with sunbathing on the upper deck of *Norland*. However, things were to liven up considerably as we sailed further south. The enjoyment of our South Atlantic cruise was tempered by the need for all seven of us to cross-deck to *Atlantic Conveyor* each day for an interminable series of briefings in company with 809 Naval Air Squadron pilots.

Our small convoy carried a lot of helicopters, and each day there was a routine Helicopter Delivery Service between the various ships of the convoy, 'organised' by the Navy. This service was an absolute shambles from start to finish. Nearly all of the STUFT ships had a hastily welded-on helicopter landing pad (*Norland* had two) for the duration. Each NP made a pretence of operating pukka 'Flying Stations' for the Helicopter Delivery Service, but there was no control of passengers, and no one was issued with a life jacket. For us, the drill was to be up beside the stern landing platform just before daybreak and await the arrival of the Helicopter Delivery Service. A 'Flight Deck Officer' would be on duty, but he never knew when the Helicopter Delivery Service was going to arrive or where it was going next. After the chopper had landed the Flight Deck Officer would go forward and ask its destination; meanwhile the passengers would rush at it and scramble in until it was full. Unlucky passengers would then have to wait several hours for the next Helicopter Delivery Service. Operating under strict radio silence, the Helicopter Delivery Service operated a sort of 'bus service' around the ships of the convoy, which were often many miles apart. There was no system of priorities – anyone could take a trip for any reason. After many days of this chaos the Navy started to issue a sort of timetable, showing when the Helicopter Delivery Service would arrive, and who was entitled to board. However, the system was never made to run efficiently.

Norland was quite a comfortable ship to sail in. Her autostabilisers gave us a smooth ride in the heavy seas we were to encounter later. The *Atlantic Conveyor* (or the 'Atlantic Convenience', as we called her) rolled badly in any sea of note because her stabilisers were U/S and she was incorrectly loaded. The Master was Captain Ian 'Birdseye' North, and I was to have many enjoyable conversations on the bridge with this extremely likeable character. On his regular North Atlantic container runs he made sure she was a bit top-heavy to ensure a smooth ride through stormy seas. Unfortunately, he had had no control over her present load, and her centre of gravity was too low for comfortable handling.

On this our first day aboard the 'Atlantic Convenience' (so called because of the quaint urinals attached to the ship's rails), we spent much of our time helping the ground crew complete the task of 'bagging' our tied-down aircraft in their custom-made plastic covers. On return to *Norland* that afternoon we discovered the men of 2 Para busy with weapon training, firing their small arms, machine-guns and the occasional Milan anti-tank rocket into the sea, the latter with an almighty bang that spoilt any idea of a peaceful nap. The weapon training was a regular daily event, and eventually we became concerned that they would run out of ammo before they got to grips with the enemy! That evening I was summoned to an 'Executives' briefing on *Norland*, at which OC 2 Para (Lieutenant Colonel H. Jones), OC 18 (Chinook) Squadron, OC 848 Naval Air Squadron and OC our own NP were present. I knew OC 18 (Chinook) Squadron, Wing Commander Tony Stables, from Cranwell days and together we were to have quite a few laughs at the content of the these briefings, the aim of which was to keep us up to date with current Naval matters and pass on any new information about the invasion plans. (At this stage we were unaware of the details of Operation *Sutton*, the plan to make a landing at San Carlos.) At this first meeting 'H.' Jones expressed his intention to try and get some of the RAF officers moved to another ship (to get more room for his subalterns, it transpired).

The next day, Sunday, was a relaxed day aboard *Norland* in idyllic weather conditions. There was no weapon training to disturb our peace and quiet, and the decks were littered with the pink bodies of personnel taking this last opportunity of relaxation in the tropical sun. At latitude 20 degrees South the temperature was noticeably cooler, although flying fish still skipped across the waves alongside. That evening I was invited to the Master's cabin for drinks and dinner with the crew, a good-hearted bunch of Yorkshiremen who seemed philosophical about the increasing uncertainty of their future.

Next day at first light we were back aboard *Atlantic Conveyor* to receive a whole day of briefings on carrier operations from pilots of 809 Naval Air Squadron. All of this was new to us, and we listened intently to the details of deck-handling operations, launch procedures and signals that would be used. Later, we were given a briefing on missile combat by one of 809's pilots, who claimed to be some kind of Weapons Instructor. His brief was full of bullshit and duff gen and we were suitably unimpressed. At the Boss's request I gave a briefing to our own guys on GR3 VIFF (Vectoring in Forward Flight) combat tactics, including use of cloud as defensive cover (strictly forbidden in peacetime) and how to get the best out of the engine without blowing it up. I recommended turning the engine limiters OFF and putting in the mechanical 99 per cent rpm stop on the throttle. By this means in an emergency you could merely 'firewall' the throttle in Low Level Air Combat and do the rest on the nozzle lever, without risking much harm to the machine. This was how you used the machine in VIFF combat.[5] I also covered Sidewinder and Guns Snapshot tactics.

In the afternoon there was a bit of drama as OC 809 Naval Air Squadron (Lieutenant Commander Tim Gedge) was ordered out to man the hastily unbagged Sea Harrier parked on the forward landing pad. We had received information (God knows from where), that an Argy Air Force recce Boeing 707 was heading our way, and the Navy were cleared to shoot it down. Very quickly, the Sea Jet was armed with Sidewinders and 30-mm cannon ammunition. A Victor tanker had been scrambled from Ascension and was on its way to refuel Tim after the engagement. Taking off only with Vertical Take-off fuel, he was going to be critically short of gravy if he had to carry out a long chase. After sitting out on deck for an hour the mission was cancelled, the threat having turned away.

The next day in the morning I paid a visit to *Norland*'s engine room with 2nd Engineer Jim Draper, who showed me round all the engine room hardware. Later on two Soviet 'Bear' long-range maritime recce aircraft turned up out of the blue and proceeded to orbit the convoy at low level for half an hour. It was a slightly uncomfortable feeling to realise that their reports of our position could easily be transmitted to Argentina. I was immediately reminded of Second World War convoys being shadowed by German Condors, transmitting their position to waiting U-Boats. Later, just to cheer us up, we heard on the BBC World Service that the Argies had declared our convoy a legitimate target. At this range we were not concerned about enemy air action, but we had no hard intelligence about the positions or capabilities of their submarines closer to the Falklands. There was a bit of a panic in the afternoon as we received a call to Action Stations because of a suspected submarine. Our briefed Stand To position was to lie on our bunks wearing steel helmets. As we had plenty of booze stowed away in our cabin this was fairly comfortable. Later, we heard that the submarine turned out to be a whale. There were to be many more of these alarms as we ploughed on ever-southward through the heavy swells of the South Atlantic. During one of our visits to the 'Atlantic Convenience' I casually mentioned the well-known 'Torpedo Crouch' to the guys. This was a Second World War sailor's trick when sailing through minefields or expecting a torpedo hit, the individual walking with knees permanently bent to absorb the shock of any explosion. This free advice was received ungratefully, I thought, the guys hobbling around the deck like a bunch of trainee Quasimodos in order to send me up a bit. In the end someone insisted that we have a squadron photograph taken with everyone standing in the 'Torpedo Crouch', much giggling all round.

At this stage of the voyage the major hazard to life and limb was 2 Para's fitness training. The whole battalion would run around the corridors and stairways of the ship on a sort of cross-country route twice a day. Each para was fully kitted-out in combat gear and they ran a company at a time. We soon learned to keep out of their way, as they were unstoppable once they got moving. I decided that it was time to do a bit of running myself. During the evenings we relaxed in the bar and by now had got to know quite a few of the officers of 2 Para, spending some time discussing our likely tactics should we have to provide Close Air Support for them when they went ashore. 'H' Jones was already a familiar face, and we also met Captain David Wood, the young Adjutant, and Captain Chris Dent, 2IC 'A' Company, among others. All three of these gallant characters were killed later at the battle of Goose Green.

By now dawn was breaking later and later each day as we sailed further south-west and into the southern winter. In the morning we awoke to find an empty sea around us; we had dropped back way out of position during the night, when all ships sailed fully blacked-out and with no radar. We had to steam at full speed for three hours to catch up with the convoy. We received the sad news on this day of the death of John Eyton-Jones and another Sea Harrier pilot – they were lost in bad weather while they were searching for an enemy ship. 'E.-J.' had been a popular RN Exchange Officer on 1(F) Squadron, having left us not long ago to return to the Sea Harrier. Later that day we watched a Refuelling at Sea evolution, with the RFA tanker *Tidespring* in close formation alongside us for hours. By now there was a definite chill in the air, and we shivered at the prospect of winter conditions after the tropical heat of Ascension.

On 13 May 1982 we celebrated the seventieth birthday of 1(F) Squadron! We celebrated in suitable style aboard *Atlantic Conveyor*, after a major intelligence briefing, which gave a rather daunting picture of what we were up against. In particular, the Argies possessed plenty of the latest SAMs and Radar-laid Anti-Aircraft guns, including batteries of the lethal 35-mm Twin Oerlikon, which already had a couple of kills to its credit over the islands. We were still not sure how many air-launched Exocets they had left, but they would surely be coming our way aboard the carriers, which were the most valuable targets. We were now within range of enemy attack, and one or two of our guys were starting to look a bit twitched. Pete Harris was particularly concerned about the lack of escorts for our convoy, becoming quite nervous during the many Stand Tos for submarine attack. Fortunately, we had John Rochfort's sense of humour to keep us amused, either taking the mickey out of the Navy or poking fun at the paras. News of the destruction of three Skyhawks by one of our Type 22 destroyers was a boost to morale. However, the fresh water plant had broken down and we were likely to start rationing soon. The weather was becoming increasingly windy, and I was able to have a play with a Blowpipe SAM simulator on deck. It struck me as a particularly user-hostile weapon system; my opinion of British missiles was not high and I didn't expect much from this particular one.

The next day was very grey, with much low stratus and poor visibility. Water rationing was in force. All personnel were ordered to wear long trousers and long-sleeved shirts at all times, as a rudimentary survival measure. We had our aircrew immersion coveralls, but there were no survival suits for the vast majority of passengers on the ships. If any ship was sunk we knew that a lot of people were going to die very quickly in the cold sea. That night at the executives' meeting I suggested to the Senior Naval Officer that we should deploy the Blowpipes plus extra machine-guns on deck to counter the threat of conventional air attack. I had discovered that their plan was to have just four machine-guns in position for this purpose. The Army argued that it would be impossible to hit aircraft from a moving deck, but I argued forcibly that this was not the point: the more tracer and SAMs you could get heading in the general direction of the attackers, the more likely you were to cause them to miss. With conventional iron bombs, I knew that it was quite possible to miss even so large a target as *Norland*. Eventually, I got through and they upped the numbers of guns on deck during a Stand To.

Later in the day we suddenly broke out of the murk into brilliant sunshine, the wind still blowing at a brisk force 8. For the first time I had managed to identify some Wilson's petrels plus the Wandering and Lesser Albatross, a magnificent sight cruising effortlessly over the waves in the wild open seas. That night we were invited for drinks with the Master again, and beforehand I went out on the bridge wing with the Officer of the Watch to observe a night Refuelling at Sea. Not a light was visible – both ships being completely blacked out. After several minutes of dark adaptation I could barely make out the dim shape of the tanker hammering through the waves, seemingly within touching distance. I went inside and asked Don Ellerby if he had ever done anything like this before. Did he know what was going on out there? His answer was that he hadn't – and he'd rather not watch, thank you very much! He was pretty cool about the whole business. Once again, at the end of the Refuelling at Sea we were left many miles astern of the convoy, and had to spend the rest of the night running at maximum speed through heavy seas to catch up.

The next day was another wasted trip to *Atlantic Conveyor*, which was now pitching and rolling alarmingly as a storm blew up. By the end of the day the wind was up to 50 kt over the deck and there was some discussion about whether or not the Helicopter Delivery Service Sea King would be able to take us back to *Norland*. Anticipating a sleepless night aboard *Atlantic Conveyor* – there was no spare accommodation – we all got out on deck in the howling gale to await the Helicopter Delivery Service. As the Sea King arrived, the wind was touching 50 kt over the deck. Things started to look a bit hairy. The winch strop was hanging at 45 degrees to the vertical, the pilot having to hover over the sea in order to position it over the deck. The deck was pitching plus and minus ten feet. The Flight Deck Officer – standing braced at an angle of 45 degrees to the vertical – was still putting people into the strop when one passenger very nearly fell out, just managing to hang on by his fingertips as the strop reached the door. The Flight Deck Officer then said that only personnel 'who had been winched before' could be taken aboard. As usual, there were no life jackets. I volunteered next, and managed to get aboard. J.R., who was next in the queue, saw the Sea King's rotor blades come within inches of striking a container. This was enough for the remaining passengers, who returned below to spend an extremely uncomfortable night aboard.

Early next morning our lost souls returned from *Atlantic Conveyor* by Helicopter Delivery Service, looking pale and wan after a serious booze-up followed by almost zero sleep. The ship's clock had now been put back an hour a night for the last four nights in order to bring local time in line with what was going on outside. Unfortunately, the ships did not all put their clocks back at the same time, which was to cause further chaos with the timing of the Helicopter Delivery Service.

A sense of boredom crept in briefly, and I made a determined start with the Rubik's cube (all the rage with the RN guys). By now, we had been told of the major change in plan whereby we were now to go directly aboard HMS *Hermes*, to operate *solely in the Ground Attack/Recce role*. Although a sensible use of our expertise, this was a bit of a blow as we had been looking forward to flying Combat Air Patrols and getting stuck into the Argy air raids with the large stock of Sidewinders we had brought with us (virtually the whole of the RAF's War Stocks). As a result of this change of plan we had hastily organised some briefings with various FACs (Forward Air Controllers) and the Air Liaison Officer from *Fearless*, an RN character who seemed to know next to nothing about Air–to-Ground operations. The more I learned about the way we were to be tasked in support of the landings, the less confident I became that we would be allowed to do anything useful. The whole set-up of command and control of Ground Attack aircraft seemed to be a shambles, the RN having been out of this business for many years now.

On 17 May we finally moved to the *Atlantic Conveyor* in preparation for embarkation aboard *Hermes*. At last there was a sense that things were getting moving – that we were going into action. Much of the day was spent helping the ground crew unbag the jets. We had our first practice with the FINRAE (Shipborne Inertial Navigator Alignment) equipment, which did not work. There was one Stand To for submarine attack, plus one Air Raid Warning Yellow, both of which turned out to be false alarms. We met up with the LSL (Landing Ship Logistics) group and our much-enlarged convoy penetrated the TEZ for the first time. By now we had been given the final plans for the landings, which were to take place early on 21 May. For the Navy, a priority task now was to sort out the loads of all the ships in order to get the stores in the right place ready for the landings. All of the humping and dumping had to be carried out by helicopter, and by now there was virtually continuous traffic between the ships of the convoy to achieve this. Fortunately the weather was fine with an easy swell, and I made a trip across to *Fearless* to collect some of our guys' baggage, which had been delivered to the wrong ship. Back aboard the *Atlantic Convenience* several of us spent some time in the cavernous cargo deck checking through our squadron operations equipment.

In the fetid atmosphere and dim light below we picked our way through a gigantic Army Surplus store, surrounded on all sides by supplies and munitions of every description. During our time below decks there was a brief Tannoy announcement from Captain Layard, which made clear who was in charge now. There had been some pilfering of essential items from some of our survival equipment, and

Layard was furious. In a low voice, shaking with rage, he announced that if he caught those responsible for the thieving he would 'personally cut their hearts out'. We believed him. That night Bob and I went through the details of our cross-decking operation with the Boss, eventually to crash out exhausted after the day's efforts.

Next morning, some three hours before dawn, we were woken by a Stand To. After a mad scramble into immersion suits, we rushed to our lifeboat stations, to be told that this was to be a full-scale practice for casualty drill after a simulated air attack. For the next couple of hours we sweated and cursed and struggled to carry 'casualties' down from the bridge, using the unwieldy Naval stretchers. Dressed in full cold weather survival gear, this was back-breaking work for a bunch of Harrier pilots unused to hard labour. After standing down from this exercise there were two more real Stand Tos for us after we had managed to grab some breakfast. We discovered that both of these alerts were for aircraft of the Task Group, now only a few miles away. Once again the weather smiled on us: unbelievably, the sea shimmered almost flat calm in brilliant sunshine as we manned up the jets in readiness for lift off. I was third in line from the pad and I saw Steve Brown (an RAF exchange pilot with the RN) nearly write off a Sea Harrier. Setting up for the Vertical Take-off right in front of me, I saw his nozzles rotate to the 40 degree check position and remain there as he slammed to full power to take off. This was the oldest Harrier mistake in the book; I had seen students and experienced pilots do it on several occasions. With the extremely rapid engine acceleration of the Pegasus, once you had slammed to full power there was no way out of the situation. The aircraft would lurch forward and upwards instead of straight up, and the pilot's instinctive reaction was to apply full back stick to get away from the ground. After skidding across the pad, Steve's tailplane missed the 4-feet steel deck rail by a couple of inches as he lurched airborne in a horrific nose-up attitude. It was not an encouraging start to the cross-decking operation. When lined up on the pad my electrical generator failed, leaving me on battery power only. In peacetime I wouldn't have gone; however, any delay would hold up the whole cross-decking operation. I could see *Hermes* just a couple of miles away and so I launched anyway, to make a very shaky first carrier Vertical Landing.

CHAPTER FOUR

Hermes

Before darkness fell that day four GR3 pilots managed to cross-deck successfully to *Hermes*, leaving two U/S aircraft to follow on later. The Boss, I, J.R. and Pete Harris flew aboard, and I recall my first ever deck landing as being 'not too shiny'. After parking on the grossly overcrowded deck, we went below to meet the pilots of 800 Naval Air Squadron who had been in theatre since 1 May. I hadn't been aboard a carrier for years, but somehow the smells and the constant hum of machinery below decks seemed familiar. Old memories came flooding back: childhood memories of visits with Dad to aircraft carriers in Devonport Dockyard after the Korean War. We were ushered into the No. 2 briefing room, which was to be our working accommodation and home for who knew how long; we were to share this small space with the Sea Jet pilots, about thirty in a room barely 20 feet square. Apart from a small adjoining 'broom cupboard' where we were to keep our target maps, this room was used for planning, briefing, debriefing, film debriefing and even for sleeping. Comfortable fixed seats were arranged in rows like a cinema and it was quite usual to find an exhausted pilot sleeping in a corner in an immersion suit.

I was struck by the haggard appearance of the Sea Harrier pilots. After five weeks aboard ship they looked exhausted, the more senior pilots in particular looking haggard and scruffy with half-grown beards and bloodshot eyes from hours spent below deck in this cramped space. To us, it was a shock to see how knackered these guys looked. They had carried out one or two Ground Attack sorties over the islands in early May, but further Low Level Ground Attack operations had been discontinued on the Admiral's orders after the shooting down of a Sea Jet in the first Goose Green attack, plus some flak damage sustained during the Port Stanley Airfield (PSA) attack. The air engagements of 1 May had not been repeated and since then the Sea Harrier pilots had been operating mainly in a purely defensive role. This had involved dozens of fruitless scrambles to chase shadows picked up on radar, and many hours of sitting on five-minute deck alert in the freezing South Atlantic night. On transit to their Combat Air Patrols they were dropping the occasional 'nuisance' bomb from 20,000 feet over Port Stanley Airfield (well clear of the defences), just to let the Argies know they were around.

Soon we were to discover why the more experienced pilots were so exhausted. On passage to the South Atlantic the Naval Air Squadron Commander had realised that not enough pilots were night qualified and had asked for permission to train up some more. This had been refused by the Navy hierarchy and now the few Night-Qualified pilots were having to do both night deck standby (sitting for three hours in the cockpit) and also daytime sorties, as there were not enough experienced pilots to lead the daytime missions. Being on duty both by night and day over such a length of time was an immense burden on even the fittest of aircrew, and the visible effects of fatigue were obvious to us, fresh from our relatively relaxing cruise.

With no time to take off our flying kit, the briefings began on operations from *Hermes'* deck. Lieutenant Commander Rod Frederikson gave a very practical need-to-know brief, leaving out all the trivia. Unfortunately, he started this excellent brief with only the Boss present. As second to land I joined the brief after about ten minutes, and the remainder of our pilots came in as they landed, to miss most of the briefing. Rod had been ordered to start the brief at a certain time and we were soon to discover that this was the Naval way of doing things. A Senior Officer would give an order, which was to be carried out *without question*, regardless of whether or not the task was feasible or necessary. Any attempt to question the order would be regarded as a form of mutiny. Before the briefing was complete, a message came through from Flyco (Flying Control) that we were to be prepared to fly all of our serviceable aircraft again on a training sortie. It was now barely ninety minutes before sunset and the Boss left in a hurry to explain to 'Wings' (the Air Commander) that in the absence of FINRAE we would be unable to align the Inertial Navigator and therefore we would have no Head up Display available, an essential requirement for a first night approach to a ship. Initially, Wings agreed that a launch at this late stage of the day was not sensible, so we relaxed and took off our immersion suits. I had a nasty suspicion that things were going to change again and sure enough within half an hour Bob, the Boss and I were told to man the GR3s immediately. (This was the Navy showing the RAF who was in charge now.) There was no time to complete the Shipboard Operations briefing or even brief among ourselves on the sortie we were to fly. The Navy were going to kick us into the air without explanation – just to show that they were in charge. The Boss made a last despairing effort to prevent the madness, explaining that as it was now only half an hour before sundown, three very uncurrent pilots would be flying at night for their second ever deck landing on our very unreliable standby instruments. *No chance*: the Navy attitude was, 'We're in charge, so get on with it'. With a sinking feeling in my stomach, I strapped into my jet and awaited the worst. We had not even been briefed on the night deck-lighting procedures. As the sun disappeared, the Boss asked Flyco if they still intended to launch us. We received the reply that was to become all-too familiar: 'Stand by.' Followed by nothing. No explanation; no decision; just 'Stand by'.

To cut a long story short, eventually we weren't launched. The only reason for this was that the deck-handling parties were unable to get the grossly overcrowded deck cleared for a take-off. By now there were twenty-plus Harriers onboard – the maximum they had ever operated in peacetime was twelve. With many helicopters also ranged on deck, the situation was shambolic, and there was no way they could get us moving. After climbing wearily out of our aircraft we went below. The Boss was looking extremely worried and I expressed my view that this kind of thing was going to happen again: we were no longer masters of our own destinies, and the people calling the tune were not only ignorant, they weren't interested in our particular operating problems. The Boss's reaction to this little pantomime worried me: he still did not seem to realise that he was no longer in control of our flying in the accepted RAF sense. On the ground he had disciplinary control of the squadron personnel, but he seemed unable to accept that he was now completely out of the chain of command as far as our flying operations were concerned. I had accepted that this was going to happen at a fairly early stage when we left Ascension, when some 809 Naval Air Squadron pilots filled me in on just how much some Senior Navy Officers hated the RAF. I already had a pretty dim view of the Navy hierarchy, and my prejudices were to be confirmed in full measure in the coming weeks.

Back in the PBF things had calmed down a bit as routine fixed-wing flying operations ceased and the ship settled into night-time routine. After a meal in the Wardroom we were introduced to some of the 800 Naval Air Squadron pilots: the CO, Andy Auld, a taciturn, lugubrious Scot; their small but noisy Senior Pilot, Lieutenant Commander Mike Blissett; 800's Operations Officer, an offhand, cynical Irishman. Amongst the others present were Lieutenant Commander Gordy Batt, a roly-poly Westcountryman of piratical mien, Flight Lieutenant Dave Morgan, ex-3 Squadron and serving on exchange with the RN, along with the ever-humorous Flight Lieutenant Ted Ball. Most of these characters were well known to us as the RAF had given initial Harrier training to all of them at Wittering.

That evening we also met the ship's Intelligence Officer, who seemed offhand and uninterested. We discovered that he was also a qualified Ground Liaison Officer, and should therefore be our direct link with the Intelligence and Air Tasking Organisations for all Attack and Recce operations. However, he was to give us no assistance whatsoever. We discovered that the only source of intelligence information was on a lower deck some considerable distance from the No. 2 briefing room; during Action Stations this room was completely inaccessible as all the intervening watertight doors were closed. I also discovered that the room contained no Air or Ground Situation map! This was a bit of a blow. Within the RAF we were used to a properly constituted Air Tasking and Intelligence Organisation at all levels, pilots being given regular intelligence updates on enemy and own troops' positions, plus the locations of all defended areas. This was the only way to run professional and efficient Ground Attack and Recce operations. For efficient operations both an Intelligence Officer and a Ground Liaison Officer were necessary to collect and disseminate vital information and to monitor incoming Air Task Messages (ATMs) for errors, which were not at all uncommon. We were to be given none of these facilities aboard *Hermes*, despite the fact that the ship was manifestly capable of providing them. What the Navy provided was an *ad hoc*, ramshackle and unprofessional set-up.

Some of the Navy pilots slept overnight in immersion suits in the No. 2 pilots' briefing room, even when not on duty. We discovered that this was because of the fear of torpedo and Exocet attacks. All of the ship's decks below the waterline were out of bounds at night (except for essential personnel), and so sleeping accommodation was at a premium for what was already a very overcrowded ship. At the time there were also many SAS and SBS personnel on board and we stepped over rows of prostrate bodies sleeping soundly on the bare steel decks of the gangways. The Navy pilots lost no time informing us of the rather anti-social characteristics of the Exocet: it homed on to the largest radar target area of the ship, and this meant that any hit on the starboard side would be smack in the middle of the No. 2 pilots' briefing room! The Sea Harrier Engineering Officer spent a lot of time with us and was much exercised by this very real threat to his pink body. We saw with some amusement that this character had his own personal scoreboard of Exocets fired by the enemy. (Everyone knew that they had a strictly limited number available.) Each time an Exocet was fired he ticked it off on the board, presumably to sleep a little more soundly as the remaining missiles dwindled in number. For a jape the Navy pilots periodically added extra missiles to the list when he wasn't looking.

We discovered the 'Greasy Spoon', a small aircrew buffet bar next to the pilots' briefing room, and also the pilots' 'heads', a fearsome device built with the accumulated experience of centuries of Naval plumbing. We soon discovered the hazards of using this device in anger. Connected to the labyrinthine complexities of *Hermes'* plumbing system, the bowl was prone to backfiring at unpredictable intervals. Like a mini Icelandic geyser, the contents of the bowl would be hurled skywards with varying degrees of violence, depending on the sea state, the revolutions of the engines and the phases of the moon, for all we knew. For me, at least, severe constipation became the norm for the duration of my time on board.

On the other side of the pilots' briefing room was the aforementioned 'broom cupboard', which we had been offered for use as a map store and planning room. There were already some of the Navy's 1:50,000 scale maps in there, and to our amazement we discovered that *none of them had any grid overprint*. This meant that they were unable to plot the position of any target other than obvious ones like Port Stanley Airfield on the coast. We resolved to get our map stocks aboard from *Atlantic Conveyor* in double quick time, or we would be unable to do any worthwhile attack missions.

The ship was permanently at Alert Condition Zulu, because of the submarine threat. This meant that many watertight doors were closed, adding greatly to the difficulty of moving about the ship. At this stage we had been told that there were two unaccounted-for enemy submarines, which would cause havoc if they got in amongst the Task Force shipping. The RN took this threat very seriously, and there was permanent Anti-Submarine helicopter activity going on by day and night throughout the war. The 'Pingers' (Anti-Submarine helicopter crews), had been flying intensively for weeks, and were even more exhausted than the Sea Harrier guys. I met one pilot who had flown over fifty hours in the previous ten days, all but two of which had been at night.

Wearily, we dumped our flying clothing in the flying clothing locker room and were shown to our accommodation below. The locker room was a bare compartment with a few tiny cupboards in the wall. With three times the usual number of aircrew aboard it was a shambles: there was nowhere to hang anything up, and each pilot's expensive outfit of wartime flying gear was just scattered in piles on the floor. Our Safety Equipment Worker, Corporal Walsh, was a dedicated and extremely competent NCO, but even he could do little to keep this lot in order. Items of kit went missing or were damaged because of the chaos, and it was obvious to us that this would become a significant limitation on our flying, as the full complement of serviceable flying kit was absolutely essential for all of us. In the hectic flying days that were to follow, there were lots of frantic last-minute searches for helmets, immersion suits, guns (Browning pistols and live 9 mm ammunition lay scattered about everywhere), and other items of kit, leading to rushed briefing and planning and some delayed take-offs. The Navy guys seemed resigned to this shambolic situation; according to them, nothing could be done about it.

In conversation with Lieutenant Commander Andy Auld, CO of 800 Naval Air Squadron, I was dismayed to see how demoralised he was about the conduct of operations so far. Andy told me that he had on several occasions tried to get the Captain to allow them to do things differently, but he had now been told to wind his neck in or he would be relieved of command and sent home. We were soon to learn just how bad things were, and what an unhelpful influence 'The Flag' had on many aspects of air operations.

Our main concern at this stage was to find out as much as possible about routine flying operations from the ship. In particular, we wanted to discover just how efficient the Navy Air Traffic Controllers would be at getting us back aboard ship in bad weather. Lacking radar – or any other navigation system for that matter – we would be relying totally on them to get back aboard; indeed, we would need constant radar guidance just to find the Task Force on the long return flights from operations over the islands. We were briefed on the system of a forecast position of the carrier for several hours in advance: this was vital information for any departing Harrier, and unfortunately it was not often accurate. According to the Naval Air Squadron pilots, we could look forward to some pretty hairy recoveries in poor weather, although by now some common sense had percolated through to the hierarchy about bad weather operations, and we were unlikely to be launched into totally unflyable conditions, as had happened on one or two occasions up to now. The Carrier Controlled Approach (CCA) was reasonably accurate for line-up, but, unlike RAF radar approaches, no glidepath information was available. In bad weather Carrier Controlled Approaches the Sea Harriers just descended to a height of 100 feet on their Radar Altimeter and then crept forward as slowly as possible until they came alongside the ship. With no Radar Altimeter and with our inferior VSTOL handling characteristics,[6] this was likely to be a pretty uncomfortable exercise for us. In really bad weather they dropped flame floats into the ship's wake, the idea being that you followed them until you found the ship! In really bad visibility there was a very real danger of colliding with the ship at the end of a difficult Carrier Controlled Approach.

That night I slept well in my camp bed on the floor of a cabin shared with an RN Lieutenant. Fortunately, this chap was to spend a lot of time on night shift, so I was able to sleep undisturbed most nights. Bob also shared a cabin, and the Boss had a cabin to himself just at the stern of the ship. Unfortunately, the Navy's habit of doing full power ground runs on Harriers in the middle of the night just above his ceiling did not allow him many comfortable nights. The remainder of our pilots camped out each night in the Wardroom Bar, the floor of which was covered in sleeping bodies by 10 o'clock. Ship's orders called for all aircrew to sleep in immersion suits. The next day, 19 May, we were to begin our first and only day of intensive carrier work-up training.

For me, the ship was a pretty comfortable place to sleep at nights and we were grateful for this as we went into intensive day operations. Reasons for this were several: in the first place, there were no practice alarms, thank god. Also, the Navy did not abuse the Tannoy system throughout the night with trivial messages, as was common practice on RAF bases during major exercises. (This merely meant that no one was able to get any sleep.) Also, the ship gave us a very comfortable ride in even the heaviest seas. She seemed very smooth running and only when full speed was ordered in an emergency did one notice an uncomfortable amount of vibration. This was in marked contrast to *Invincible*, which vibrated severely at any speed above about 18 kt, making sleep impossible for everyone. The average knot-tying matelot treated this kind of thing as routine, as the danger of extreme fatigue was not unacceptable. However, for aviators the need to be at maximum pitch of concentration meant that any sleep deprivation was dangerous in the extreme. More than once we were to be grateful that our primitive GR3s had no night-attack capability. As it was almost midwinter, our productive flying day was a maximum of ten hours, even allowing for pre-dawn launches and night landings.

This lack of night flying for us provided another bonus in that our hard-pressed ground crews had extra time available in which to repair our jets as they were damaged in action. We were short of ground crew anyway, and had to rely on a lot of assistance from the equally hardworking RN ground crews. Because of our initial role allocation as *attrition replacements* for Sea Harriers, we had brought only eighteen ground crew to look after the relatively few items of our equipment that were not common to the Sea Harrier. Naturally enough, if we were only brought aboard carriers as replacements, then there would be enough ground crew to look after the ship's unchanged complement of jets. However, finding out at a late stage that we were to be used a *reinforcements* in addition to the normal complement of Sea Harriers meant that we were immediately desperately short of ground crew.

This was only to be relieved by the loss of 50 per cent of our aircraft strength over the next two weeks. Led by Flight Lieutenant Brian Mason, 1(F) Squadron's Junior Engineering officer, our ground crew were to perform superhuman efforts of maintenance, battle damage repair and arming during the period of operations. Brian was a quiet and determined Geordie; he was a popular character with both aircrew and ground crew alike, and we had the utmost respect for the leadership he gave our hard-pressed ground crew in unique circumstances. The RAF was already trying to get a reinforcement group of ground crew to us from the 1(F) Squadron back-up team sailing from UK aboard the MV *Sir Edmund*, under the command of Gavin McKay. After many adventures – having been delivered in error to several wrong destinations – only a handful of this travel-weary group were to arrive aboard *Hermes* just before the end of the war.

Next morning we discovered that our aircraft had been armed with Sidewinders plus a full load of live cannon ammo in preparation for the day's training, which could of course at any time turn into operational flying on Combat Air Patrol if the Task Group was attacked. We briefed up for three-ship Air Combat training sorties, and had an excellent day's flying in fairly good weather. The deck was still pretty shambolic and during the day our fifth aircraft was ferried aboard from *Atlantic Conveyor* – now 100 miles away – after a refuelling stop on *Invincible*. This brought the total of Harriers to twenty-one on board. The deck crews worked miracles of jet-shuffling to get our formations lined up closely one behind the other for the launch. Although we were used to Harrier confined site operations in the fields and woods of UK and Germany, this frantic manoeuvring only inches from lashed-down aircraft was a bit of a challenge until one learned to trust the deck marshallers completely. Your aircraft was kept chained down (as a precaution against the ship's rolling) until it was time to taxy. Straight away some pilots were introduced to the joys of taxying in reverse, an essential skill required when moving back from a parking slot near the bow, or with the nose of the aircraft parked out over the side of the ship. This was a daunting exercise at the first attempt. It felt unnatural and demanded total trust in the marshaller. Unfortunately, my first practice at reverse taxying was to be in total darkness ...

When finally lined up for launch, each aircraft sat less than 10 feet from the aircraft in front, and you were buffeted severely as he ran up to full power for take-off. The Flight Deck Officer stood a few feet abeam your cockpit, his legs braced wide apart and his body angled at almost 45 degrees to remain standing in the gale blowing down the deck. The red light turn to green above Flyco, the Flight Deck Officer's flag touched the deck and you were off, slamming to full power immediately. You relied entirely on Flyco getting the ship's heading and speed right to give enough wind over deck for you to stay airborne after leaving the ramp. A series of marshallers were ranged down the deck behind the Flight Deck Officer, and their job was to bring the following aircraft forward to the launch spot without delay. As the preceding aircraft rolled for take-off these guys often lost their footing in the jet blast, despite leaning backwards at impossible angles. When this happened, they merely lifted their feet off the deck and continued to give the correct marshalling signals from a prone position. At all times there was a very real danger that they would be blown into the unyielding sharp metalwork of a parked aircraft or, worse still, over the side. After a couple of days of deck operations we realised that we had a dedicated bunch of professionals working on deck to get us airborne. Struggling by day and night in the freezing wet conditions, these guys certainly earned their pay.

After leaving the ramp, the secret of success was careful handling of the nozzles to achieve a smooth transition to fully wingborne flight. Any attempt to rush this when heavily loaded would lead to disaster, your aircraft mushing into the sea with insufficient wing lift. Fortunately on this, our first, day the aircraft were lightly loaded and required the minimum deck run to get airborne. It was good to get airborne again and practise some full-blooded combat manoeuvring. We were all very aware that we were flying fully armed aircraft; nevertheless it was necessary to arm up the missiles fully to get the 'growl' of acquisition. Any mistake with the firing button would have led to the shooting down of one of our own aircraft. Some excitement was generated on the Boss's first sortie of the day when he and Jeff Glover were directed to intercept an Argy Boeing 707, which had been picked up on radar at maximum range. In the event they never made contact: the target was too far away for a successful intercept. On our recoveries to *Hermes* we took the opportunity to practise some Carrier Controlled Approaches. The weather was fine but we wanted to find out how good the Navy Controllers were. Fortunately for us, in Lieutenant Tim Kelly we had an absolute ace as 'D' (Approach Controller), and we were to be grateful for his skill and flexibility on many occasions in the coming weeks.

Back on board, another hazard to life and limb was the stack of live weapons stored ready for use all around the deck between parked aircraft. Sidewinders, 1,000-lb bombs, depth charges and all manner of items formed an obstacle course for both aircrew and ground crew alike as they picked their way around the deck. Most of this ordnance was to be stowed away below decks after a few more RN ships had been sunk, their demise hastened by the detonation of deck-stowed munitions.

On station just a short distance 'Up Threat' from *Hermes* was our permanent 'Goalkeeper'', HMS *Broadsword*. This Type 22 frigate, armed with Sea Wolf SAMs, was our last line of effective defence against incoming Exocets and enemy fighter-bombers. The Sea Wolf computers considered anything moving faster than 250 kt as a hostile target – and the system had a very rapid reaction time. In consequence, we were told to keep our groundspeed below this figure at any time we were in range of the system. There were other Air Defence ships within the Task Group and straight away we discovered that they were an extremely trigger-happy bunch. We had to be very careful to use the correct IFF (Identification Friend or Foe) codes and the correct procedures to avoid being shot at. We were soon to discover that the two Type 22s were just about the *only* effective Air Defence ships in the whole Task Force. As one of these frigates was to be permanently stationed in the Falklands Sound area, our chances of avoiding enemy air attacks looked slim. *Hermes'* own defences were little short of pathetic: apart from an antique and useless SeaCat SAM installation, our only other armament consisted of a number of rifle-calibre machine-guns strapped to the rail (with canvas straps) at various points around the ship. The majority of warships were hardly better armed, the Navy having virtually abandoned dedicated anti-aircraft gun armament in favour of Sea Dart and Sea Wolf SAMs. Sea Wolf was to achieve moderate success in action, but the cumbersome Sea Dart achieved little by the end of the war, having shot down one or two attacking jets, a high-altitude Lear Jet and a couple of helicopters (one of which was an 'Own Goal'). These few missile kills were in stark contrast with the unprecedented performance of the reliable, American-built AIM9L Sidewinder, which was to achieve phenomenal kill rates during the air battles to come. There were a few old-fashioned 20-mm and 40-mm guns scattered about the Task Force, but there not anything like enough to put up an effective defence against a determined air attack, as the Navy had already discovered. Sadly, it seemed that the RN had remembered few of the bitter lessons of their disastrous Mediterranean campaigns of the Second World War, when scores of inadequately defended ships had been sunk by air attack.[7] Now they were to reap the reward for decades of neglect of weapons capability in favour of 'crew comforts' – in particular, officers' crew comforts. As described in *Heart of Oak*, Tristan Jones' stunning and venomous portrait of the rigours of lower-deck Naval life in the Second World War, RN officers had always insisted on relatively palatial living conditions for themselves at the expense of their noncommissioned crews. In 1982, an impartial observer visiting a Soviet and a British warship in turn could be forgiven for assuming that one of the prime tasks of the latter was to provide ample space for the officers to entertain visitors at lavish cocktail parties, rather than go to war.

There were more briefings for us on the 19th and we got to meet some more of the characters aboard ship. We met the Ship's Operations Officer and 'Wings', the Chief of Flying Operations, who seemed an amiable enough cove at this stage. It was somewhat disconcerting to discover that no one in Flyco had ever flown the Harrier. Syd Morris was already busy making contact with the various components of the Air Tasking Organisation, which was based aboard HMS *Fearless*. The ship's Intelligence Officer made an occasional appearance, but he seemed more intent on impressing us with the fact that he was equal in rank to the Boss, than on providing us with any actual assistance. I paid a visit to his intelligence briefing room on 4 deck and discovered that it took nearly ten minutes to get there, after climbing through the tiny 'kidney hatches' of many watertight doors en route. Copies of intelligence signals arrived at the No. 2 pilots' briefing room and were read by anyone who happened to be interested. They were then placed in a bulldog clip on the wall. There was no proper intelligence map of the Falklands displayed, and we asked the Navy pilots how they had dealt with this for the few attack sorties they had carried out up to now. They just read the signals as they came in and plotted what they thought was relevant information on the maps they used for that particular sortie. We discovered that there were two Photographic Interpreters aboard, and they had been given a small makeshift photo processing compartment in the bowels of the ship some five decks below us. The basic principle of efficient Photographic Interpreter work was a rapid system of film processing and interpretation, followed by rapid delivery of the intelligence to the agencies that needed it. Additionally, it was essential for the pilot who had taken the photos to be present with the Photographic Interpreters as the film came out of the processor. Only the pilot could tell the Photographic Interpreters which piece of ground was covered by a particular strip of film: without this information the Photographic Interpreters could grope around for hours trying to match the film to a map in order to get an accurate location for the targets shown. In addition to the obvious delays created by this ramshackle set-up, the debriefing requirement was difficult to fulfil when the Captain insisted that all pilots who had made contact with the enemy should debrief with him first, before doing anything else. It was becoming increasingly apparent to us that the Navy had forgotten the basic principles of fixed-wing attack and recce flying, having been so long out of the business by now.

I paid a visit to the Photographic Interpreters' film processing compartment and was depressed at the ramshackle set-up. They had just one film processor, a single manually operated light table, one printer and a bucket of distilled water for washing prints! To process one film took thirty minutes (in the RAF it was done in a fraction of this time) and to produce prints took another hour. One of the Photographic Interpreters was Sergeant Bowman, seconded to the RAF from the Army, whom I knew from his work at the Reconnaissance Intelligence Centre at Wittering. This splendid character worked tirelessly for us, trying to get the maximum amount of intelligence from every film received. Despite his commitment to the Captain, he still managed to find time to get up to the No. 2 pilots' briefing room to brief us personally on anything he thought was important (it usually was). The journey to and fro took even longer than the time to reach the intelligence room. The Photographic Interpreters' main problem was that the Captain did not trust their assessments of film negatives. On RAF recce squadrons all intelligence is gleaned from the study of stereo pairs of negatives; to produce prints merely slows the down the whole procedure, and they are only produced for special purposes. Unfortunately, not only the Captain but a load of other Naval Senior Officers demanded their own personal sets of prints. Thus, having produced nine or ten sets of prints, the hard-pressed Photographic Interpreters would then have to act as postmen, delivering them all over the ship. This was little short of pointless, as most of the officers demanding prints didn't understand the first thing about intelligence and had no need of them to carry out their tasks anyway.

In the No. 2 pilots' briefing room we found a drawer full of prints of various parts of the islands, including high-level shots of Port Stanley Airfield and Goose Green. The prints were not indexed or filed in any order, just thrown in the drawer at random. With assistance from the Sea Harrier pilots, we dug out the most recent and important ones and studied them with great interest. Taken in the main from an altitude of about 20,000 feet, they did not show detailed defence positions, although the effects of the Vulcan raids were clearly visible. Straight away the uncomfortable thought crossed my mind that pretty soon somebody would have to get down among the flak and SAMS and take some proper Low Level oblique shots of all these areas. As the squadron Recce Specialist, this job would almost certainly be coming my way ...

Later on, when Air Tasks came in for us, we would rummage frantically through the photo drawer in the hope of finding a recent print of the planned target area. We knew already that the maximum effective altitude of the Roland SAM was about 15,000 feet, and we understood why the Navy would not fly any lower in these areas. The Sea Harrier carried the same F95 recce camera as us (albeit with a 3-inch focal length lens), and their pilots had been briefed to take regular pictures of anything interesting during their high-level Combat Air Patrol sorties. Within a short time, on my suggestion, some of the 6-inch focal length lenses were removed from our little-used recce pods and used in place of the standard 4-inch lenses of our F95s. During our high-level photography the extra magnification of the 6-inch lens gave quite a bit more detail for the Photographic Interpreters to study.

We were also introduced to the smoothly superior Commander Walton, describing himself as an Air Adviser on the Admiral's Staff. However, with the Captain so close to the Admiral, it seemed obvious to us that any advice from Walton on air matters would not count for much. In the mercifully few dealings I had with him, Walton appeared flippant and uninterested in our suggestions. His standard response was to shrug his shoulders and say that was how things were being done and there was nothing he could do to change it.

We were amazed at the content and style of the daily 'Operations' briefing in the pilots' briefing room. The only highlight of this performance came when the ship's Senior Met man (an Education Officer) gave his daily brief. This cove was a laugh a minute; he knew his job well and gave pretty accurate forecasts, bearing in mind the dearth of information available to him. There were obviously no Met reports from the islands, so they were initially a meteorological 'black hole' as far as we were concerned. He was also a wag, keeping us constantly amused with his extremely unmeteorological banter. One of his favourite descriptions of a typical South Atlantic low pressure pattern was 'The Zebra's Arsehole', which phraseology went down very well with our guys. After this diversion there would be a brief by the Junior Operations Officer. He wore a flying suit with more badges than a Boy Scout – presumably the more to impress us with his aviation expertise. He would give us a long and particularly useless brief on the dispositions of our own ships, the expected 'threat direction' for the day, the submarine threat (always the same), time of sunrise and sunset etc. The few really necessary parts of this stream of information were already displayed on the briefing board of the pilots' briefing room, and were regularly updated during the day. He would then give us what was his idea of an intelligence update, always in a very offhand and flippant manner. The information given was invariably so broad-brush and out-of-date as to be useless to us, and we became increasingly irritated by his take-it-or-leave-it attitude to questions.

We had to sit through this briefing about two hours before sunrise every morning from then on. After giving this briefing the Navy considered that every pilot knew sufficient to be thrown off the front of the boat at any time to attack a heavily defended target without any further instructions or explanation. This was their approach to wartime Ground Attack operations. That evening we found out some details of our first operational mission: an attack on a fuel dump at Fox Bay on West Falkland. The weather forecast was not at all shiny for the morrow and before we stacked we planned as many details as possible in preparation for a very early launch. Initially the task was for just two aircraft, but I asked the Boss if I could tag along and make it a three-ship. This was agreed. The Navy had some recce photos of the Fox Bay area, where they had strafed a merchant ship at its berth. We dug out the photos and nearby the small hamlet were clearly visible many rows of fuel containers lying unprotected in the open. There was also some evidence that the Argies were in the process of burying the fuel to protect it, and so there was some urgency about attacking it straight away.

CHAPTER FIVE

First Operation – Fox Bay

Only three of our aircraft were going to be serviceable the following morning and we were unlikely to get any assistance from the FINRAE equipment. Colin, our tame FINRAE expert, had managed to get the equipment aboard (it consisted of an inertial platform plus associated computers all mounted on a tea-trolley sized carrier), but he and his team of two NCOs were having a lot of difficulties in getting it to work. The main problem was that the deck was far too crowded to lay out the necessary wiring for the alignment of our Harriers' inertial platforms. The three of us spent some time studying the 1:50,000 map of the area. The Boss decided to attack from a north-western direction, involving an Initial Point run through the high ground to the north-west of the settlement. From the photos it was going to be an easy target to find, lying as it was on a peninsula of land in open, flat terrain. We asked the Navy pilots about defences: they said they thought there might be a gun position to the east of the target area, but they weren't sure. The place did contain military units, and common sense told us to expect some kind of defences – hence the need for a single-pass co-ordinated attack. As far as the Navy pilots were concerned, the whole of West Falkland was an unknown area as they had not operated there – apart from this ship attack. Expecting little help from our own inertial navigator gear because of the FINRAE problems, we were anxious to make sure we made a reasonably accurate landfall in the anticipated poor weather conditions. Hence, working on the KISS (Keep It Simple, Stupid) principle we planned a route that let us down right on the northern tip of East Falkland, close to Cape Dolphin, a long peninsula that stuck out in a north-western direction at the north end of Falkland Sound. The Navy advised us that there was an Argy lookout position on the peninsula, and could we have a look at it en route. After landfall we planned to run across to the northern tip of West Falkland and then fly at Low Level through the mountains to approach the Initial Point from the north-west. Our formation was to be the standard 1(F) Squadron Escort Formation, in which the leader flew up front followed by two aircraft in line abreast forming an arrowhead formation. The weapon load was to be three cluster bombs each.

That night I crashed out on my camp bed with my mind in turmoil. This was it: our first operation, and it had to go well. I tried not to think of all the things that could go wrong. Would I go U/S before even getting airborne? Yes, knowing my luck. This would mean having to go through all the first-op tension all over again. What if the weather was impossible? There was no doubt in my mind that we would be launched regardless, but how on earth were we going to find the target if we couldn't even find the islands? Eventually, I accepted that fate could not be anticipated: what would happen would happen. I fell asleep and slept soundly until my alarm clock woke me some three hours before dawn. At breakfast there was grim news, which brought home the sad realities of wartime flying, where tragic accidents occur even more frequently than in peacetime as everyone tries their hardest under the most difficult circumstances: during the night a Sea King had been lost on an operation with twenty SAS aboard, plus Garth Hawkins, the best FAC I knew. Twenty-two had been killed, including Garth.

The weather forecast was pretty bad. A low-pressure system was centred over the islands and heading towards our position, over 100 miles to the east. By the time we reached the islands it was hoped that the weather would have improved a little, but by then the worst of it would be over the Task Group. Our actual cloud base was about 700 feet, with poor visibility underneath, and the forecast for the area of the Task Group was for visibility down to 300 metres with a cloud base of 100-feet.

'Oh they'll launch you in this – no problem!' said Tony Ogilvie, the Duty Sea Harrier Ops officer. The Boss suggested to Wings that a delay in launch time would give us a better chance of getting to the target (and of getting back aboard). Predictably, the answer was, 'Get on with it'. However, the Navy decided graciously to send a Sea Harrier with us as a guide, using his radar to make sure we at least let down in roughly the right place. Lieutenant Commander Neal Thomas was to be the man. Things did not go too well on deck. As expected, FINRAE was playing up and Bob and I got no alignment at all for our Inertial Navigators. The Boss managed to get some kind of alignment and so he at least had Head up Display instruments available. Bob and I had only our cheap and unreliable 'Woolworth's' Artificial Horizon as attitude reference, plus the equally useless Head-Down C2G compass to navigate with. The compass would swing wildly with any change of bank angle, making accurate flying difficult.

In worsening weather conditions we were launched into the murk, joining up with some difficulty in the treacherous haze below cloud. Our aircraft lurched uncomfortably at 210 kt with the unaccustomed heavy load. We had to fly this slowly in order to guarantee not to exceed 250 kt groundspeed, thus exciting the ever-vigilant Sea Wolf operators. The deck crews were very slow to get Neal airborne and, assuming he wasn't going to come with us, the Boss turned on track and began the long climb into the murk, Bob and I hanging on grimly as the world turned a dirty shade of grey in the hostile cloud. This was a typical low-pressure system cloud structure: thick, wet and clammy – and lots of it between us and the target. In the climb we eventually heard Neal check in on the departure frequency far behind us. He never managed to catch up, but soon had us locked-up on radar, keeping us covered for the letdown point. Not knowing the height of the cloud base, the Boss had planned to let down well out to sea so that we could go as low as we dared on instruments without risk of running into high ground. In the long, slow descent we received a laconic call from Neal that our track looked good for the letdown point. He wished us luck and turned back. We were grateful for the help.

Below cloud the weather was better than expected; by 1,500 feet we were already clear of the main cloud layers, with just a few patches of stratus below. Conditions below cloud were dark and ominous, a sudden increase in turbulence signalling a strong low-level wind, which sliced the tops off the steel-grey waves as we turned south-west towards the thin, dark line of the Cape Dolphin peninsula. An eerie feeling came over me as we coasted in over enemy territory for the first time. We knew already that small parties of SAS and SBS were ashore carrying out reconnaissance in preparation for the landings. The thought that those gallant and hardy characters were somewhere out there restored some of our confidence. Moving out into Escort formation, I felt more comfortable and settled into the old routine of searching forward and back for possible enemy activity. We did not expect to be bounced; however, the ingrained habit of constant vigilance occupied the mind and boosted your confidence.

As we coasted in again over West Falkland I was trying to check on the navigation pretty carefully. This first mission had to go well and we couldn't afford to get lost. With no inertial navigator this was not too easy, as our cheap 'Woolworth's' C2G compass swung wildly with every change of direction. In addition, we all had to work fairly hard to fly a sensible height above ground. For the first time in our flying careers we could fly as low as we wanted. However, there was no point in overdoing it yet, and I had to make several conscious efforts to pull up and give myself a bit more separation from the wild terrain. The land was very similar to the Flow Country of northern Scotland, with flat marshy areas between large tracts of smoothly undulating tussock grass studded with boulders. Closing up into a more compact formation, we flashed across a few low peaks and then dived into the broad valley between Mt Robinson and Muffler Jack Mountain. After passing abeam Chartres settlement we made a 90-degree turn to port, moving out into Attack Formation as we approached our planned Initial Point below Mt Sullivan. For this attack I was to follow the Boss's track and drop my weapons last, after Bob had crossed in front of me. Traditionally, the last man over the target is supposed to collect most of the flak, and so I was wound up to a fair peak of tension as we pushed up to the attack speed of 480 kt. The 'rusty baconslicer' whine of the Pegasus faded amongst the deeper and more powerful rhythms of the airflow, now thundering and buffeting outside the stubby airframe.

Suddenly, we were flying in bright sunshine as we hammered down the valley towards the target, each aircraft trailing occasional pulses of condensation in the moist, turbulent air. The visibility had improved and the tiny doll's houses of the Fox Bay settlement appeared right in front of us as planned. I was flying as low as I possibly could: the ground became a blur in my peripheral vision and my concentration was riveted on the Boss's aircraft just a mile in front of me as he eased up to drop his cluster bombs. The fuel dump was easy to see, just like the recce photos, and I saw an oily fireball exploding behind the Boss's aircraft as his cluster bombs hit the target. Bob flashed across my field of view from right to left – also a good hit – and I concentrated hard on my attack in the Pop-Up manoeuvre to attack height.[8] Aiming a bit beyond the flames I pickled, shoved the throttle into the corner and pushed the stick forward violently to get as close to mother earth as possible, expecting return fire at any moment. Within a few seconds I was over the bay and nearly dragging my wingtip in the water as I turned to follow the others behind the steep headland of East Head. Only when the headland was between me and the target area did I relax. I had to force myself to climb to a safer height: I had been over-cooking it on the low flying and felt rather lucky not to have clipped a wavetop. Throughout the attack, none of us saw any sign of flak. The attack had been the most exhilarating experience: the combination of extreme low-level flight, successful hits on the target and the all-pervading tension made you feel like a superman. Off-target I had felt capable of anything – adrenalin had taken control and I learned that you had to make a very firm effort to stay cool and retain a margin of safety, however small.

We joined up into close formation to enter cloud for the climb to height. There was still a lot of cloud and, like the outbound flight, we flew in instrument conditions for most of the way home. Approaching the Task Group, we split up to make individual recoveries. In spite of the forecast, the weather was only a little worse than on our departure and we all recovered aboard with the minimum of hassle. The Boss was immediately summoned to the bridge to debrief the Captain on the mission. However, this was pointless as the Boss could only say we had found the target; only the last man over the target (me) could confirm whether or not the target was hit.

Some more sorties were planned for us that day, but because of the deteriorating weather they were cancelled. However, we were able to see already some of the problems of the Air Tasking set-up, as several messages came in for us during the day. We had expected a fully manned Tactical Air Operations Centre to be available aboard *Hermes*, which ship was supposed to bear the brunt of Offensive Support (Ground Attack) operations. As well as the lack of Intelligence/ Ground Liaison Officer facilities already mentioned, we were taken aback to discover that the ship's Operations Officer was our only available link in the tasking chain. This merely meant that he passed on Air Task Messages to us as they came in, after first clearing with the Captain that he wanted them flown. This was only a part-time job for the Operations Officer, as he had many other responsibilities within ship's operations. The Air Task Messages reached the pilots' briefing room in a variety of ways. Usually they were phoned through, to be taken down on the back of a fag packet by anyone who happened to be standing near. Naturally enough this often led to mistakes; however, attempts to query possible errors were almost invariably ineffective. As far as Ship's Ops were concerned an Air Task Message was an Air Task Message, and you just went out and flew it, even if it was patently obvious that the task was nonsense. No intelligence back-up was given with any Air Task Message. Occasionally we received the luxury of an Air Task Message signal, and straight away we realised that we had another problem to deal with. In many cases we were sent *Air Requests* by Ship's Ops, in their mistaken belief that they were Air Tasks. *Soon we discovered that the Navy didn't know the difference between an Air Request and an Air Task.*[9] This of course generated endless confusion for us as an Air Request was not necessarily going to be turned into an Air Task, causing us much wasted planning, to be cancelled only at the last minute. Eventually, we were being tasked by three separate agencies: the Admiral's Staff, the Ship's Staff and by Forces Ashore. Some Air

Task Messages were sent in error to CTG 317.8 (the Amphibious Landing Group), and hence never reached us. In our innocence at this stage, we did not appreciate how on-board generated missions were to be tasked. We were soon to find out that these were to be even more shambolic, the RN hierarchy ordering us into the air at the drop of a hat without a shred of explanation or any sort of intelligence briefing.

Later in the day John Rochfort turned up with the last of our U/S aircraft from the *Atlantic Conveyor*. It was good to see him aboard as we were going to need his caustic sense of humour in the next few days. That night we all briefed among ourselves for the planned operations of the next day, the pilots involved in the first wave having already been nominated. The amphibious landings were due to commence before dawn and we were to be on standby the whole day for Close Air Support tasking in support of the landing troops. I was not looking forward to this one little bit, as we would have to operate well within our own SAM engagement zone, the plan being to put Rapier batteries ashore as soon as possible. I anticipated a lot of mistakes with such a rapidly set-up system, and I had no faith in the briefed procedures to penetrate our own defences in the landing area. Our missions would be directed by FACs, and we were in no doubt among ourselves that this would also turn into a shambles for all the usual reasons that we had experienced in countless peacetime FAC exercises (see Appendix 7 – Forward Air Control). We didn't mind failing to hit a few enemy targets, but the thought of an 'Own Goal' on our troops filled us with apprehension. I was told that I would be leading Mark on the first push at dawn. After a few 'horse's necks' in the bar that night I was ready for an early crash out. I lay awake for a while trying to think of how it would be after the confusion of the landings – the loss of Garth was going to make a big hole in their FAC capability. As far as I was concerned, he was the only FAC we could have trusted. We had already met the RN chief Air Liaison Officer during our voyage south. This character had been given this vital job on the strength of his having just completed the basic training course for FACs at RAF Brawdy. This was the limit of his experience of FAC work. Garth excepted, there was any number of extremely experienced RAF and Army Primary FACs who could have been sent in place of this character. This was just one more example of the RN providing 'Jobs for the Boys' – however inexperienced – in order to keep the other services away from the action.

That night as I lay awake in my camp bed the large Amphibious Landing Group of warships and troop transports was already moving towards the islands in the dark, mysterious seas far to the west of us. This was the beginning of the great adventure: the first large-scale amphibious landing carried out by British forces since Suez. During the day there had been a quiet air of determination and confidence as people went about their tasks, the ship literally humming in anticipation of guaranteed action in the morning. In addition to my misgivings about the prospect of flying Close Air Support sorties, we had no doubts that the landings would be certain to goad the Argy Air Forces into furious retaliation. Doubtless, some of the heat would be coming our way, and the non-flyers on *Hermes* would receive their first real taste of the action. I had severe doubts about the vulnerability of the troop transports and warships in the confined waters inshore. To me, the terrain surrounding the landing area seemed tailor-made for sneak air attacks, using the cover of the hills to approach unseen. It was certain that the Sea Harriers would have their work cut out to provide protection, and I wondered idly if our GR3s might be quickly re-roled to give them some assistance. This would be a relatively simple evolution all round: for daylight Combat Air Patrol work one GR3 could work with one Sea Harrier. This would have meant six extra Air Defence aircraft available to the hard-pressed Task Force. In the guaranteed aerial bunfight due to start at daybreak, this seemed an eminently sensible back-up plan. However, it was not to be. There was not even so much as a mention of the possibility when we stood down at the end of day flying on 20 May.

CHAPTER SIX

Invasion – 21 May

Some three hours before dawn Mark and I were busy planning the first mission of the day. The Air Task Message gave details of an Argy dispersed helicopter Landing Zone about 10 miles west of Stanley in the high ground. Expecting further attacks on the Port Stanley Airfield area at any time, the enemy had wisely decided to deploy their helicopters out into the hills. An exact location was given in the rough terrain just below Mt Kent, a name that meant absolutely nothing to us at this stage. I planned a run in from an Initial Point on the coast to the north-east, near MacBride Head, so that the early morning sun (if there was any) would be over my left shoulder as we approached the target. Target acquisition was going to be a major problem with such an early Time on Target – we were due to launch about half an hour before our sunrise and it would be barely light when we reached the target some distance to the west. We went through all the details of the sortie carefully, and I briefed various options for the attack, bearing in mind that this was going to be a particularly high-value target. (Like us, the enemy was desperately short of troop-carrying helicopters.) We knew that there was a radar-laid gun position not far to the east, but I calculated that it was probably out of range, and that therefore we could afford to make more than one attack in the target area. We knew that parked helicopters – even uncamouflaged ones – were notoriously difficult to see even in daylight; they were also likely to be well spaced-out so that we couldn't hit more than one per attack, hence we might need more than one attacking pass to achieve success. Having completed planning and briefing, Ship's Ops changed the task. We were now to fly to the area of the landings and call *Fearless* for possible Close Air Support tasks in support of the landing. Our planned task was scrubbed completely, and there was no mention of what we were to do if *Fearless* had no task for us. Having seen this kind of thing all too often in exercises at home, I told Mark to hang on to his maps – I planned to have a go at the helicopters anyway if there was no other trade for us. We then went

56

through another complete sequence of planning and briefing for the new task. As I suspected, just one minute before we walked out to fly, Ops came through and said that we could have a go at the helicopters if there was no other task for us!

Out on deck it was as dark as a witch's armpit. The ship was completely blacked out, and it was impossible to see more than a few feet. With the unyielding sharp edges of a score of Harriers lashed down at all angles, the deck was hazardous enough in daylight; by night it presented a lethal version of blind-man's buff. From the exit door in the island I took a rough bearing on the position of my aircraft, which was parked up near the bow. Stumbling over aircraft tie-down strops and feeling my way from wingtip to wingtip, I eventually found my aircraft and shivering ground crew. After a careful walk-round check I climbed in and began the brief routine of the pre-start check. The canopy was smeared with salt deposits and a lot of salt water had got into the cockpit, making it particularly difficult to set up some items of equipment such as the IFF (Identification, Friend or Foe) – of vital importance on every sortie. After a lot of fumbling with a torch I hoped I had managed to get the correct code into the IFF box (as usual, some of the integral lights were U/S, making it almost impossible to read the code). The start signal was given and my aircraft came to life as the engine wound up to idle rpm. The ship was rolling smoothly in a moderate swell, and by now my eyes had adapted sufficiently to make out the movement of the waves passing uncomfortably close beneath the cockpit (the nose of my aircraft was over the side of the ship). The signal to taxy was given after a brief radio check with Mark, who was parked further aft.

This was it – my first attempt at taxying in reverse – and I almost made a complete cock of it. I managed to back out of my slot on to the centreline of the deck, but now I was faced with a backwards run almost the full length of the deck between the encroaching tails of the other parked aircraft, dimly visible to me in the gloom on either side. Taxying backwards was a completely unnatural exercise. Like riding a bike back-to-front, it was easy once you knew how, but the first attempt was a major problem in self-confidence. In reverse, the Harrier nosewheel steering system gives an initial false impression that you are using the correct rudder, when in fact you aren't. Every time I started to move back I ended up going in the wrong direction and was forced to come to a juddering halt with my aircraft at an angle across the deck. There was precious little room for manoeuvre on either side, and with rising panic I began to fear that I would never be able to get back to the take-off point. The marshaller became increasingly frustrated. I tried again and again to remember the briefed technique but it was no use;

every time it went wrong and I had to stop after only a few feet. By now my hands were gripping the controls fiercely and I was in a frenzy of anger and frustration at my incompetence. At last, someone in Flyco recognised my problem and came up with some calm words of advice on the technique: 'Push the rudder in the direction you want the *tail* to go.'

That was the trick! Why didn't someone tell me that before? At last I got the hang of it and brought my aircraft to a stop in the correct launch position, my legs shaking almost uncontrollably from the tension and anticipation. What a start to the sortie! I forced myself to calm down and think clearly; this was going to be my first night launch and there was no room for any more errors. The launch was uneventful and with Nav lights on DIM setting we climbed away in improving weather to the west, the sky already showing signs of lightening behind us.

From 25,000 feet the northern coastline of East Falkland stretched clear in front of us. At that height dawn was breaking directly behind us, although the land was still a mass of shadows. It would be at least another half-hour before the sunlight reached ground level. On the radio I was in good contact with *Fearless* and – to my delight – they had no target for us at that time.

'Thanks very much – we've got an alternate target,' I replied, changing frequency quickly before he changed his mind. As we dived towards the coastline we passed from full daylight into twilight again and I checked Mark in on the new frequency.

'Green, check in,' I said.

'Green Two.'

'Loud and clear.'

That was it: the game was ON.

By the time we passed the Initial Point at Low Level, the ground was indistinct, and we kept our height up for the first few miles of the run until we became accustomed to the conditions. With mounting excitement, we approached the target area. The low conical shape of Mt Kent rose in front of us and I concentrated hard on the briefed target area, just below and to the left of the hill. We had eased up a little to give a better chance of seeing targets, but despite this we were almost abeam the position before I recognised what we were looking for in the half-light of dawn. Well spaced-out in the rough tussock grass were several large helicopters. I recognised a Chinook as the biggest, plus a couple of Pumas and also a Huey a little way further to the west. The Huey already had its rotors turning, having just landed – there was no time to lose if we were going to clean this little lot up.

We had seen them far too late for a first-pass attack. In order to find them again easily in the gloomy conditions, I decided to set up a left-hand racetrack pattern around the back of Mt Kent, keeping as low as possible to stay out of sight of any troops in the target area. A curt few words on the radio established that Mark had also seen the targets. After one run around the mountain, I was lined up with the target area again, running in to attack the Chinook with cluster bombs. In the poor light I was suckered into flying too low and the voice in my brain spoke too late: 'Too low you fool! You'll never hit them from this height!'

Too late. I pickled and turned hard left around the mountain again. Looking back over my shoulder, I saw the whole pattern of bomblets exploding just beyond the Chinook. Now it was going to be guns only for both of us. Mark's attack had also failed, his cluster bombs hung up uselessly on the pylons because of an electrical fault. Now I was getting a bit annoyed: I was determined to strafe the lot of them and on the next pass I rolled out on the juicy target of the Chinook. We were both flying pretty low and had to pop up a couple of hundred feet just before firing in order to avoid flying into the ground during the firing pass (see Appendix 6 – Strafing Techniques).

My first guns pass was no good in the poor light, leaving me well pissed off. Fortunately Mark was still in the ball game and smashed the Chinook on his first guns pass. It was still burning as I attacked again. This time everything went right and my long burst left a Puma in flames. Firing on inflammable targets in the poor light was extremely spectacular, each individual round exploding in a brilliant white flash of light at the rate of 40 per second until the target itself exploded violently in a ball of orange flame. On the next pass Mark also hit a Puma, maybe the same one that I had hit. By now we were running out of targets except for the Huey, which I had picked up very late in each firing pass on the other targets. So far, no one had fired at us that I had seen: however, I was getting pretty constant Radar Warning Receiver indications from behind me during each turn in to the target: the evil rattlesnake chatter of a fire control radar. I was pretty sure they were out of range, so I tried to ignore it and pressed on with the attacks. Now I was after the Huey, the last undamaged target. Unfortunately, its camouflage was the best of all, it being impossible to pick out until very late in the attack, so I had to guesstimate an initial aiming point each time. Infuriatingly, I had already commenced firing when I would pick up the movement of the rotor blades just to one side – too late to correct my aim. Apart from my initial call, the action so far had taken place in complete radio silence. However, after my second or third attempt to get the Huey there was a very snappy call from Mark: 'Green Two's taken a hit!'

I called him to turn away to the north and ran out after him to see what the damage was. I was frustrated at having to leave the Huey.

However, much later I discovered that I had managed to get some hits on it, causing damage to the rotor blades.

In the climb to height heading east, I formated closely on Mark to check him for damage. All I could see was one small hole in the bottom of the fuselage through which some fuel was leaking. Mark confirmed that he was losing fuel from one side, but I was confident that he had enough to get home provided we didn't mess about. I reminded him to jettison his hung-up cluster bombs to save on fuel consumption. At 15,000 feet the light was still poor, and I was much impressed by the pyrotechnic spectacle as the cluster bomb bomblets deployed, many of them detonating from mutual collisions. Like a clip from *Star Wars*, each detonation sent a laser-straight bolt of lightning thousands of feet down towards the sea. After a fairly short return flight (the Task Group had moved closer inshore to support the landings), Mark landed on with about 500 lb of fuel remaining. After landing, I hurried over to see him and apologised for making so many passes on the target, explaining the problem of seeing the Huey.

'Oh, that's OK,' said Mark. 'Didn't you see them shooting at us?'

'What do you mean?' I asked.

'Those troops by the Pumas – they were firing at us on most of the attacks.'

'Look old sport, do me a favour and tell me about that sort of thing next time, will you!'

We had a close look at the damage. There was a small-arms round through a wing fuel tank, plus the hole I had seen. The engineers were not too bothered, and assured me that they could fix it within a couple of hours. With mixed feelings I then reported to the Captain, who had the Admiral standing behind him with a superior smirk on his face. As expected, the Captain ranted on a bit about making too many passes over the target: 'Well done, but never forget – only *one* pass in future, OK?'

The Admiral – the Great Submariner – added his twopenneth with a sneer, never having flown an aeroplane in his life: 'I think you've learnt a very cheap lesson.'

These two appeared to be living in a dream world. It was all very well for them to moralise from the air-conditioned comfort of the bridge: with only one pass we wouldn't have hit anything at all. The Argies would then have been left with some useful helicopter lift capability to counter the seaborne landings that were in progress. I could excuse the Admiral's ignorance, but I was taken aback at an ex-Buccaneer pilot's lack of appreciation of the brutal realities of Armed Recce: all Ground Attack against defended targets was a lottery, and only the pilot on the spot could decide how many passes were necessary, depending on the value of the target and the difficulty of destroying it.[10]

Down in the pilots' briefing room I found the Boss and Bob in deep gloom. There had been a terrific balls-up on the last launch, which was to have been the Boss leading Jeff Glover on Jeff's first operational mission over the islands. Bob told me the story.

'Jeff's gone on his own,' he said tersely.

'What do you mean?' was my bewildered reply.

We had an unwritten agreement among the Flight Commanders that we would not allow anyone to go alone on any operation yet – certainly not our most junior pilot, as Jeff was. The Boss's wheels wouldn't retract after launch, so he had to dump fuel and land back on. At the same time, he had told Jeff to carry on alone with the mission – Close Air Support in the landing area. I was absolutely furious about this: to let Jeff go on his own on such a difficult mission was unforgiveable. The Boss was wandering about looking sick and I sat back with foreboding to await the outcome. Unable to sit still, I went up to Flyco to be told that he had been airborne for over an hour already and there was no contact with him on radio. With a sinking heart, I realised that he wasn't coming back.

I hung around in Flyco for a while to await further messages. Within half an hour there was a signal from the Commander Amphibious Warfare (COMAW) aboard *Fearless* in which he complained about a Harrier mission – Jeff Glover's – which had used the wrong IFF procedures on entering the Amphibious Operations Area, thereby nearly getting himself shot down. This was bad. Straight away I feared the worst – that Jeff had been shot down by our own forces. By now the ship had signalled *Fearless*, telling them that Jeff was overdue. The reply was quick: they claimed to have heard him briefly on the radio, but had then lost track of him. There was nothing for it but to get on with the rest of the day's flying and try to forget about him. In war you can't afford the luxury of worrying about the ones who don't come back – for whatever reason. Back in the pilots' briefing room there were many grim faces. I didn't speak to the Boss, who was looking devastated. The rest of the day's tasking was a shambles. Communications with *Fearless* were hopeless and only two more missions were flown. Pete Harris and John Rochfort were tasked to fly around in the area to the east of the landing area and 'see what they could find'. They went off just after losing Jeff, and Pete was looking rather anxious. After landing he told me that they had flown up and down right at ground level, expecting heavy flak at any moment. Naturally enough, with the necessary concentration on low flying they saw nothing on the ground. On landing, John made a slight error of judgement during touchdown on the difficult No. 5 spot (the deck was narrowest at this point). He drifted left and bounced sideways into the catwalk, his wing hanging over the ship's side. Things looked tense for a moment but the Flight Deck crew reacted splendidly, a dozen of them jumping on the inboard wing while a veritable army of beefy matelots appeared from nowhere to manhandle the 8-ton jet back to safety. This was an occupational hazard of landing towards the stern, and a Sea Harrier pilot was to repeat the performance later. Several months after the war I visited RNAS Yeovilton Air Museum and I was disgusted – although not surprised – to see that the only photo of RAF GR3 Harrier activity during Operation *Corporate* was one of John's aircraft lying in the catwalk. For me, this was to sum up clearly the Navy's contemptuous and childish dismissal of the contribution made by the RAF's GR3 Harriers.

Very late in the day Tony Harper and I carried out an Armed Recce mission to Dunnose Head airstrip, a grass airfield on West Falkland. This was a bit of a milk run, and after the tension of the morning it was pleasant to cruise around the relatively peaceful skies of West Falkland. This was the first of a series of tasks to search for enemy transport aircraft, which were suspected of using many of the small grass airfields to bring supplies and troops into the more isolated settlements. Already our radar picket ships had been seeing a lot of this kind of activity at night over the islands, but so far no one had been able to intercept them or catch them on the ground. Much later we learnt the full story of the heroic exploits of the Argy transport aircraft crews, who managed to fly to and from the islands almost every night, bringing in ammunition and supplies and flying out casualties. Operating from inadequate airstrips and in appalling weather conditions, they managed to slip past our much-vaunted Air Defence ships and Sea Harrier patrols time and time again, without any sophisticated night flying aids or instrument approach equipment. They knew full well that they would be hamburger meat if caught by a SAM or a Sea Harrier on Combat Air Patrol (there was zero chance of successful escape from a Herc shot down in Low Level flight). In spite of this they kept on coming back right up to the last night of the war. At least we fighter-bomber pilots had ejection seats and cannon armament, plus our speed and manoeuvrability. The Argy transport crews didn't even carry parachutes: they had nothing but their courage and flying skill, and I admired their exploits without reservation.

While our operations had been beset by problems, the Navy was having a grim time in the Falkland Sound area. Waves of Argy aircraft had swept in to attack the ships protecting the landing troops. By nightfall no fewer than five RN ships were sinking or damaged, the

Argy pilots having pressed home their attacks with almost suicidal courage. Much has been made of their so-called 'poor tactics' in attacking too low to allow their bombs to explode. In my view this is typical of the worst kind of 'armchair criticism', made with 20/20 hindsight by people who have never been involved in a shooting war and have even less idea of the practical problems of sticking a bomb in a ship (see Appendix 4 – Bombing Techniques). Two major factors are overriding here. First of all, it is *much easier* to hit any target with a bomb if you fly very low and get as close as possible before weapon release: 'scraping the bomb off on the target' was an RAF expression for the technique. Additionally, when the adrenalin flows at maximum rate the natural tendency of any attack pilot is to get lower. Obviously, a low-delivery bomb is unlikely to explode – if it does then the attacking aircraft is as much at risk as the target. However, a salvo of unexploded half-ton steel bombs travelling at 800 feet per second possess the impact energy of an express train, and can do tremendous damage to any target they hit. The RN was discovering this, the Argy unexploded bombs tumbling end over end like gigantic Dum-Dum bullets as they smashed through compartments, cutting vital fuel lines, weapon control system wiring and leaving an Unexploded Bomb hazard for the hard-pressed Bomb Disposal teams to deal with. Any fighter-bomber pilot is fully aware of this and – after fighting his way to the target through enemy fighter Combat Air Patrols, flak and SAM defences – he will have an almost irresistible urge to HIT the target, whether or not the bombs explode. If he misses – and both sides managed to miss quite large ships – then the question of whether his bombs explode or not is almost academic. All his efforts have been wasted, and he might as well have stayed on the ground. Finally, in the quite likely event that a retarded bomb fails to retard and falls 'slick', then there is still a chance of a hit if the pilot is making a point-blank attack. In the desperate confusion of fire surrounding the landing area, only a small proportion of the most experienced and cool pilots could be relied upon to achieve the exact bomb-release parameters necessary to achieve both a hit *and* successful detonation. When this was achieved, the reason was more often luck than skill. Killing people from the air was never a very precise business.

On this day we also instituted the procedures for Deck Alert for our GR3s. Aircraft and pilots were kept at various states of readiness to be launched quickly in support of our forces. The two main states were: Alert 20, in which the pilots could sit around fully kitted-up in the pilots' briefing room; and Alert 5, in which we had to be strapped-in on deck. On Alert 5 you could be sitting in the cockpit for three hours at a stretch. After the first couple of hours the cold would really get to you through all the layers of flying clothing. Still, it was better than doing it at night. Naturally, the Navy didn't understand the first thing about the requirements of short-notice Offensive Support tasking – they thought that a 'Launch the GR3s' order from Flyco was all that was necessary. During land-based operations we operated a fairly sophisticated telebrief system, in which all aircraft on ground alert were kept permanently in contact with Ops, the Ground Liaison Officer and Intelligence. Between them, they gave regular situation updates and passed on details of the Air Task Message, if necessary sending out a runner with target maps. (Your chances of hitting any target without a 1:50,000 map were pretty slim.) In addition, without a map you had to fly higher to pick out a target described by an FAC, with a much higher chance of missing on the first pass anyway, necessitating an extremely hazardous second pass. (The Navy didn't seem to understand this: as far as they were concerned, finding and attacking heavily defended targets on land was no more difficult than scrambling to intercept incoming air attacks under radar control.) Expecting zero assistance from Flyco, we set up our own system whereby our Duty Commander Flying (DCF) would get as many details of the incoming task as possible, plot targets and Initial Point runs on a map very quickly, and then rush up on deck to brief the crews before start up. This irritated Flyco and meant some slight delays on launch, but we didn't care about that. (There were already so many delays in the ramshackle tasking system that a couple of extra minutes on deck weren't going to make any difference.) That night we had a hot debrief on the day's flying. The Boss gave us the very necessary pep talk we had heard several times en route south: 'Whatever happens – be *professional* in all things to do with our flying. We know that the Navy don't understand the problem and don't want to listen, but whatever happens don't let it get to you. I know it's hard, but we've got to keep cool and do our best in spite of all the cockups.'

We were then told about the ongoing cockup with IFF. As well as the Rapier crews' problems with friendly IFF responses (which prevented some engagements), we heard for the first time that if both aircraft in a formation used IFF, the response would be corrupted and you would be identified as hostile by our SAM operators. What a time to find this out!

After our debrief we heard that the first task in the morning was to be a four-ship attack on Goose Green. I was to lead, with Bob, Pete Harris and John Rochfort in the formation. The four of us looked at each other without saying anything for a few moments. Goose Green was where Nick Taylor had been shot down by the 35-mm Oerlikon flak battery on 4 May. He had been hit by very accurate radar-laid fire before he even reached the target, crashing on the beach with no chance to eject. This mission was going to need a lot of careful planning, and we set to work straight away (see Appendix 2 – Single-seat Low Flying). We dug out the existing photos of the area, all of which were from high level. The Navy confirmed that it was a flak-trap, and not a healthy place to hang around (Ted Ball had been comprehensively shot at during a High Level overflight of the area). Our Air Task Message called for an attack on two locations about 2 km apart: one of these was a supply dump and communications centre on the airfield itself and the other was a suspected military encampment just to the south. I spread out the 1:50,000 map of the area on the floor in our minuscule planning office.

The first thing we needed was a decent Initial Point and pre-IP. There was precious little terrain cover from any direction, and I decided to approach from the east where there appeared to be more undulating ground. I knew also that the attack on 4 May had not come from this direction. As an Initial Point I picked a corner of Laguna Isla, a largish lake about 15 nm from the target. As a pre-IP I chose Colorado Pond, a lake in a prominent gap in the main east-west mountain chain, just below Mt Wickham. I was careful to avoid planning over high ground in case we encountered low cloud. Starting from the northern tip of East Falkland, we would run some 30 nm across the middle of the island to the pre-IP, the only highish ground being the 200-feet high Malo hills, about halfway across. The mountain range would shield us from detection by the Goose Green radars until the last couple of minutes; in addition, I had already decided to fly all the way to the islands at Low Level, to minimise the chance of being picked up by the radars at Port Stanley Airfield. (We were already having severe doubts about our easily tracked High Level departures from the Task Group. At this time *Hermes* was still close enough to the islands for us to fly a LO-HI profile – very soon we were to lose this option altogether.) It was also obvious to me that we would all have to attack together: I had no intention of using the tactically suspect 'Pairs Trail' formation, in which aircraft attacked targets about 3–4 nm in trail behind each other. Once we had woken up the flak crews all hell was going to break out and any stragglers would get blown away. This was going to be a Simultaneous Attack in old-fashioned Battle 4 formation all the way: I had a good team and I was confident they would cope with it.

CHAPTER SEVEN

Four-ship Attack on Goose Green

Saturday, 22 May 1982

Sunrise was bright and clear over the Task Group. In the Met briefing we heard that there were no major problems over the islands, except for possible low stratus over high ground. On deck the FINRAE team was by now working at a pretty high standard, and all of us received what we thought was a good alignment from the kit. At this stage I was under the impression that FINRAE was giving us at least a good heading alignment – essential for accurate map-and-stopwatch navigation at extreme Low Level. Up to now there had been no inkling of any problems in this area; however, later in the sortie I was to discover that my Head up Display heading was over 3 degrees in error.

We got airborne in good order armed with cluster bombs, which we all agreed gave us the best probability of success during very Low Level attacks. The four of us settled down in a smart-looking formation, flying at about 1,000 feet above the steel-grey sea. Flying lower at this stage would merely result in too much salt deposit on the windscreen. I listened intently to the confusion of bleeps and squeaks on my Radar Warning Receiver as the radars of the Task Group faded below the horizon behind us. Later on, as we recognised the first 'chirp' of the enemy's long-range search radars, we descended until the four of us were skimming the wave tops. After about thirty minutes we saw the islands, an ominous dark shadow on the horizon slightly to port. As we closed with the land, a nagging doubt about my compass entered my mind. We should have hit the tip of MacBride head smack on, but it was obvious that we were going to be several miles off to the north. A compass error? Unlikely, I thought. Most probably the initial ship's location had been given wrongly. There was no way of checking this before launch: we relied entirely on the Navy to give us good gen.

66

Coasting in over East Falkland, we ran into a lot of low stratus straight away. As briefed, the formation closed up automatically into Fighting Wing formation and my confidence was boosted somewhat to see the others in my mirror as the lower patches of stratus forced us ever closer to the ground. Uppermost in our minds was the thought of the Malo hills, just a couple of miles ahead. If we could get past this obstacle I was sure we could get through to the target. The gap between the base of the stratus and the ground looked impossibly narrow. However, we all knew from experience that if you could see a gap, you could probably get through it – as long as you kept your nerve and aimed as close to the ground as you dared in the gap. Absolutely the last thing you wanted was to enter cloud near the ground: in that event your only safe way out was to climb until you were in the clear on top. Any attempt to dive down out of the cloud was exceptionally dangerous, and had been the cause of countless fatal crashes over the years. Text-book formation was out of the question and the formation spread laterally as we approached the slot. I held my breath and flashed through the gap, the cloud brushing impossibly close above my cockpit, the desolate terrain close enough to touch. A small boulder would have been a significant obstacle.

Thankfully the way was clear ahead and with a sigh of relief we settled back into formation as the cloud base lifted sufficiently to see the gap in the hills just a few miles ahead. Approaching the gap, once again I was a bit right of track. Obstinately I refused to blame the compass: in the poor weather I hadn't been able to fly at all accurately across the islands. 'That must be the reason for the error. Now, let's concentrate on finding the Initial Point. It should be easy, damn it, you took long enough to choose it last night,' I thought ...

The gap at Colorado pond was clear for us as the adrenalin started to pump stronger in anticipation of the attack. There followed a run of about 15 miles across gently undulating terrain to the Initial Point. We opened out into attack formation, with Pete Harris and J.R. wide on the port side. My track should have ended up right over the lake, however, as the Estimated Time of Arrival came up no large lake was in sight – just a small pond dead ahead.

This was extremely tedious. We were less than three minutes from the target: any second now we would be in their radar cover and surprise would be lost. *Where was the Initial Point?* Looking back over my left shoulder I caught a glimpse of a large expanse of water momentarily visible between two low hills. We were all flying as low as we dared: now I cursed myself for not recognising the compass error for what it was. For the third time I was off track to starboard. Once again I felt an old panic rising. I forced myself to keep calm, my thoughts racing. Should I try to 'eyeball it' back on to the Initial Point run from our present position – with the risk of missing the target altogether; or should I turn the whole formation around and line up again properly, with the very real risk of being picked up by their radar in the turn? The decision was made within a fraction of a second; my thumb was already on the transmit button and I heard myself call the Turnabout manoeuvre. We flew east for about a minute before I called another turn back on to the correct track for the Initial Point, which I now recognised clearly. Everyone seemed to sense what was at stake, and in the turn wingtips were almost scraping the ground as we sought cover in every fold in the almost-flat terrain, desperate to hide ourselves from the enemy's radar cover for as long as possible. We all knew what was waiting for us over the target. As I rolled out before the Initial Point I saw that Pete was almost in position on my left, with John trailing a bit after the hard manoeuvring. Now we had to go for it. I called this on the radio and set off for the target, still shaken and angry with myself for the error. The various checkpoints of the Initial Point run flashed past me and I made the smallest track corrections necessary to keep on the line. Not trusting my Head up Display compass, I was 'feature crawling', a technique I had learned from some old Dutch recce pilots at Volkel. The whole run-in was firmly imprinted on my memory from thorough map study before the flight. There was no need to refer to the map in flight. I knew that it was impossible to use a hand-held map at this height and speed. It was vitally important to be exactly on track in the last few miles of the run, as you came into visual range of the target defences. Any unnecessary 'wing flashing' to regain track was a clear giveaway to the defenders, their radars alarming on the incoming targets which were just breaking out above the radar horizon.[11] With my reactions screwed up to fever pitch, I steeled myself for the final Pop-Up to weapon-release height just a couple of seconds before the target. We flashed across the short stretch of clear water that was Darwin harbour and just beyond the tiny village I picked out the expanse of the airfield, still dotted here and there with the odd wrecked Pucara. We knew that they had been left out by the enemy as decoys, to tempt us into range of the flak batteries.

So far there was no sign of gunfire and my Radar Warning Receiver had been silent throughout the run-in. 'Things are too quiet,' I thought, 'We're going to get clobbered very soon.'

I snapped up to about 100 feet above the terrain, feeling horribly exposed to every gun position on the isthmus. Ignoring the Pucaras, on the north side of the airfield I recognised some camouflaged vehicles by a hedge. This was my target. I pickled and dropped the right wing to look back towards Bob and see the fall of shot of my cluster bombs.

As my head turned somebody switched all the lights on. The sky around me lit up with multiple flashes, a dozen huge flashbulbs going off almost simultaneously. The accompanying crackle told me that this was heavy calibre flak, and they had got my range. 'Jesus Christ – these guys take offence easily!'

I pushed both throttle and stick forward violently and cringed as low as I could in the cockpit, expecting a hit at any second. (Later, Bob told me that he was sure I had been hit; the shell bursts had been all round my aircraft and he couldn't see how I would get away with it.) As I scrambled for cover down in the tussock grass I had another problem: my electrical generator had just dropped off line with a distracting shower of flashing lights and audio warnings in the cockpit. For a moment I was sure I had taken a hit, but after a few seconds the warnings disappeared; the violence of the bunt manoeuvre must have triggered them off. After about a minute of frantic low flying at 550 kt, nothing else had happened and I realised that we were now out of range.

'Red – Check in,' I called.

'Red 2.'

'3.'

'4.'

Rock on! They were still there, and I gave a loud cheer to a startled group of sheep as we flashed past. We were now flying at a more conservative height and roughly back in formation again. In the climb to height up Falkland Sound we checked each other for possible damage. We had been carrying chaff stuffed in the airbrake and both Pete Harris and J.R. had dropped theirs.[12]

Back aboard ship I discovered that Pete Harris's aircraft (No. 14) had failed to drop weapons again. This was the same aircraft that Mark had flown with me yesterday, and the engineers obviously had not cured the fault. Pete Harris was not at all happy about this after what we had been through at Goose Green. Our debrief with the Captain was pretty friendly, and he seemed reasonably satisfied with our efforts. For the rest of that day there was not a lot of activity for us.

In the afternoon Rod Frederikson and his wingman of 800 Naval Air Squadron were flying at medium level over Choiseul Sound, to the east of Goose Green, having completed an uneventful Combat Air Patrol mission. Cleaving the blue waters of the Sound they observed an enemy Armed Coastguard Patrol Boat, the *Rio Iguazu*. Following the distinguished aggressive traditions of the Fleet Air Arm, Rod promptly pitched in with his wingman to strafe it with 30-mm cannon. (Incidentally, Rod had no Head up Display for the attack; however, he still managed to achieve some hits.) The Argy commander of the vessel –

realising that for him the war was over – promptly headed for the shore, where he beached himself and departed hot foot with his crew into the hinterland. This was all well and good and we all had a good laugh when Rod described the action to us after landing. Within twenty-four hours we received an intelligence report that some Argy troops had been seen reoccupying the beached vessel; more ominously, they had been seen to carry some portable SAMs. We promptly drew a red ring around the position of the boat on our situation map to warn off further unwary Harrier pilots and thought no more about it. Some two weeks later, the FLOT (Forward Line Own Troops) had moved some 30 miles to the east, and the area of the beached *Rio Iguazu* was securely under British control. We heard that a party of British Sappers had been sent aboard the boat to see if they could patch it up. They were to receive a big surprise, not from the enemy but from our own buddies from *Invincible*. We heard that some *Invincible* pilots were given clearance to attack the grounded boat, much to the disgust of the Sappers on board. Apparently those on *Invincible* were unaware that the *Rio Iguazu* had already been put out of action. This was just another example of the poor intelligence liaison between the two carriers.

Fortunately no one had been hurt. The pilots were ribbed a bit about this incident but this was a bit unfair in my view, as they were the unfortunate victims of yet another example of Naval incompetence in intelligence management. (*Invincible* pilots never saw a FLOT during the whole campaign.)

Two of our formations sat on deck for hours of Alert 5 without being scrambled, and I was amazed to see that later in the day the Boss and Tony Harper were launched to carry out Ship Affiliation with HMS *Exeter*. Tony's aircraft went U/S anyway and he came back early. Almost at dusk, the Boss and Tony launched again for an Armed Recce mission, during which they found nothing of interest. Their landing back on in the dark was pretty interesting. The ship had a system of deck floodlamps, which shone down below the level of the pilot's eyes in the hover; these were switched on just before landing. That part was not too difficult, once you had established a steady hover alongside the ship. But decelerating to the hover over the dark and featureless sea took a lot of concentration with just a few faint points of light from the ship in your peripheral vision. This same night there was to be a sobering demonstration of just how dangerous night flying from a ship could be.

CHAPTER EIGHT

Sea Harrier Night Raid

L ater in the afternoon the Captain turned up in the pilots' briefing room – an almost unheard-of event. He wanted an attack on the Port Stanley Airfield runway straight away, and the Sea Harrier pilots were going to get the job. Somewhere, he had obtained intelligence information that the Argies intended to fly some fighter-bombers into Port Stanley Airfield, using it as a forward base to attack the Task Group. Using 1,000-lb free-fall bombs, the idea was for the Navy to use their much-vaunted toss bombing attack profile, using an offset[13] on the coast to the east of the airfield. It took a long time to get the four aircraft bombed-up, and it was obviously going to be dark before they could get airborne. Night attack without Night Vision Goggles was no joke in any single-seat aircraft, and the Navy only had three pilots available at that moment who were both experienced and night current. They needed a fourth man and, true to form, Gordy Batt volunteered. Gordy was a super character who had been very helpful to us in our uncomfortable initiation into Navy-style aviation. An ebullient, barrel-shaped West Countryman, his outspoken approach and splendid sense of humour set him apart. He was an experienced F4 carrier aviator, but he had never done a night carrier launch in a Sea Harrier. He was one of the guys that the RN Squadron Commander had wanted to get night qualified on the journey south . . .

The Boss and I were sitting in the pilots' briefing room while the Captain was briefing the guys on the raid: he was obviously a bit wound up about the threat, and he wanted as much damage to the runway as possible. As an aside to the Boss, I rashly offered to go along on someone's wing for the attack, to add a few extra bombs to the salvo. I was fairly confident that my night formation was up to it. The Boss thanked me for the offer but vetoed the idea. Before we stacked I ran into John 'Leems' Leeming. Originally a Lightning pilot, he and

I had flown together for a while in Belize a couple of years before. Leems had been looking pretty pleased with himself all day, and this was my first chance to ask him what was up.

'Yesterday I gunned a Skyhawk,' he said, with a fierce grin.

'Jammy fucker! What happened?' (I still hadn't caught up with who had shot down what the previous day.)

> Yesterday on Combat Air Patrol I had a good 'growl' from this Skyhawk but couldn't get the damn missile to go. In the Lightning, if the missile growled it would fire, but the switchery's different in this shit heap: stupid really. Anyway, I was determined to get him so I switched to GUNS and hosed on into point blank range; I just held the trigger and stirred the stick and rudders around until he blew up around me – I wasn't really aiming properly, there wasn't much point at that range.

(Sadly, Leems did not long survive the war, being killed in a horrific mid-air smash some six months later. I was Duty Commander Flying when it happened.)

Green with envy, I retired for a couple of horse's necks in the bar with the guys before the Navy launched. There was nothing more for us to do that day and there was some noisy banter about the Goose Green attack that morning. I had to take a bit of stick about the failure to find the Initial Point (IP) first time, and my excuses about the compass fell on deaf ears – quite rightly too. I couldn't complain: we had hit the target and survived. I crashed out early and slept soundly, much to my surprise.

After returning from the Armed Recce mission the Boss stayed up a bit longer to talk to Wings about something or other, also to watch the night launch of the Port Stanley Airfield bombers. Gordy was the second to launch and the poor bastard went in like a dart not far off the bow. There was a huge explosion, and then silence. The launch was continued, and a rather shaken formation joined up for a successful attack on Port Stanley Airfield. (Successful in that all three aircraft released their weapons: next day there was no evidence of any bomb impact on the runway.) Only now did we learn that – in spite of the peacetime boasts of the Sea Harrier operators – their weapon system at that time was not capable of hitting a runway 4,000 feet long and 90 feet wide from a toss-bombing attack.

So died Gordy. At breakfast next day we heard the news from the Boss. In addition, a few more rumours had come in about Jeff. We had already heard the Argy claim to have picked up a couple of dead pilots, one of whom they said was a Harrier pilot. That seemed to be it for Jeff. Then we heard another rumour – that he had been shot down by a Pucara. None of us believed this – it seemed too unlikely.

The flying programme for us on 23 May would consist mainly of 'milk runs' to West Falkland. The general opinion was that there were few defences on West Falkland, except for the Port Howard area, which we had been able to avoid thus far. Hence, the introduction of a 'Counter Air' programme to attack airfields promised a bit of relaxed 'gardening' for a while.

CHAPTER NINE

The Counter Air Programme

And so it almost turned out. The first mission was a four-ship, comprising Pete Harris, Mark, the Boss and Tony Harper, who were to attack Dunnose Head airstrip. (Tony and I had recced this strip on 21 May and found no evidence of recent air activity.) Pete briefed the guys carefully about the need to avoid hitting the tiny settlement nearby and they all set off in good order after a textbook launch. The attack went as planned except for Mark, who somehow managed to get the wrong aiming point. His stick of bombs went right across the edge of the settlement, demolishing their food store; in addition, a Mr Tim Miller was blinded in one eye by a bomb splinter. (Fortunately, one of Mark's bombs failed to explode.) The locals abandoned the settlement after this and fled to the hills in fear of further attacks. Much later, when the war was over, a group of 1(F) Squadron pilots visited the settlement to apologise for the error and assist in rebuilding the food store. Mr Miller was philosophical about his injury and did not bear any hard feelings. He realised that mistakes would happen in war. However, the locals did ask why the hell they hadn't been asked whether or not enemy aircraft were using their strip – they could have given a negative answer straight away, without the need for any bombing. (The strip was really too short and too isolated to be of much use for the defence of the island.) The locals assured us that if anyone had asked they could have put the strip out of action quite effectively using their own farm machinery! Apparently, the SAS had been lurking in that area and had seen enemy aircraft flying 'in the vicinity' – not actually landing at Dunnose Head. None of them had gone into the settlement to talk to the inhabitants. This was a typical example of the poor-quality 'intelligence' upon which the RN commanders on *Hermes* based their decisions. The whole affair had a rather more happy ending some months later, when Mark was best man at Tim Miller's wedding back in the UK.

In the afternoon John Rochfort and I received an Air Task Message for an Armed Recce of the Port Howard area, looking for the usual troop and vehicle activity. We studied the 1:50,000 map of the area carefully, and I noted that the tiny port area was contained in an elongated natural harbour screened on the south-eastern side by a narrow ridge some 400 feet high. This ridge lay only about 3 km from the port, and I planned to use it as cover for a 'stand-off' photo of the whole area. The south-east was an ideal direction from which to attack a well-defended target area like this, as the attackers would be shielded from the port area until the last moment as they popped up over the ridge. However, for any chance of success at picking out camouflaged targets, a Target Acquisition photo taken from about 3 km out in the direction of the run-in would be very useful.[14] To take this picture we needed only to stick our noses above the ridge line during a fast run in a north-east direction up the western side of Falkland Sound. Having done this, I calculated that it would still be a reasonable option to return about ten minutes later and fly right through the middle of the target area on the deck, still taking photos, but also looking for any Opportunity Targets to attack. I had no illusions about the likelihood of carrying out successful attacks out of a single high-speed pass over a well-defended target. From my experience of Recce and Armed Recce, I knew only too well the difficulty of picking up camouflaged targets at high speed at really Low Level – your chance of achieving a successful first-pass attack was minimal. For this reason it was not a very sensible Air Task Message, hence my determination to get the maximum possible photo coverage from both aircraft. Such coverage was not a requirement of an Armed Recce mission; indeed, the manoeuvres required for good photography were incompatible with those needed for a successful first-pass attack. As more and more Armed Recce missions were tasked, it became apparent that neither the Navy nor our tasking agencies were aware of this fact. However, the task was for Armed Recce, and so we had to give it a shot.

After an uneventful transit John and I let down at the southern end of Falkland Sound, after warning the LAAWC (Landing Area Air Warfare Controller) of our presence. This was essential to avoid being bounced by the ever-vigilant Sea Harrier Combat Air Patrols, eager to notch up more easy Sidewinder kills. As usual, radio communications were lousy and we kept a wary lookout for our Combat Air Patrols, unsure that our message had got through to them, or to our trigger-happy SAM operators and flak gunners in the Sound area.

We ran up the western side of Falkland Sound at beach level, the tension mounting as we approached the target area, concealed for the moment behind the grey, forbidding ridge line that dominated the coast. The uninviting winter-grey sea carried that vicious short 'chop' so characteristic of the Sound with its fickle winds and strong tides. When I judged we were abeam the target we both popped up just high enough to see and photograph the port area. We saw no flak, and the area looked bare of activity from this distance as we dived back down behind the ridge line. After flying some distance to the north-east, I found my Initial Point and 'stooged' for a while to kill time before the final run through the target area. During the approach run I almost collided with the wreckage of a fighter-bomber sticking up out of the ground, right on track (the camouflage was very good). It was undoubtedly one of the Argy Mirages or Skyhawks shot down during the recent attacks on the fleet assembled in the Sound, just a few miles to the south-east. As we crested the last low ridge before the target area, both of us were screwed up to a fair pitch of tension. This was where Jeff Glover had been blown away, and we still had no clue as to how it had been done. I dropped into the well-rehearsed routine of the recce pilot: look well ahead, identify the target area as soon as possible and start scanning for military activity. You knew what you were looking for: irregular dark shapes of camouflaged vehicles and gunpits, and any subtle difference in the colouring of a hedgerow or building that would betray a carelessly draped camouflage net. (No army in the world had 'cam' nets that exactly matched their surroundings.)

There's got to be something here – where the hell is it? As we raced closer, I forced myself to keep up the steady, economical scan pattern: never back to an area you have already covered; don't move your eyes too fast, or you know damn well you won't see what you're looking for. When was the flak going to start?

Although we were approaching at nearly 800 feet per second and right on the deck, the scenery seemed to move in slow motion, the few tiny houses of the port area standing peacefully in the gentle sunshine, like a picture postcard.

Come on! There's got to be something here; we're nearly in the middle of the target area and you still haven't seen anything. Call yourself a recce pilot? Jackpot – there it is!

Abandoning the steady search ahead, I had dropped my eyes for a moment to the road underneath me, which led into the settlement. I caught a glimpse of two or three olive-drab figures frozen in disbelief, their white faces staring almost eyeball to eyeball as I flashed over them. I had seen something else. In a line along the low stone wall bordering the road many bivouac tents were visible through gaps in carelessly arranged camouflage nets. Within a couple of seconds we were through the houses of the village and racing away down the narrow sea-loch to safety. I was feeling pretty pleased with myself that

I had seen something. John had seen nothing. Resisting a strong temptation, I decided not to return to attack the troops I had found. With luck there would be a many more visible on the film we had both taken. And so it proved. After an uneventful return journey our films showed a large troop encampment camouflaged just half a kilometre from my track. Their tents were cunningly blended into the hedge-rows, and I could see why I had not picked them up visually. More sinister, the photos also showed several well-concealed flak guns around the port area. I was glad we hadn't gone back.

The Boss and Tony Harper were already planning another airfield attack mission as John and I landed, and we were both on it. The mission was to attack Pebble Island airfield and recce Chartres landing strip: there might be enemy aircraft parked on the ground; if not, we were to drop our bombs on the runways. Pebble Island had already been attacked by the SAS a couple of weeks before and the Navy thought it might be in use again. The Boss was to lead, with me as No. 3. Nos 1 and 3 had cluster bombs, 2 and 4 carried 1,000-lb retard bombs. We launched in good weather about an hour before sunset. Mark's gear wouldn't retract, so he had to jettison his bombs and land back on, leaving three of us to continue.

Approaching Pebble Island in glorious evening sunshine, we split as planned for the co-ordinated attack. The sea was picture postcard ultramarine, the strong surface wind dashing each wave crest brilliant white. Over the island the airstrip appeared to be littered with various aircraft, mostly Pucaras, and I aimed my cluster bombs at the middle of the largest group. Off target, I looked back for John to see him lob all three bombs plus his underwing tanks into the sea just beyond the target. Knowing he was flying the notorious No. 14 and thereby expecting another hang-up, he had done his best to get weapons off. Having unsuccessfully tried the stick top button, he immediately stabbed at the jettison buttons on the weapon control panel. Unfor-tunately, in the heat of the moment he hit the wrong button (they were small and fiddly to operate), and everything came off the wings. Losing the tanks was a bit of a blow, as we were running out of spares. I really felt for John – he had done his best in a difficult situation and it had all turned to worms. En route for Chartres airstrip the Boss suffered main radio failure. After a lot of messing about we finally got together on our standby radios for the recce of the strip, which lay in the middle of West Falkland. Absolutely nothing was visible at Chartres, which didn't even look like an airstrip. We climbed and set course for the ship with the sun setting brilliantly behind us. With the radio problem the sortie had not gone too well and the Boss was grumpy during the debrief. Apart from one pair on deck alert for Close

Air Support, this was all the activity we carried out before we stacked for the day.

Later in the evening we received a tremendous piece of news. Wings paid a visit to the pilots' briefing room and told us that he had received a report that the Argies were holding an injured Harrier pilot. This could only be Jeff: no other Harrier pilots had been lost recently and the news was a magnificent boost to our morale. Jeff was an exceptionally popular member of the squadron and the hoot and roar that greeted the news showed just how much we felt for him. Apparently, he was being held somewhere on the islands and our immediate response was, 'The bastards had better look after him'.

That same evening we were told that tomorrow we were to make a Low Level attack on Port Stanley Airfield. This was going to be a difficult target and the first thing we needed was some up-to-date photo coverage of the airfield from Low Level, all previous photos having been taken from 20,000 feet or more. The Navy had carried out their Low Level attack there on 1 May, and no one had taken a close (Low Level) look at it since. As far as we could see there was no point in rushing in with an attack formation without some photos showing the defences and worthwhile target areas. As I was supposed to be the recce specialist, I suggested that first of all I should fly through fast and low on my own and bring back photos for the attackers to study. This plan was agreed by all concerned, and we started planning that night. Wings immediately said that the attack would have to take place first thing in the morning. This was no good, I explained patiently. We had to do the recce first, for which we needed decent photographic light (at least two hours after dawn), and then we had to get the film processed before the attackers could complete their planning. Grudgingly, Wings accepted this plan.

I was amazed that the Navy still had not grasped the basic principles of photographic reconnaissance. Unfortunately, the Captain never did understand the problem. On several occasions he was to send aircraft off on fruitless sorties to take pictures in unsuitable light conditions – despite protests that we were wasting our time. On one occasion he had demanded the usual prints from a dusk sortie on a particular target. Sergeant Bowman rang him up and told him that (as expected) nothing was visible on the negatives. A Senior Naval Officer's reaction to this kind of 'insolence' was predictable: Sergeant Bowman was ordered to keep his opinions to himself and send prints pronto. (This was to enable the Navy hierarchy to make their own deductions, despite the fact that none of them had the faintest idea of how to interpret a recce photo.) Wearily, our long-suffering Photographic Interpreters went through the process of producing prints from useless negatives, which were then delivered to the Captain. Naturally enough they were almost blank, with not the slightest detail visible. This kind of childishness on the part of the Flag caused little harm (except for wasted sorties and waste of the Photographic Interpreters' time) if the photos were going to be taken from 20,000 feet, well clear of all the defences. However, a singleton Low Level recce pass over a heavily defended target was a different ball game altogether, and I knew that I would have to use a few tricks to avoid being blown away.

Unfortunately, like much of our equipment, the Harrier recce pod was poorly designed, with little thought for the likely problems of real warfare. Its specification was to take good photos from a speed of 420 kt at the optimum height of 250 feet agl (above ground level) – perfect for peacetime training. The camera fans were so orientated that coverage was severely limited at heights below this. In addition, at higher speeds the film suffered excessively from blurring. As a result, I couldn't plan to fly too fast, and I was going to have to pop-up to at least a couple of hundred feet right in the middle of the airfield. I had practised the pop-up recce technique many times with the Starfighter in the sparsely populated Ardennes on disused airfield targets (which could be approached at 'realistic' heights).

We picked the brains of the Navy pilots about the best way to approach Port Stanley Airfield. Their attack had been from the north and from the east, approaching over the sea. A sea approach was naturally a good option for them, as they could use their radar to identify positively their correct landfall. This was ruled out for us as there was no way we could guarantee an accurate landfall with map-and-stopwatch navigation. The west looked a better option to me and I planned a route through the hills, approaching the airfield down the Murrell river. This route had the additional advantage of offering plenty of terrain cover from flak and SAMs until I was almost at the airfield.

Straight after the early briefing next morning a message came from Flyco to say that my pre-attack recce mission was cancelled. They wanted the attack carried out asap. The Boss went back to Wings and asked to be allowed to launch the recce mission, emphasising the importance of the photos for subsequent attacks. (We were pretty sure that we would be returning to Port Stanley Airfield.) This was all to no avail. The only concession was that two Sea Harriers were to join in the attack with us as defence-suppression aircraft. They were to run in from the north and carry out a stand-off toss attack with airburst bombs just before our team arrived over the target. I asked the Boss if I could go along on the attack, having had such detailed involvement with the planning, but he turned me down. I had a strong feeling that a lot of luck had been riding with me over the last few days and that it was not due to run out just yet. A lifelong atheist, outwardly I professed scorn at all superstition: however, deep inside I felt that luck was on my side for the time being.

I waited nervously in Flyco while the mission was airborne, having sneaked out on deck to take some 8-mm film of the launch. They all came back with only minor damage after a reasonably successful attack. However, the second pair had got too close to the front pair over the target. They had planned the standard 'peacetime' thirty-second spacing between pairs, but over the target they were at about half that distance. Mark brought back some superb Head up Display film showing Bob's 1,000-lb retard bombs going off just in front of him, causing no real problems for Mark. (I had long suspected that the standard separations were far too tame for use in wartime: to me, the real hazard of loss of the element of surprise for the second aircraft over the target was in no way compensated by the increased separation from the fragmentation envelope.) There had been considerable flak over the target; in Mark's view most of this had been stirred up by the Sea Harriers' attack – as far as he was concerned they would have done better without them. In addition to the cluster bombs the guys managed to get at least one 1,000-lb bomb on the runway, although the crater it made was quite small. Later we discovered that the Navy had selected the wrong bomb fusing, thus considerably reducing their cratering effect. Standing in Flyco to watch the recovery of this formation, I was taken aback to hear that a Sea Harrier would have to land on with an airburst-fused bomb hung up on the centreline pylon – uncomfortably close to the deck on touchdown. The pilot, Neal Thomas, had been unable to jettison it and as he began the slow descent to land just outside Flyco, our small group of spectators ducked slowly below the window frame, in the vain hope that the thin plating would protect us should the bomb detonate on touchdown. After the uneventful landing we all breathed a sigh of relief, self-consciously standing upright again.

By now we had become aware of the severe limitations of the system of ordering up correctly fused bomb loads from the ship's magazines. Basically, the Captain was the first to be shown any incoming Air Task Message, and he immediately gave orders to prepare what he thought was the appropriate bomb load, including details of fusing. Naturally, in true Naval style, this was done without reference to the pilots who were going to deliver the ordnance. On receiving the Air Task Message in the pilots' briefing room some time later, we would make our own decision on the weapon load and send the request via Ship's Ops for transmission to the Bomb Bosun. Finally, our permanent ops officer in the pilots' briefing room would ring the Bomb Bosun direct to confirm exactly what it was we were getting, and try to get him to change it if it wasn't right. We tried to change this ludicrous system with only limited success, but several times we found ourselves attacking targets with unsuitable weapon loads which were wrongly fused. Once again, the Captain's overconfident belief in his own expertise led to a lot of wasted effort on our part.

Later, four of us were to sit out on deck for several hours awaiting Close Air Support tasks from *Fearless*. None were forthcoming and so we did no more flying that day. At least it was a chance to get out into the fresh air for a while, even if it was pretty cold. As aviators we were fortunate to get a glimpse of the sun occasionally. I felt sorry for the rank-and-file matelots who spent day after day below decks. With virtually constant Harrier and helicopter activity, access to the deck was strictly limited. However, as aircrew you could always find an excuse to get out to an aircraft and have a chat with the ground crew. Fortunately, the weather had been holding out quite well for us. Despite doom-laden forecasts back in the UK, the weather had been quite respectable so far. There had been no gales in our time on *Hermes*, and on most days there was usually a bit of sunshine. There was a permanent long, rolling swell, which so far had not hampered our deck operations unduly. With an unmodified nosewheel, unlike the Sea Harriers, we had strict limits on the amount of deck movement we could take for a launch. If you hit the ski-jump with a heavy load as the bow was rising there was a very real danger that the nosewheel would collapse, with disastrous consequences. Even in moderate sea conditions there were hazards to deck movement at any time when the ship was manoeuvring sharply. This was demonstrated dramatically when Mike Broadwater's Sea Harrier simply slid over the side of HMS *Invincible* during a change of the ship's course. Mike ejected successfully but had to be casevac'd (casualty evacuation) home.

We had also learned that South Atlantic weather patterns produced markedly different conditions to those experienced at home. As an example, at first we all expected that a high-pressure system would bring good weather and a low-pressure system would bring the opposite. In practice, the reverse was usually true. The low temperature of the surrounding sea had an overriding influence on the local weather, causing large patches of sea fog to form whenever the skies cleared. In contrast, even quite an active-looking low-pressure system would produce nothing more hazardous than a low cloud base – of little consequence when operating over the sea. Over the islands such low stratus often hindered operations, but there were few low pressure days when we were completely unable to fly. Apart from the unpredictable weather and the enemy defences, the next most important danger came from our own forces ...

CHAPTER TEN

Blue on Blue

There were several occasions on which Harriers came within an ace of being shot down by our own forces. On 28 May, Ian Mortimer (Morts) and Sharky Ward from *Invincible* were on Combat Air Patrol and spotted a formation of three aircraft below them over Falkland Sound. According to Morts, they turned in behind with all switches LIVE and were just about to take a shot when Morts suddenly had a suspicion that they weren't enemy. He shouted at Sharky to lay off. Fortunately no missiles were fired and the Harrier GR3 formation escaped unharmed. (This was almost certainly the Boss, Tony Harper and Pete Harris.)

Another example involved Lieutenant Alan Bolton, a newly qualified Sea Harrier pilot sent straight from the Yeovilton course to the South Atlantic. During a hasty launch from *Invincible* he forgot to input the ship's heading to his Nav kit. In these circumstances the 'kit' automatically assumes that launch heading is north, whereas the ship was actually heading south-east. As a result, instead of following the remainder of his formation to the west, Alan departed to the north-east, only realising his mistake when some distance from the ship. To compound the error, he did not immediately declare a compass unserviceability. Turning through 180 degrees he headed back towards the Task Group, to be locked up as a hostile by *Invincible*'s Sea Dart radars. The Principal Warfare Officer was just about to push the button on Alan when someone realised the error and stopped him. They had only twigged when someone noticed fewer Sea Harriers heading west than there should have been.

That night Bob, Pete Harris and I had a hard-hitting discussion with the Boss about the way we were doing these airfield attacks. We already knew that the retard bomb was not a very effective weapon against a runway – even if the Navy could manage to fuse them correctly. Bob and I were convinced that the Admiral would be sending us back to Port Stanley Airfield time and time again on Low Level raids, until we had got what he considered to be enough bombs on the runway and we were bound to take a lot of hits in the process. We were depressed to hear the Boss's adamant defence of the Party Line. 'We are here to do as we're told, etc., etc.' At least let us try some other form of attack, I suggested. The less-hazardous toss attack – if carried out by enough aircraft – would eventually get some deep-penetration free-fall bombs on the runway. I suggested we could fly on a Sea Harrier's wing for the manoeuvre, making use of its toss-bombing computer and radar to achieve accuracy.

If we took the 100-gallon tanks off the aircraft each of us could carry five bombs, i.e. fifteen bombs per attack with a three-ship formation. At least let us try to make the point to the Navy, I argued. The Boss did not accept my arguments, and I'm afraid tempers were worn thin by the end of the discussion. I was keenly aware that the lives of our pilots hung on our Attack Policy. I turned my back abruptly and walked away to avoid saying something I would regret.

The next morning I was delighted to see that we were to carry out some toss-bombing attacks on Port Stanley Airfield, in company with Sea Harriers! At the briefing the Boss said nothing about my suggestion of the previous night. We launched a six-ship formation to attack as two three-ships at one-minute intervals, each aircraft armed with three bombs. I discovered the Navy's reasons for not giving us five bombs each: firstly, it would take too long to arm the formations (they had had all night to get ready); secondly, *there was no safe storage for our removed 100-gallon tanks on deck*. I would have been prepared to store my tanks in my cabin if asked – they were that easy to handle. For the mission I was tasked to lead four of our aircraft, which were to split into two pairs en route and join two Sea Harriers for the combined raid. The brief was dead simple: there was no need for any radio calls, all we had to do was hang in close formation on the Sea Harrier as he flew the toss manoeuvre, releasing our bombs as his came off the wing. I briefed that after the attack I would climb back overhead the target at a safe height to spot fall of shot for both formations. We were armed with a mixed bag of bombs, some of them direct-fused and some with delayed-action fusing. The delayed-action bombs were a harassment, designed to deter the enemy from bringing any fighter-bombers into Port Stanley Airfield.

The most hazardous part of this mission was the join-up after launch. Having got airborne in good order under a low cloud base, there followed an uncomfortable period of 'milling' as we tried to get the formations joined up correctly. At low speed this was not easy so close to the sea in our heavily loaded aircraft. The constraints of deck operations meant that we were rarely afforded the luxury of a launch in the correct order. Pete Harris and I joined up on Neal Thomas, and the Boss and John Rochfort were led by 'Spag' Morrel. Spag, a swarthy and piratical Lieutenant of 800 Naval Air Squadron, was a veteran of exchange tours both on the Starfighter and on an RAF Harrier squadron. A good flyer and a wag to boot, he was one of the many familiar faces we had been pleased to see on joining ship.

After a high-speed run-in over the sea we pulled up about a mile from Cape Pembroke, the radar offset. We had been flying under a fairly continuous layer of stratus and I hoped that it was not going to be too thick. In spite of our heavy load the manoeuvre was easy to follow and we paused in a steep climb for a few seconds, thumbs tensed over the bomb-release button as we flashed through the cloud layers. My eyes were fixed on the big green bomb just a few feet away on Neal's outer wing pylon. This being my first-ever toss attack, I was a bit wary of all this high-explosive that we were about to lob into the air. As Neal's bombs came off I 'pickled' and could not resist the temptation to hold the wings level for a second to admire the impressive sight of 9,000 lb of bombs in loose formation heading for the sky.

Let's get the hell out of here!

My Radar Warning Receiver had suddenly come to life and I broke hard away to the north at full power, dodging the stratus patches in the preplanned escape manoeuvre. Below cloud at maximum speed I dodged among the peaks to the north of the airfield just out of missile range, at the same time looking for the bomb impacts. I saw a cloud of dust appear at the western end of the field – unfortunately, just beyond the end of the runway. I climbed steeply through the gaps again and turned back over the airfield, where I was delighted to find a large hole in the clouds. I heard Spag's call of 'Bombs gone!' and then all hell broke loose below me. With our bomb impacts their chain had been pulled well and truly. I saw at least three SAMs fired off in various directions.

'Hey Spag – SAM coming your way!' I called, watching the smoke trail running straight and fast across the airfield towards Cape Pembroke. Shortly afterwards this missile fell into the sea about a mile offshore, and I passed this information on to Spag. By now there were lines of tracer and twinkling flashes at random around the area as the defenders vented their fury on the fleeting targets all round them. Soon the rest of the formation was well out of harm's way and I felt pretty safe at altitude above the hornet's nest. In the middle of the mayhem I observed Spag's bomb impacts not far off the side of the runway – not a hit, but close enough to be a big nuisance. The next thing I saw as I banked steeply around was a Roland SAM heading straight for me. I assumed that it was Roland because I had seen a flash of flame from the known Roland launch site near Sapper Hill. Gritting my teeth, I turned beam on and dropped the nose for more speed just in case we had made a horrible miscalculation about the performance capabilities of the French-built missile. With a sigh of relief I saw the smoke trail peak out and fall away several thousand feet below me. I had seen enough and it was time to go home. Feeling pretty pleased with ourselves, we returned aboard in high spirits in the hope that this kind of high-tech 'gardening' was going to become a regular feature. Some hopes. Once again the Master Tacticians of the Flag had other ideas.

The rest of the day was not particularly demanding as far as we were concerned. The Boss and John Rochfort were scrambled for a CAS mission, but did not find any targets. Pete Harris and Mark were sent off to do toss attacks on Port Stanley Airfield with no supporting Sea Harrier, a particularly useless exercise and waste of time for all concerned. We had not the remotest possibility of carrying out accurate toss attacks on our own. The only other option was to perform extremely high-level dive-bombing, staying above the Port Stanley Airfield defences. Unfortunately, none of our weapon instructors was able to calculate the required aiming picture for this exercise! After a quick turnround, Pete Harris went off again on his own to Port Stanley Airfield to repeat the toss-bombing exercise, with no observable results.

With the advent of these less-risky Stand-Off Attacks, it seemed as if life would become a little more comfortable for 1(F) Squadron for a while. However, the Argentine Naval Air Arm was about to make a dramatic first appearance in the area of the Carrier Task Group, re-minding us just how vulnerable we were to a determined Argy air attack.

CHAPTER ELEVEN

Exocet Attack

Late in the afternoon we heard that HMS *Coventry* had been sunk by a formation of Skyhawks. Later on the story filtered through to us. Ted Ball had been on Combat Air Patrol in the area and described seeing the ship capsize. There had been tactical errors by the Navy during the engagement, not least of which had been too much reliance on Sea Dart (which did not work), instead of letting the lurking Sea Harriers deal with the attackers (using the 90 per cent reliable Sidewinders). At the end, *Coventry* herself had got between her escorting Type 22 and the attackers, thus negating interception by Sea Wolf. As *Coventry* sank, the next Argy air attack was already en route to our location. We were the next target.

Just before dusk the *Atlantic Conveyor* was hit by an Exocet in a very short-notice attack. As usual, she had been cruising close by to act as an 'Exocet Sponge', i.e. to attract any missiles aimed at *Hermes*, the most important ship in the Task Group. During alerts – unlike the RAF – the Navy had a rather unnerving habit of broadcasting *exactly* what was going on throughout the action. For us, cowering below decks, it would have been preferable to have heard about it once it was all over. The chilling alert klaxon sounded, along with the broadcast: 'STAND TO, STAND TO! WE ARE PICKING UP SUPER ETENDARD RADAR TRANSMISSIONS AT CLOSE RANGE TO STARBOARD.'

'Oh shit – here we go!' We rushed to don anti-flash hoods and gloves. Several pilots were struggling into immersion suits as a precaution against an involuntary swim. I couldn't be bothered with this: if we took an Exocet hit on the starboard side none of us would be swimming anywhere.

My blood froze with the next Tannoy broadcast: 'NOW HEAR THIS. A MISSILE HAS BEEN LAUNCHED TOWARDS US!'

'Fuck this for a game of soldiers!'

There was a series of loud bangs as the ship launched the huge chaff rockets arrayed on the superstructure. After a brief silence, there were two more loud bangs in close succession. This came from HMS

Invincible, which was passing very close by. Although we didn't recognise it at the time, the sound we heard was a double Sea Dart launch from her bow launcher – presumably carried out in order to impress the Admiral, as the Super Etendards must have been well on their way home over the horizon. After a few seconds of silence there came a single, laconic comment from the bridge: *'ATLANTIC CONVEYOR HAS BEEN HIT, AND SHE'S BURNING.'*

The whole business was over within a couple of minutes, but we were to remain at Action Stations for many hours, in case of further attacks. I was determined to get a view of the action and take some film. I knew of a back way to the upper deck, past the Met office, and I sneaked upstairs in the gathering gloom to see what was going on.

Cine camera at the ready, I climbed through the hatch and out on to the island behind the funnel. I could see *Atlantic Conveyor* lying just a short distance away with most of her hull obscured by thick smoke, through which occasional flashes of flame were visible. Several helicopters were already hovering in the edges of the smoke, but I could see no life rafts in the water. Although I realised that the light was really too poor to take film, by now I was taking shots of the burning wreck. (On processing, as expected, the film was completely dark.) I thought of the poor sods who had been aboard: Captain North and his crew, plus quite a few personnel from 18 Squadron, who were at that time still trying to get their four Chinooks into a flying condition. One of the Chinooks was airborne on an air test when the ship was hit. With no fuel to go anywhere else, the pilot was forced to land on *Hermes*. Claiming that there was no room, the Navy gave serious consideration to pushing the Chinook over the side, until common sense prevailed. I went below for a short while to see what information had come in about the attack. A little later I returned to my vantage point on the upper deck to watch *Atlantic Conveyor* burning in the dark. By now we had moved closer in to assist the helicopters, and the scene was hellish. Lying as we were, downwind of the burning wreck, her hull was almost completely obscured by smoke. Flames occasionally leapt skywards, illuminating the sea for some distance around. At times I could see several helicopters hovering in and out of the smoke, their searchlights probing the darkness for signs of life. With anti-collision beacons flashing they seemed to be hovering dangerously close to one another, and I was mildly surprised that there was no collision to add to the carnage below. Unable to tear myself away, I stayed watching the ship die for a couple of hours until the smoke and flames started to fade away. We moved away from the scene and finally I went below, shivering uncontrollably from the cold. By now many of the survivors had already been brought aboard.

A little later we heard with great sadness that nine people were missing, including dear old Birdseye North. We heard from Captain Layard that they had been the last two to abandon ship. They had swum to the life raft with Captain North following and on reaching it Layard had swum around to the far side to board. He never saw Captain North again. So died one of the most likeable and laid-back unsung heroes of the war. Captain Ian North had survived wartime torpedoings during gallant service with the Merchant Navy, only to die in the freezing waters of the South Atlantic, his ship and his life sacrificed without complaint in order to protect us. Our spirits were raised on hearing that all of our colleagues on 18 Squadron had survived unharmed. We heard a graphic eyewitness account given by an airman who was below decks and saw the burning remains of a missile fly the full length of the cargo hold.

A Sailor

He knew the icy loneliness and saw
The dreadful affinity of sea and sky
Close grey upon him; heard the weird wind's cry
Shrilling mad descant to the brass of war:
The cold white latitudes of despair that freeze
Blood, dreams, enlightenment in the Arctic day
Called, down the thunderous corridors of spray,
His flesh of youth bruised by irreverent seas,
No fame or ribbon sing of those whose graves
Like his, litter the ocean, though he flung
The sea his breath and had no more to give:
Only the immortal and unfeeling waves
Moan his wild threnody. He was so young,
He died before he had begun to live.

D.S. Goodbrand
January 1944, Russia

This very near miss brought home forcibly our vulnerability to determined air attack and the Admiral immediately ordered the withdrawal of the Carrier Group a further 100 miles east. This increased distance from the islands was to add yet more problems to air operations. Before I continue with the next phase of the Ground Attack war, it might be useful to describe some of our routine day-to-day operational procedures.

CHAPTER TWELVE

Routine Operations

After our hectic introduction to shipboard operations and the cultural shock of working with the Navy, we had settled into a sort of routine aboard ship. First of all, at an early stage the Flight Commanders and the Boss had agreed that we should operate a system of leaders and wingmen for the duration – unlike peacetime flying, when the roles were often switched to maximise training value.[15] After the first couple of days of flying two things became painfully apparent: first, that there were a lot of lessons to be learned and we had to learn them fast to survive; second, that the tasks of leaders and wingmen were quite different, such that it would be wasteful of experience to keep on switching roles. This was a hard but necessary decision to take. Some pilots nominated as permanent wingmen felt that they were being treated as second-class citizens. However, after the trauma of the first few days' operations, I believe that most of our pilots accepted that the concept was reasonable. Basically, the leader's job was to plan and brief the mission, cope with all the domestic hassle of getting the formation off and back on to the deck again, and navigate the formation accurately to and from the target.[16] The wingman, his mind uncluttered with domestic trivia, was expected to monitor the leader, keep a good lookout at all times and attack whatever the leader attacked. It surprised me constantly that wingmen were often able to see things that the leader missed through the necessary concentration on map reading. Over the target, our wingmen were often able to achieve a better result than their leader, being able to see his fall of shot and then correct on it. Our attacks were always planned with the minimum separation over the target. Nevertheless, the inevitable time separation often led to the wingman seeing more flak than the lead. All of our leaders were painfully aware of this: however, because of various twists of fate only our formation leaders or singletons were to be shot down.

Next, we decided also to run a system of Duty Flight Commanders, who would be either the Boss, Bob or me. The Flight Commanders'

tasks were varied, and on his shoulders lay a great weight of responsibility – literally, the lives of the squadron pilots. Once we
appreciated the hopelessly shambolic way that Navy air operations
were organised, the Duty Flight Commander's main job became that of
Ground Liaison Officer/Intelligence Officer/Operations Officer combined. He would read incoming Air Task Messages, or try to take them
down personally when they were phoned in from Ship's Ops. Often, a
rapid visit to Ship's Ops would be required in order to attempt to get
more information or some associated intelligence, very little of which
was usually available. Having got as much information as he could,
he then selected a suitable team to fly the mission. In doing this he
had to take into account the difficulty of the task and the strength of
the defences. Very soon it became apparent to the Duty Flight Commanders which leaders and wingmen worked best together and, more
important, which pilots were best capable of carrying out particularly
difficult tasks. Most of us eventually felt the strain of constant danger
in the air. However, by contrast one or two pilots – Bob, for example –
showed little trace of fear at any stage, even after the most hair-raising
experiences. Bob seemed to amble between disasters at his usual
languid pace, as if he was putting up with a tiresome station exercise.
For me, J.R. provided the essential replacement for the ever-cheerful
Jeff Glover, now languishing in an Argy POW camp. J.R. seemed to
be the most infuriatingly 'normal' member of our small group. He
showed genuine fear after a dangerous mission, and indulged in
hilarious exultation after a success. His increasingly manic sense of
humour was never dimmed, even in the most desperate circumstances,
and he could always find some witticism to cheer us up. (It was J.R.
who coined the term 'Rat-Infested Rust Bucket' to describe *Hermes*.) He
knew he wasn't the greatest VSTOL pilot, but to me he was a first-class
wingman, worth half a dozen prima donnas. When the chips were
down in the air he could size up the situation quickly and make sound
tactical decisions.

In order to achieve maximum operational effectiveness, the Duty
Flight Commander sometimes had to make extremely difficult decisions about who was to fly a particular mission. Inevitably, for the
more demanding sorties the same people were chosen again and again,
exposing them to an ever-increasing risk of being shot down eventually. As a Flight Commander, I had to be prepared to lead any mission;
there was no choice about that, it came with the job. But making the
choice as to whom I should send on a difficult task was probably the
hardest thing during my time in the South Atlantic, knowing that
while they were airborne I could sit back in relative safety aboard ship.
For all of us, potentially the worst missions would be those flown from

Alert 5 on deck. As already described, during these missions our pilots were sometimes being launched to attack the most difficult targets after a totally inadequate preparation.

Although we were under immense pressure, at no stage did I see any of our pilots show any sign of dissent when given a task to fly. However, hard-hitting discussions were common at the end of the day's flying, and I for one encouraged our guys to vent their feelings freely in company with the Flight Commanders. Rank was put aside as far as I was concerned during these discussions: I was secretly glad that the guys had enough sense to discuss our very real problems 'in house' rather than shouting our differences around the bar.

Another of the Duty Flight Commander's essential duties was to calculate the VSTOL figures for the aircraft in use that day, making allowance for their various weapon loads. In the pilots' briefing room we had a series of complicated 'chase round' graphs on the wall for this purpose. You started off with the air temperature for the period of operation and then used the total weights of the various aircraft and their individual engine performance characteristics to come up with a series of deck take-off distances required for different values of Wind over Deck. Each aircraft and weapon load required a different take-off run, and it was vital to get the correct figures passed up to Flyco in time to be relayed to the Flight Deck Officer, whose responsibility it was to ensure that each aircraft was lined up for launch at the correct distance from the ski-jump. The Duty Flight Commander also calculated hover performance figures, of vital importance when landing back on again. As we were quite often landing back on with full weapon loads, hover performance was often marginal. We did not jettison unused weapons unless it was physically impossible to get them back aboard again. *Atlantic Conveyor* had been carrying a large quantity of our weapon stocks and from now on we were to be critically short of some items, particularly cluster bombs. Having passed on the VSTOL figures, hopefully Flyco would get the ship pointed into wind with sufficient Wind over Deck to ensure a safe launch. The system worked reasonably well, except for one occasion described later.

A typical preparation for a day's operational flying would be as follows: I would be out of my camp bed about four hours before dawn so that I could have a good breakfast without having to hurry. The main ship's briefing took place some two and a half hours before sunrise, and before this the first wave of our pilots would have met up in the pilots' briefing room to be teamed up as pairs ready for incoming tasks. The Duty Flight Commander would already have some idea of the likely area of operations, and formation leaders would take the opportunity to do a bit of map study and updating on the known intelligence features of the area. One of the major holes in our know-ledge was the position of our FLOT (Forward Line Own Troops), an essential piece of information. Try as we could, we could not get reliable updates of this, and on one occasion our FLOT position was five days out of date. (In this we were better off than the pilots aboard *Invincible*: they received no FLOT information at all.) Next, as we had practised many times on exercises and Tacevals at home, we would get together as a formation and carry out a 'Pre-brief' on the likely sortie and weapon loads. This involved a thorough briefing on all the aspects of the sortie we could cover without actually having seen an Air Task Message. By now we would have received the ship's briefing – for what it was worth – and we could already draw up our transit route to and from the islands. For this purpose we had printed some small Transit Maps showing the islands and a large sea area to the east in which we were cruising. Use of these maps saved using up precious larger-scale maps. Unfortunately, after the sinking of *Atlantic Conveyor* the Admiral had ordered the whole Task Group another 100 miles further east. This had two consequences for us: first, we were now going to be critically short of fuel on some missions; second, we had to get a new lot of Transit Maps printed as we were now off the edge of the old ones!

All of this map preparation depended on accurate information from the Navy as to the ship's likely position at launch time, and more important, her position at our likely recovery time. As we could never be sure of these times or positions there was always some uncertainty in this planning. It was vitally important to agree tactics with your wingman. Each leader and wingman had subtly different styles and preferences for the wide variety of tasks we might be called upon to perform, and we always spent time briefing this. All of this Pre-briefing time was money in the bank when – as was all too often the case – an Air Task Message came in with an 'impossible' TOT (Time on Target). Because of the appallingly bad communications, Air Task Messages often carried a TOT that could only be met if the aircraft had taken off ten minutes ago! In this case there was little point in signalling for a delay in TOT as the message would not get through in time for the receiving ground forces to change their plans. We just had to go for it as fast as we could, hoping that we would not be too severely shot at by our own defences if we turned up late. Fortunately, this kind of rushed planning and briefing was all too familiar to us from our experience of peacetime exercises. The unofficial motto of the RAF Harrier Force could well have been, 'If it's not done fast, it's not worth doing!'

Harrier-deployed site operations had never been conducive to a gentle and measured approach to aviation, and those pilots who were unable to keep up with the brutal pace of operations soon found themselves posted elsewhere.

Having carried out as detailed a Pre-brief as possible, time would then be spent in checking and donning full wartime flying gear. At this stage there would be the occasional panic as kit was discovered to be damaged or missing. Lastly, we each had our preferred location for the trusty but cumbersome Browning automatic and spare mags. Many pilots carried them in the immersion suit leg pockets, but I was pretty sure that these would be ripped off in an ejection. (This was in fact the case.) On receipt of an Air Task Message the pair would discuss it with the Duty Flight Commander and try to resolve any outstanding queries. Arriving in raw signal format, our Air Task Messages were often riddled with errors and omissions, not having been checked by anyone aboard ship before being passed to us. (This was one of the essential tasks of a Ground Liaison Officer in RAF Attack squadrons.)

Now came the important part of the mission preparation. I used as much time as there was available to study the terrain around the target area. I was looking for the most suitable attack and escape direction, taking into account the defences, type of target, surrounding terrain, position of sun, wind and many other vital considerations, the optimum interpretation of which could make the difference between success and failure. For me, the most important aspect was always the terrain around the target. With practice, I had got the feel of the Falklands terrain based on the 1:50,000 maps, and I was always looking for the smallest variation of contour which would conceal our approach from the defences. Even the lowest hillock just a few metres high on the map could be used. The ability to fly almost at ground level turned such seemingly insignificant features into valuable cover. Like the sniper, creeping unseen across apparently open terrain, we planned to make use of every scrap of cover to conceal our approach to the target. Equally important, off target it was vital to plot the nearest piece of terrain cover that would shield us from the fire of the defences as we ran out. Our tactics were a straight run-out off target at maximum speed and as low as possible towards the nearest terrain cover. I was contemptuous of the '3D Guns Weave' tactics so popular amongst pilots back in UK who had never been shot at. As far as we were concerned, 'jinking' to put off gun aiming merely made your aircraft a bigger plan target, forced you to fly higher, and kept you in range longer. The argument was simple – there was not a SAM or a gun in the world that could shoot through a hill.

Conscientious map study brought an extra bonus for the formation: every minute spent studying the terrain and discussing ingress and egress tactics helped to imprint the essential details of the attack on the brain. Even when planning was complete, if there was time to spare we would continue to study the maps and memorise every detail. We knew that when the adrenalin started to flow, time spent looking in the cockpit was at a premium; your actions were carried out in accordance with a pre-planned routine that you just had to remember. There was no room for a second's hesitation when the shooting started. With the map study it was important to brief exactly what the target area would look like once we unmasked from behind the last ridge line. This was not always easy, and I often fell back on the well-remembered advice of Ernie van den Heuvel, my erstwhile recce mentor on the Starfighter in Holland. Ernie was a genius at 1:50,000 map reading; a recce pilot of some twenty years' experience, he taught me more about map inter-pretation and target planning than I had ever learned with the RAF.

In the South Atlantic many things conspired to make planning and flying more difficult than European operations. The sun, as an obvious example, was in a completely different position in the sky. Years of northern hemisphere habit patterns gave one a sixth sense of esti-mating aircraft heading from the position of the sun at any given time of the day – essential for target planning and Low Level Situation Awareness. In the Falklands, I found time and time again that I had to sit and work out where the sun was going to be from first principles. Having spent most of the time on target area planning, it was now time to fine tune the High Level transit part of the mission, as by now a more accurate launch time was known. Details of the mission were passed up to Ship's Ops and we would finish off with a fairly short brief on the sortie, the majority of points having already been covered in detail.

Our last call before the flight deck would be the Aircraft Servicing Office, a tiny compartment just opposite the main exit door to the flight deck. This was manned invariably by Brian Mason and Chief Tech Fred Walsh, always with a grin and a joke to send you on your way. Naturally, aircraft documentation had been drastically cut down for wartime operations. The aircraft servicing form merely carried details of the weapon load, plus a few comments as to what the previous pilot had found wrong with the aircraft. We were already carrying quite a few major snags on items for which there were no spares. The delivery time for spares could be as long as several days from the UK. After Ascension, the spares would be parachuted into the sea nearby from a Hercules, flying a marathon return sortie with flight refuelling of twenty-eight hours. Our aircraft were flying with booster pumps U/S (which caused major fuel asymmetry problems); suspect hydraulic systems that lost all pressure as the gear was retracted; plus several other major technical defects that you would not dream of flying with in peacetime. Along with this was the usual array of battle damage repairs, indicated by patches of metal and silver 'speed tape' stuck over the various bullet and shrapnel holes. The next most vital piece of information was the location of the jets. Our machines were parked at random amongst the Sea Harriers, and we didn't want to spend half an hour stumbling up and down the deck looking for them. Before stepping outside, helmets were put on, mainly to avoid losing them on deck. In the prevailing gale force wind over deck, anything dropped was over the side in an instant. There had already been a couple of heart-stopping moments when pilots had managed to drop their carefully prepared maps and were forced to chase them among the tied-down aircraft. By Sod's Law there was usually a Harrier taking off as you stepped outside, adding a hurricane of jet blast to the wind over the deck. Having found your jet and faithful ground crew, the next priority was a thorough pre-flight walkround. We had been told to speed up on these in order to get started up quicker: I quietly ignored the instruction as I wanted to have a damn good look at what I was flying. Quite often a considerable part of the airframe would be hanging out over the side of the ship, adding to the difficulty of carrying out an inspection. Finally, the Navy had an endearing trick of parking jets with the nosewheel a couple of inches away from one of the deck lifts, which would be lowered without warning, leaving a 30 feet deep hole right where you were about to tread. On more than one occasion I nearly fell backwards down one of these lifts, not having heard the bell that warned of its movement. It was also important to make a thorough check of all the weapons hung on the aircraft. I made sure that the bombs were correctly crutched, arming leads properly connected up and both guns loaded, cocked and plugged in.

After climbing in, the next thing to do was to get rid of the fine deposit of salt, which invariably covered the cockpit transparencies. This had to be done before launch as it would not come off in flight, leaving you with severely impaired vision. Cleaning was achieved by the simple expedient of throwing a bucket of distilled water over the canopy. Naturally enough, like all other ship's activities, the Navy had to make a pretence of carefully organised control of everything to do with aviation. A system of tannoy broadcasts was used to hustle us into the cockpits and start and launch our aircraft at the appropriate time. For the purpose of these broadcasts our aircraft were called 'The GRs'. So, at twenty minutes before the planned launch time Flyco would call 'MAN THE GRs'; ten minutes before launch they called 'START THE GRs' etc. They were totally inflexible, and we discovered with some amusement that we were actually expected to obey these instructions as soon as they were given – whether or not the aircraft were in a fit state to be either manned or started. On several occasions we would be sitting twiddling our thumbs in the pilots' briefing room after a 'MAN THE GRs' call; an irate caller from Flyco would demand why we had not manned this or that particular GR. 'Because the bloody thing's still in pieces – can't you look out of the window?' would be our reply.

They never really got the hang of this in Flyco, and right up to the end of our operations they were still calling 'START THE GRs' even when the GR in question had all its panels off and was covered in a swarm of technicians. The problem was that Flyco found great difficulty in breaking out of the peacetime shipboard flying attitude, when launch and recovery times were strictly controlled. Absolute adherence to these times was demanded of pilots who, we had already discovered, were treated with less consideration than that given to a Sea Dart round on a launcher. This was a hangover from the old catapult-and-wire days of naval aviation, when launch and recovery evolutions made very different demands on deck space, with the ship at a good speed and pointing into wind at all times. For recoveries we regularly made approaches to land from over the bow if this gave a more convenient heading for the ship, and the wind was strong enough. The ease of launch and recovery of the Harrier gave a flexibility to carrier operations that was only slowly being recognised by Flyco. In our operations so far the Navy had learned with reluctance that it simply had to make allowances for things like changed TOT, U/S aircraft, changes of target etc., or by now we would have carried out hardly any effective Offensive Support operations. By now we knew that Flyco could rant as much as they wanted: either we launched at a time that was convenient for us (and not for the ship), or the mission was likely to be a failure. Even the most dim-witted of Naval officers understood this simple fact by now. However, many sorties were still turned into near-disasters by the sheer incompetence of Flyco, under the iron hand of the Navy hierarchy. Having spent many hours observing flying operations from Flyco, I felt that I had a pretty good picture of how things were run in there. Basically, everyone working in Flyco lived in fear of the Captain – for good reason – his temper was awesome to behold and he would rant and rage about anything that appeared to be going wrong on deck and slowing up the launch. He seemed to be constantly engaged in a competition with *Invincible* to get aircraft airborne quickest. We couldn't see the point of this. Inevitably, mistakes happened fairly often in such a complex and demanding flying and Air Tasking operation. To me, what was so obviously lacking was to allow people (pilots, the Flight Deck Officer, the engineers – whoever had the problem) just a few moments to sort out the problem for themselves, assisted by some kind of analysed decision from Flyco. This rarely happened. Expediency was all, and the orders flashed down to those toiling on deck were simply, 'Do this' or 'Do that', seemingly without the slightest consideration of whether or not such an action was feasible or even necessary. At other times – when a crucial decision *was* required – nothing but silence came from Flyco.

After this digression, our valiant GR3 pilot is still busy in the cockpit with the most important pre-launch task: setting up the correct IFF squawk for the take-off. Our IFF control box, designed to be mounted vertically in a large, multi-crew aircraft, was mounted horizontally on the right console, in the position where it collected the maximum amount of dust, dirt and sea water, which inevitably found its way into the cockpit. The tiny windows showing the code selected were invariably partly obscured by dirt, which ground its way into the digits themselves, steadily erasing them to make them even less legible. At sea the whole equipment would be liberally covered in sea water and evaporated salt spray. In the dark it took me on one occasion nearly five minutes to dial in the correct code, grimly clutching a torch between my teeth to light up the panel. Like many of our cockpit control panels, its integral lighting consisted of individual bulbs behind each digit; naturally, if just one bulb failed (there was usually one U/S –this was a totally moronic design feature), it was impossible to read the code without recourse to the torch gripped in the teeth. Time and again we cursed the bloody-minded incompetence of the people who could have put such a system into a cramped single-seat cockpit, which was never better than an ergonomic slum even under the most favourable conditions. There was no alternative to this tedious procedure: a serviceable IFF was the only guarantee not to be shot down by our own Task Group in the quite likely event of a completely U/S radio during our return to the ship. There had already been several major cockups and technical failures involving Navy SAM operators, which had led directly to the loss of ships to enemy air attack. It was clear to us that they were now out for blood, and not too particular whom they fired at. With the obvious distaste for the RAF demonstrated by the Navy hierarchy, I could not imagine them showing much remorse in the event of shooting down one of our GR3s by mistake – no doubt they would have blamed it on us anyway.

In parallel with this activity, the pilot is also trying to get the best inertial navigator alignment possible from the FINRAE trolley, parked in front of the cockpit. There were several tricks involved in getting the best out of the kit, and we all strove to achieve this in order to avoid the dreaded 'Auto Rev 1', in which the inertial platform toppled irrecoverably in flight, leaving you with no accurate attitude or heading reference. Worse still, as I had discovered at Goose Green, was the insidious compass error you could do nothing about. The radio would be on by now, and the leader would have carried out the briefest check-in with his formation. There was usually very little routine radio traffic involving our Harriers during deck ops, although most of the Sea Harrier guys seemed to use normal radio procedures in the visual circuit, calling 'In the Wait' and 'Final, Gear down', etc. We had not been briefed on any particular radio silence procedure; I decided early on to have none of this and made no radio calls at all that were not absolutely necessary once I had got the ship in sight. Most of the radio calls were to do with helicopter traffic, which was virtually constant. The reader must bear in mind that, in addition to constant anti-submarine work, large numbers of helicopters were permanently busy during daylight hours, operating the usual Helicopter Delivery Service between the ships of the Task Group. As usual, this demanded a considerable amount of radio traffic to get the correct loads to the correct place. We did have our own squadron 'natter' frequency, which we used to sort out various clank-ups that had only become apparent after strapping in. Next would come the start instruction, to be followed by the fun and games of deck manoeuvring, already described in a previous chapter. En-route tactics will be described in Chapter 13.

CHAPTER THIRTEEN

En-route Tactics

*Courage, these days is a minor talent. No man is braver than the next ...
the air raid wardens in Coventry or Plymouth, these men do things under
fire which we fighter pilots can only regard with awe. A fighter pilot
doesn't have to show that kind of courage. Unreasoning, unintelligent,
blind courage is in fact a tremendous handicap to him. He has to be cold
when he is fighting. He fights with his head, not his heart. There are three
things a first class fighter pilot must have. First, he must have an
aggressive nature. He must think in terms of offence rather than defence.
He must at all times be an attacker. It is against the nature of a Spitfire to
run away. Second, both his mind and his body must be alert and both
must react instinctively to any tactical situation. When you are fighting
you have no time to think. Third, he must have good eyes and hands and
feet. Your hands, your feet, your mind, your instincts must function as
well, whether you're right side up or upside down.*

Sailor Malan
1942

After the launch came the usual low-speed 'milling' before the
join-up, followed by a climb to altitude for the outbound
transit. The vast majority of missions were flown on a HI-LO-
HI profile, especially after *Atlantic Conveyor* had been sunk. During the
climb, the most important thing was to get a comprehensive check-out
of each aircraft's IFF squawk (the automatic coded reply signal), using
the ship's radar. Often it was discovered that the IFF was squawking
something other than what was dialled up, and there followed an
awkward period of rough flying as the pilot struggled to set in another
code that gave the right numbers. In cloud, this was well-nigh impossible. At times the set was completely U/S. This meant an immediate return to the ship as the IFF was the only safeguard against being
shot down by our own defences. The loss of Jeff had reinforced our
determination not to send single aircraft on a mission, except in the
most exceptional circumstances, and so the not-infrequent IFF faults

led to several total mission failures. After several of these in quick succession, later in the campaign we were forced to accept a U/S IFF in the formation. Time and again we cursed the poor design and lousy reliability of this vital equipment: very fortunately none of us suffered a 'Blue on Blue' as a result.

En route, I always used to level off below contrails with my formations. Old habits made me wary of flying in contrails, where you could be seen for miles around. We did not seriously expect to be 'bounced' by Argy fighters, either at High or Low Level: we knew that they had far greater priorities than chasing the odd Harrier, their low fuel states precluding anything more than a quick attack followed by a run for home. The 'D' aboard *Hermes* would know our intended letdown point and, often without prompting from us, would give a reassuring 'Pigeons' (range and bearing) call to that point. Although at this stage in the sortie we were maintaining our own radio silence, as we approached within 100 nm of the islands we could hear the telltale 'chirp' of the enemy surveillance radars as they picked us up. They were well equipped with the most modern search radars, and it was always an uncomfortable feeling to know that the air raid warnings were sounding already in all the important target areas on the islands. They could start their stopwatches at this moment of first detection and within about thirty minutes our formation would appear over the target area.

The descent to low level was often made through cloud, and during this stage of the flight I would usually apply the well-known *Francis Chichester* principle of navigation, i.e. laying off your course to the safe side of your objective so that you would know for certain which way to turn when the Estimated Time of Arrival came up. Invariably we wanted to break cloud well out over the sea, and this was usually done to the north of the islands. Below cloud we would turn south or north as required to make our landfall. Unfortunately, both the north and south coasts of East Falkland were low-lying and correspondingly featureless when seen from a distance out to sea. It was impossible to plot exactly where you were until you coasted in, when the many obvious inlets and lakes would give you a reasonable pinpoint.

After the Low Level portion of the mission and the attack itself, we would start our climb for home as soon as we were out of range of the local defences. Levelling off once again below contrails, we would carry out a brief mutual inspection for battle damage. There followed an uncomfortable period of transit towards our ship, over 200 miles away in the wastes of the ocean. Still under radio silence, we were always acutely conscious of the fact that there was nothing but 4,000 miles of lonely sea if we did not make contact with the Carrier Task

Group. When the time came to call for identification, there was an almost audible sigh of relief to hear Tim Kelly's reassuring voice on the radio. Recoveries to the ship were often fairly tense, especially if a member of the formation had been hit and was losing fuel. Very fortunately for us, we never had to make approaches to the ship in really bad weather (i.e. thick fog). My most interesting recovery was with a four-ship when the cloud base was about 400 feet at the ship's position. This was the only occasion I recall when 'D' almost lost a grip on the situation, unwisely splitting our two pairs into four separate speaking units. We ended up with all four aircraft being directed to all points of the compass, with a lot of fuel and adrenalin being expended before we were all safely on deck. Of course, recoveries like this had to be radar-controlled. We could perfectly well have made our own free letdown in the area of the Task Group. However, from more than a couple of miles away *Hermes* looked just like any other ship in the group. You might break cloud 10 miles away from her, and then run out of fuel investigating every ship you could see to check if it was 'Mother'. Naturally, both radar cover and radio communications were severely degraded once you had descended to Low Level, so we knew that we had to grit our teeth and rely on complete radar control until we were lined up with the ship.

Because they knew that we were usually short of fuel, the ship made great efforts to be pointing in the right direction when we reached her. The most important piece of information was the landing course (on which you made your final approach), and the relative wind, which had a great influence on your actual landing. If weather conditions permitted, we would break as a formation over the ship, to make a turning final approach. During this, Flyco would give your deck landing spot, which was usually the only piece of spare deck available. The favourite spot was just aft of amidships, where the deck was widest. Further aft, the landing space was uncomfortably narrow. As long as the sea was not too rough, the deck landing was pretty straightforward. From a steady hover, in which you were 'formating' on the the metalwork of the ship's island, you moved across towards the landing spot and then began your descent following the hand signals of the Flight Deck Officer, who would give signals right down to deck contact, in spite of the hurricane-force jet blast. Accustomed to RAF landing procedures, where no person or equipment was allowed anywhere near a landing Harrier, it was a little disconcerting at first to be landing within a few feet of so many apparently unconcerned people – and right next to other parked aircraft, a bit like vertical landing in your parking slot on the Wittering flight line. Occasionally the deck moved away from you just before impact, but this was easily compensated with a touch of power. After touchdown, you were back into the frantic marshalling discipline again as often there were other aircraft 'stacked up' behind you in the hover, waiting to get onto your spot. Only when you were securely chained to the deck and the signal to shut down was given could you afford to relax a little, a sickly smell filling the cockpit as the ground crew sprayed gallons of WD40 down the intake. On some occasions we made landing approaches from over the bow. This was only done in fairly strong winds, when the Navy had good tactical reasons for not turning the ship into wind. This was great sport, presenting quite a challenge to the landing pilot. The ship would be moving at some speed, and so the main briefing point was, 'Never look down at the sea in the hover, you'll get very disorientated if you do!' During the deceleration to the hover, you 'formated' on the island as usual, and ended up in a hover with the sea rushing past your aircraft from behind; hence the advice to avoid looking down. I tried this for myself at one stage and it felt pretty odd. The landing itself was carried out facing aft.[17]

Wednesday, 26 May 1982

John Rochfort and I were scrambled from the first five-minute deck alert, after sitting for just over an hour on deck. Our task was an Armed Recce mission, and during the departure we discovered to our disgust that neither of us had a serviceable IFF. We turned back and landed on with our weapons. Bob and Tony Harper were next off, with a task to attack the troop concentration that John and I had found and photo-graphed at Port Howard on 23 May. We had been trying without success for some days to get permission to attack this lucrative target – the response from Flyco had been zero. Of course, it was ludicrous to wait so long before attacking such a target – by now the troops could have gone anywhere. After a successful sortie Bob reported an easy attack, making use of my 'stand-off' photos to aid target acquisition. Tony said that the whole thing had been far too easy and clinically efficient: 'A bit like murder' were his words. Less concerned with the moral aspects of killing an enemy who was so obviously determined to kill us, I was angry that we were not able to take more photos of targets before we attacked them. We had learned long ago that just one recce photo of a target was worth its weight in gold when it came to putting the weapons in the right place. Once again, it seemed to us that both the Navy and our tasking agencies had forgotten a basic principle of Ground Attack operations.

At about 1500 hours John and I were tasked to carry out an Armed Recce of a mostly flat area on East Falkland in front of our most forward troops. The only information we had was that our troops had advanced 'several kilometres' eastward from the Ajax Bay landing area and that they wanted any enemy artillery found and neutralised in the area immediately in front of them. The area to be covered was given as a square with 10 km sides, a ridiculously large area in which to search for camouflaged targets. (In peacetime exercises you would be tasked for Armed Recce on an area one fiftieth of this size: this was all you could be expected to cover in one pass. It would have been much more sensible to have tasked a photo recce mission on this area.) During the mission there was no choice but to keep on flying up and down on parallel tracks until we had covered the whole area. The flying was exhilarating but tense, as we were both uncomfortably aware of our vulnerability to ground fire, with no element of surprise on our side. Flying as low as we dared, we could skyline the most insignificant feature on the horizon. Every small lump on the ground ahead was a possible target and we called to each other constantly on the radio as each suspicious feature was investigated. As you approached you climbed to release height, finger poised over the bomb button. Was it enemy or not? Surely they would start firing back now? Damn it, another bunch of sheep! The hills were the most difficult: we searched the rear slopes of all of them in the hope of finding artillery, but no joy. As our fuel ran low I called it off and we returned aboard for a quick turnround for the final mission of the day.

On this mission I was teamed up with Mark again. This was another Armed Recce task. By now we were certain that they were confused about the terminology: some Air Task Messages had already come in using the term 'Armed Photo Reconnaissance', which by the book was a non-existent form of warfare.[18] Fat chance of the Navy knowing that. So far, we had not been tasked for any pure photo recce missions at all, even though the tactical situation cried out for them. The task was to search for troop and vehicle activity along a 50 km route from some distance west of Estancia house, finishing up close to Stanley town! Straight away, I decided that we were not going to blunder into the town on a linesearch. The town and airfield together were the most heavily defended areas in the Falklands, by this time encompassing more than sixty flak guns and seven SAM launch units. There would obviously be troop and vehicle activity in the town itself, but we had already agreed among ourselves that whatever the Navy said we were not going to fire 'unsmart' weapons into the town under any circum-stances: the cost in civilian lives would be too great. Additionally, to achieve successful Low Level oblique photography of the town demanded an entirely different approach, making maximum use of diversionary tactics so that the recce aircraft had a chance of getting back with the film. As a result, on this task I planned to terminate the linesearch short of the town's main defences. There was stratus on the hill tops in the area, but otherwise the weather was fine as we set off eastwards along the line. As usual, information on our own troop positions had been out of date for days, so I had briefed carefully on the need for positive identification of targets before we fired on anything. The muddy track that served as a 'road' was clear as far as the Murrell river below Mt Longden; here we made a hard turn back to the west as we passed within range of the Stanley defences. Flying back along the track up from Moody Brook, we approached the Mt Kent area again, and my eyes were drawn instinctively to the scene of our successful attack of 21 May. A couple of miles to the south I glimpsed what could be a helicopter, standing on its own in the middle of the boulder-strewn tussock grass ...

I called on the radio to Mark, who had also seen it. We turned towards the area to take some pictures – maybe there were other targets as well. Flying close past the target there was a fleeting glimpse of a pile of burnt wreckage and rotor blades, which must have been the Chinook we destroyed on 21 May. I took photos and recognised what looked like a fully serviceable Puma. Damn it! Why hadn't I just attacked it the first time? I was still filming when something else caught my eye away to port. A SAM smoke trail disappeared somewhere above and behind me. Someone didn't want us around, that was sure; however, the shot had been a pretty desperate effort from so close in and at that angle. Mark reported that he had also seen tracer coming from the Mt Kent area, so we departed to the west right on the deck. My brain was working hard as we flew low and fast over the ridge just to the west of the target area. Obviously, this was a valuable target; however, we had flown near it twice already and I knew what Mark was going to say if we went back. As a result, I told Mark to stay about 10 km west of the target in a safe area. Leaving him in an orbit, I set off back at high speed for an attack. Staying as low as possible until the last second, I hoped that I had 'eyeballed' the return track correctly: there was going to be no time for a track correction once I was over the ridge.[19] Just short of the protective crest I popped up and immediately bunted like crazy, the cockpit filling with dust and debris as I strove to keep from ballooning too high. My track had come out in exactly the right place, and I could see the Puma just a kilometre in front of me. I could see tracer on my right – it was too late to dodge and I kept my eyes firmly on the approaching target. I managed to bracket the Puma squarely with the two cluster bombs. Looking back over my shoulder as I turned off target, the familiar carpet of explosions developed around the Puma, then obliterated it in a hail of smoke and shrapnel.

After a half-second delay the Puma exploded in a searing orange flame. I dodged through the hills to the north and then headed west to pick up Mark and return home.

En route home, I passed the usual In Flight Report to *Fearless*, reporting the successful attack. After landing I discovered a bullet hole in my drop tank; obviously the shooting had been a bit more accurate than I thought. During the debrief Mark carried on a bit about the fact that we overflew the target area three times. I didn't understand his concern, pointing out that the first time we had been some distance away, and that anyway the 'third' pass had been made on my own. Mark insisted that we had taken unnecessary risks, and would not accept my argument that risks had to be taken in order to get results. Losing patience, I left him muttering and departed to the bar. After dinner that night I was cornered in private by John Rochfort and Tony Harper, to whom Mark had apparently poured out his heart.

'Look Jerry', began Tony: this was obviously serious, if first names were being used straight away. They asked what was going on, suggesting that I might be taking a few too many risks with the young guys. I gave my version of what had happened, to discover that Mark had embellished his story somewhat, giving a rather over-dramatic impression of the mission. I told Tony and J.R. that I thought Mark was getting a bit anxious. After the conversation I felt glad that these two stalwart squadron pilots had the guts to speak up in a forthright manner. Unfortunately, by now I was pretty sure that however we approached our task someone was going to get badly hit very soon as our targets became more and more difficult. Later in the evening we were told that the attack on Goose Green by 2 Para was about to start, and that we were to be on standby to give them Close Air Support under the direction of Forward Air Controllers (FACs) in the morning. On hearing the latter my heart sank. As we well knew, any kind of FAC attack was going to be extremely risky even under the control of the best of FACs. Now that Garth was dead and Jock Penman was casevac'd out of the battle, we would be left with the usual rag-bag of barely competent Secondary FACs to control us. I had been practising FAC attacks for the past twelve years and had come to the conclusion that it was absolutely the last thing we wanted to do in wartime. There were innumerable problems involved (see Appendix 7 – Forward Air Control), which were dutifully recorded and reported on by us after each peacetime FAC exercise: lousy Air-to-Ground communications; poor choice of Initial Points by FACs; lack of target marking; but most important of all, the low standard of training and ability of the average Primary FAC (the Secondaries were invariably useless). I had found that, apart from Garth, the only FACs who had the remotest chance of organising a successful attack were those who had recent experience of Fast Jet Ground Attack *from the cockpit.* Unless you had experienced the sheer difficulty of locating a target from an aircraft travelling at Low Level at 500 miles per hour, then you had little chance of giving effective control to such aircraft. Depressingly, little was done during my twelve years of FAC experience to improve on this situation, except for the introduction of the cumbersome Laser Target Marker (LTM), which had its own severe operational limitations (in the Falklands the battery was usually flat). For the FAC operations at the Battle of Goose Green there were to be no Laser Target Markers available for us.

Hunters in the Gulf. The author in the cockpit of DF/GA Hawker Hunter of No. 208 Squadron RAF at Muharraq, Bahrain in 1970.

A camel train photographed from 50 feet by the author from a Hunter FR10 in Northern Oman in 1971. *(Crown copyright)*

The Harrier GR1 course at RAF Wittering in 1971. From left; Author, Pete Harris, Syd Morris, John Thompson, Steve Wakely and Pete Martin.

The author's first solo in a Starfighter RF104G in 1977 during an exchange tour with the Dutch Air Force. 'A mean machine!'

A GR3 Harrier of No. 1(F) Squadron landing on *Atlantic Conveyor* on 6 May 1982.
(Crown Copyright)

Atlantic Conveyor at Ascension Island in early May 1982, her deck crowded with RAF Harrier GR3s, Sea Harriers and helicopters. The containers provided rudimentary protection against the elements.
(BAE Systems)

The original group of No. 1(F) Squadron pilots southbound aboard *Atlantic Conveyor* in early May 1982. From left: Pete Harris, Jeff Glover, Mark Hare, John Rochfort, author, The Boss (Pete Squire), Bob Iveson and Tony Harper sitting.   *(Crown Copyright)*

Atlantic Conveyor burnt out and sinking after the Exocet attack.   *(Crown Copyright)*

Hermes' deck crowded with GR3 Harriers of No. 1(F) Squadron plus Sea Harriers of No. 800 NAS in the South Atlantic during May 1982.   *(Crown Copyright)*

Refuelling at sea in the South Atlantic in a 'bit of a chop' as the Navy would say.
(Crown Copyright)

HMS *Hermes* in May 1982.

(Crown Copyright)

The author's first attack. This is Fox Bay landing and fuel dump, the lines of fuel containers can be seen at the far right of the photo. The attack was with CBU (Cluster) bombs and flown by The Boss, Bob Iveson and the author.

(Crown Copyright)

Jeff Glover being rescued by Argentinean troops who had shot him down at Port Howard on 21 May 1982. The damage to Jeff's face was caused by his oxygen mask attachments, ejecting at 500 knots. *(Kind permission of Jeff Glover)*

A dead Puma helicopter destroyed by the author on 21 May 1982 on Mount Kent. *(Crown Copyright)*

Another dead helicopter, this one a Chinook, attacked by the author and Mark Hare at dawn on 21 May 1982 on Mount Kent. *(Crown Copyright)*

Goose Green from 20,000 ft showing Pucara aircraft just above centre of the photo. This was a target area on several occasions. *(Crown Copyright)*

The crowded deck of HMS *Hermes* in good weather with RAF GR3s in the fore-ground armed with CBUs and a Recce (Reconnaissance) Pod and Sea Harriers aft.

(Crown Copyright)

The author's F95 photo of Port Howard taken on 23 May. He saw the tents and personnel at the bottom of the

The same photo annotated after the Photo Interpreters had studied them.

(Crown Copyright)

John Rochfort in the catwalk – an unlucky bounce on landing. The deck crew are rushing to manhandle the aircraft back on the deck. The engine is still running and puts the crew at risk.

Pebble Island airstrip, attacked by the RAF on 23 May 1982.

Head-up-display film of the Port Stanley attack by No.1(F) Squadron on 24 May 1982. 1000lb HE bomb exploding ahead.
(Crown Copyright)

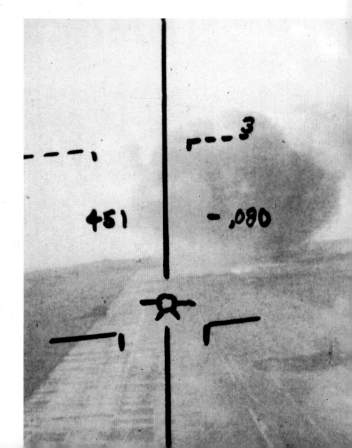

The same attack a few seconds later, another bomb exploding ahead.
(Crown Copyright)

A reconnaissance photo taken by Mark Hare, showing enemy troops wrestling with a Blowpipe missile launcher and trying to get a shot at him. Poorly camouflaged bivouac tents can be seen amongst the rocks. This is typical Falklands terrain - very difficult to locate targets from a distance. *(Crown Copyright)*

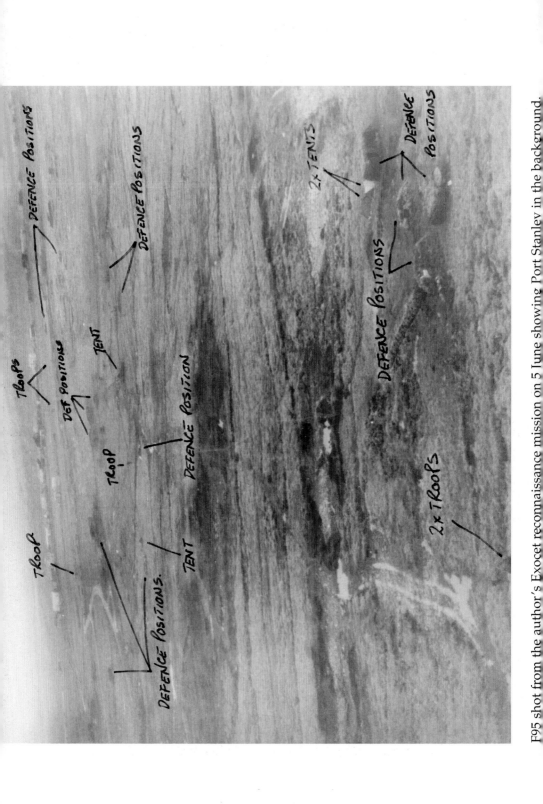

F95 shot from the author's Exocet reconnaissance mission on 5 June showing Port Stanley in the background.

HMS *Hermes* in the South Altantic in June 1982. Three RAF GR3s are nearest the camera on the left. The first is armed with Paveway Mk 2 LGBs (Laser-guided bombs). *(Crown Copyright)*

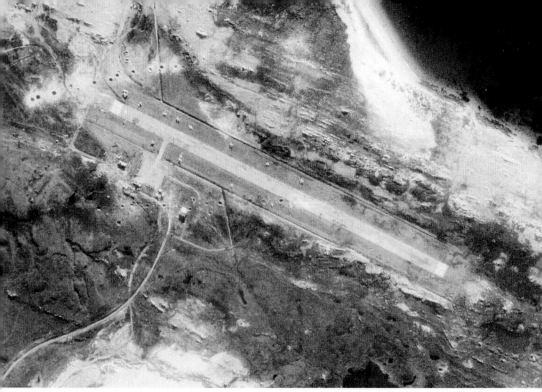

Port Stanley runway taken from 20,000 ft after the second *Black Buck* raid. The last bomb of the first stick hit the middle of the runway (crater already filled) and the second stick missed. *(Crown Copyright)*

HMS *Glamorgan* after an Exocet hit. *(Crown Copyright)*

Harrier GR3 with 2 inch rocket pods.

A Tigercat launcher, found post-war. *(Crown Copyright*

A captured Roland SAM (Surface to Air Missile) launcher at Port Stanley in June 1982. *(Crown Copyright*

The author standing-by on QRA (Quick Reaction Alert) at Port Stanley airfield in July 1982. The Harrier GR3 was armed with Aim9L missiles and 30mm cannon. Pretty boring stuff.

Port San Carlos forward landing strip, under the command of Squadron Leader Syd Morris in June 1982. A pretty bleak place. *(Crown Copyright)*

Home Sweet Home! Port Stanley airfield accommodation tents of 1(F) Squadron in June 1982. Typical winter weather. *(Crown Copyright)*

Jeff Glover on his return from captivity in Argentina. *(Crown Copyright)*

Bob Iveson, Jeff Glover and the author back at Wittering celebrating Jeff's return.
(Crown Copyright)

The author and Bob
Iveson at post-war
Wittering.
(Crown Copyright)

30 May 1982. A restorative beer in the Wardroom bar of HMS *Hermes*. Bob Iveson
right, just returned aboard having been shot down at Goose Green, evading capture
for 3 days. Self, shot down that afternoon, damage from ejection visible on my face
and neck.
(Courtesy of David Morgan)

CHAPTER FOURTEEN

Goose Green FAC Shambles

Thursday, 27 May 1982

In the early hours the BBC committed a disgraceful act of treachery by broadcasting that British paratroops were approaching Darwin in preparation for an attack. On hearing of this World Service broadcast, we were sure that the enemy would now be fully aware of the threat and thus we could expect even more determined resistance during the coming battle. (The CO of the Argy defenders was interviewed on a BBC Equinox programme in August 1998 and stated that he believed the broadcast.) To start the day off the Boss had nominated me as the Duty Flight Commander, as I had flown three times on the previous day. This was ironic: having been the most ardent critic of FAC work throughout my tour on 1(F) Squadron, I was now left conveniently on the ground when the squadron was about to put FAC into practice for the first time in wartime. I had a bad feeling about this: deep inside I was ashamed to discover a feeling of relief that I would not have to fly just yet. I saw this as the beginning of cowardice on my part. With a shudder of distaste I got on with the duties of the DCF and tried to pretend that the thought had not occurred. Just before the main briefing the Boss gave us his customary daily 'pep' talk. I had spoken to him the previous night about the problems with Mark. During his briefing he said that things were probably going to get a lot more difficult from now on, and that risks would have to be taken to achieve results, particularly during the likely FAC tasks to come. We were soon to learn just how close to the truth he was. The first pair off that day comprised Pete Harris and Tony Harper, on the by now well-practised milk run to toss bombs in the general direction of the Port Stanley Airfield runway, as usual without Sea Harrier support and therefore with no chance of any useful results.

107

I was beginning to hope that 2 Para were going to manage OK without us when the next task came in – attacks under the direction of an FAC in the flak-trap at Goose Green. Aboard *Norland* we had discussed FAC techniques at length with 2 Para and they had agreed that they would only call for our support as a last resort, knowing full well that we would take a lot of hits carrying out the attacks. Bob and Mark were next in line, and they launched in a rush to Goose Green. Their sortie was a bit of a shambles, as expected. Communications with the ground were almost unreadable and they could barely understand the target details. Additionally, the weather was not too sharp, with low cloud obscuring the hill tops. By chance they came across a suitable target and got rid of their cluster bombs. In fact, Bob was not talking to an FAC at all. The FAC, Captain Peter Ketley of 2 Para, had gone forward to recce Argy positions without his radio as he had not been told that the Harriers were coming. During his return drive he encountered a recce element of the local Argy defences, travelling in a civilian Land Rover. After a brief firefight – in which no one was injured – the astonished Argies surrendered to the FAC.

Next, the Boss was launched with John Rochfort for more FAC work at Goose Green. Straight away they encountered poor weather, and they were unable to use the only Initial Point the FAC had available because it was at the top of a mountain obscured by cloud. (This was a result of having no Primary FAC available: normally an FAC would always have an alternative Initial Point run up his sleeve.) Additionally, in order to hear the FAC they had to orbit above 5,000 feet, in clear view of the enemy radars. Being unable to start from the planned Initial Point meant that the Boss had to 'eyeball' his way on to the planned track to the target given, which inevitably led to failure to find anything to attack. The Boss and John returned in deep gloom, not having used their weapons. Captain Ketley had replaced poor old Jock Penman, casevac'd home after collapsing with an injured ankle during the approach march from Ajax Bay. Although reasonably fit, Jock was no spring chicken. He had had no assistance in carrying his heavy radio and batteries, plus personal gear.

Bob and Mark were still sitting in their aircraft on deck when the next Air Task Message came through. I can't remember the exact wording, but the request was for another FAC mission at Goose Green, where the situation was described as 'urgently in need of Air Support'. I raced up on deck and passed this on to Bob – like me, he interpreted it as an urgent call for help, requiring desperate measures if necessary. Unbeknown to us 2 Para's battle for Goose Green had not even begun yet (as usual, the Navy had not seen fit to inform us about developments ashore) and this 'situation urgently in need of Air Support' was merely the initial deployment of observation parties by 2 Para in preparation for a full-scale attack in the early hours of the following morning. The mission ended in disaster. Experiencing the same old problems with the FAC, Bob eventually managed to find a group of enemy troops on a road, which they both attacked with cluster bombs. There were a lot of other targets in the area and tracer was flying in all directions as Bob turned back for a couple of strafing attacks, before succumbing finally to a storm of flak. Bob's description gives a vivid impression of being hit by a burst of 35-mm flak:

> I was just pulling out of my last strafe pass when I felt two or three violent explosions in the airframe behind me. Immediately the controls became very stiff and a whole load of warning lights lit up on the Central Warning Panel. The engine was still running and I wasn't descending, so I decided to stick with it a bit longer to get as far as possible away from the people I had just strafed. By now I could hear all sorts of strange noises down the back and the controls had become completely useless. I could see the flames in my mirror and suddenly they flashed over into the cockpit. I pulled the handle straight away.

You could afford to wait a bit with the Mk 9 ejection seat: there was zero time delay on pulling the handle. By hanging on in his mortally stricken aircraft, Bob had managed to fly nearly 10 km west into relatively safe territory, where he landed heavily after the briefest of parachute descents.

Back aboard ship, I knew nothing of this until I received the dreaded telephone message: 'Flyco here: you've lost a GR3.'

Before Mark landed we heard from *Fearless* that the FAC had seen a Harrier shot down and that he had seen the pilot eject. This was a crumb of comfort, but what we really wanted to know was whether or not the FAC had seen a parachute. This was desperate news for me. All my worst fears had been realised and Bob was gone, probably killed. Mark was in a pretty bad state when he came in. He was banging on a bit about the flak and crazy formation leaders – as far as he was concerned Bob had committed suicide. He hadn't actually seen what had happened to Bob, so we were still ignorant of his fate.

Two more pairs of our aircraft were already planned to go off for more FAC work, but both missions were cancelled by Flyco after the bad news. As soon as I had got the message about Bob, I hurried to Flyco and asked Wings about the possibility of laying on a Combat Search and Rescue (S&R) mission to try and pick him up. There seemed to be a good chance that he was still alive. The answer came back shortly: no Combat S&R. The Admiral had vetoed it. They were just too nervous about the chances of losing more helicopters to ground fire. Right at this time an electrifying piece of information came in that a patrolling Sea Harrier pilot had heard a desperate-sounding voice on guard frequency using Bob's mission call sign. This was great news. I was convinced that Bob had survived, and I racked my brains for any means by which we could help him out, now that the Navy had washed their hands of him. The Sea Harrier pilot had tried to talk to Bob but there had been no reply. I had a plan, which I hoped would convince the Navy to allow me to try to make contact with Bob. I argued that it was absolutely vital now to get some air-to-ground photo coverage of the Goose Green area. We were scheduled to return there for more attacks the next day. After the success of the Port Howard attacks, I pleaded to be allowed to fly a recce mission. I managed to convince the Boss of the sense of this; at the same time I would be able to attempt to contact Bob on his emergency radio. Flyco didn't really want to let me go on what they thought was a wild goose chase; more important, we had only one serviceable aircraft left to fly. I would have to go alone. Eventually, after a lot of argument I was allowed to climb into the aircraft on deck, where I sat fuming at the delay that followed. The Navy took a long time to make up their minds, and it was not until 1900 hours, just an hour before dusk, that I was allowed to launch. Obviously, at this late hour I wasn't going to get any photo coverage, but I wasn't too bothered about that. My main concern was to get over to where Bob had been shot down.

Approaching the islands at high level the skies had almost cleared of cloud, leaving me with a splendid view as far as the western shores of West Falkland. The late evening sun was momentarily concealed behind a cloud bank in the north-west, the familiar isthmus in dark shadow as I slowly descended. For the last few minutes there had been tension on the LAAWC's frequency (Landing Area Air Warfare Controller), as an enemy air raid was inbound. I could hear the LAAWC controllers giving their laconic instructions to the Sea Harriers as they were directed to intercept the incoming raid.

Not for the first time did I feel a twinge of envy at the Sea Harriers' cushy job, now that they had given up Ground Attack on the Admiral's orders. No interminable hassling with an idiotic Air Task organisation for them, and no sordid grovelling about in the weeds to attack unseen targets while their aircraft were shot full of holes by every man and his dog. No: it would be the Air Defender's life for me in the next war – if I survived this one. Plenty of hanging about admiring the scenery from a safe height, punctuated by the very occasional burst of excitement when you were directed on to a 'bogey' – usually some panicky attack pilot running for his life after a desperate attempt to hit the target.

After a brief stern chase just a press of the trigger was enough. No map reading at zero feet, and no return fire. Just the roaring smoke trail of your American-built 'Lima' as it sped unerringly on its way to your helpless target. Finally, the animal thrill of elation as the brief fireball smashed your enemy into the sea. Shoot someone down and back home you would be sure of the medals and the adulation of the girls – after all, only *real* fighter pilots get to shoot down aeroplanes don't they? Those GR3 pilots just moved dirt around – anyone can do that.[20]

I returned to reality with a call from the LAAWC that an air raid was in progress at Ajax Bay, now clearly visible some 15 miles to the north-west. As if on a cue the setting sun had just broken out below the cloud to light the scene perfectly. I could see the bay clearly from 20,000 feet and now the dramatic backlight lit up the expanding clouds of dust as bombs exploded on the shore at the landing site. I could see the smoke trails of several SAMs as they flashed to and fro across the water; it was too far away to see what they were firing at. The action looked closer than it was, and for a moment I toyed with the idea of asking the LAAWC if I could join in the chase for the bad guys, who would soon be running for it down the Falkland Sound just to the west. I thought to myself: 'Forget it sport – you've got something else to do.'

I changed frequency to Guard and began the first photo run at about 15,000 feet, a height at which I thought I was reasonably safe from the defences. There was absolute stillness below. In the twilight a couple of pinpoints of light showed occasionally, the only evidence of the enemy troop positions on the isthmus. I made a couple more calls on Guard frequency using Bob's call sign, but received no reply. If Bob was down there, he obviously had his receiver switched off to save his batteries. I decided to go just a little lower. I had given up taking pictures: in the prevailing light it was pointless. Perhaps a bit lower Bob would see and hear me and switch on. Suddenly, on my Radar Warning Receiver I heard the sinister rattle of a locked-on Skyguard radar. Almost immediately I got a hell of a shock as a neon-red burst of heavy-calibre tracer passed extremely close to my cockpit. *Fuck this for a game of soldiers!*

Fortunately I had kept my speed up, and at full power I broke hard away to the east. *What a fool.* The tracer had been going extremely well as it passed me: we had no hard intelligence about the maximum height capability of the 35-mm guns, but from this experience it was obviously some way above my altitude. (Later we learned that the *Invincible* pilots had seen 35-mm shell bursts up to 20,000 feet. Naturally enough this information had not been passed on to us.) After a few more unanswered calls to Bob I set course for the ship, where I landed on in almost complete darkness.

Early in the morning of 28 May there was a lot of low cloud in our area, and much low stratus was forecast over the islands. The first task was an attack on a suspected ammunition storage area at the back of Mt Kent, to be led by the Boss in company with Tony Harper and Pete Harris. Reports of this target had come in from some SAS who were lurking in the area. A six-figure map reference of the target had been given, and we hoped that it was reasonably accurate. The target lay in a shallow ravine about halfway up the mountain. There were no distinguishing features nearby and so target acquisition was not going to be easy. The formation was armed with 2-inch rockets. On their return the Boss reported very poor conditions at the target in mist and rain. Only he and Pete Harris had managed to fire and they saw some secondary explosions, indicating that they were on target. The weather had hardly improved when the next task came in and J.R. and I set off at about 1600 hours on an Armed Recce of a long route starting at Douglas Settlement on East Falkland and finishing at Green Patch settlement. As usual, there was no information about our own troops. Once again, I briefed that the priority was to get good pictures of all suspicious areas: under no circumstances were we going to fire into any of the settlements. Flying under a very low stratus base we set off along the muddy track from Douglas Settlement which, unbeknown to us, had just been occupied by forward elements of 45 Commando. We saw no one. After Teal Inlet settlement we approached the Malo hills, where the cloud was on the ground. We had to do a certain amount of milling about to the east to get round this obstacle, and I lost contact with J.R. briefly in one of the turns. However, we found each other again at the bridge on the south side of the hills where we rejoined the linesearch. From then on we were able to complete the route without incident. Apart from a couple of settlers waving to us enthusiastically from their farms, we saw no trace of enemy activity. Back at the ship we landed back on after a Carrier Controlled Approach in improving weather conditions. For me, the day's flying was to end in a spectacularly successful mission, which I joined almost by accident.

CHAPTER FIFTEEN

Dusk Strike at Goose Green

I had been back in the pilots' briefing room for about half an hour when Pete Harris and Tony Harper were called back in from Alert 5 on deck to plan an attack on Goose Green. There had been a brief outbreak of common sense, and the Navy had allowed them to come in and plan properly for a mission into what everyone knew was a very 'hot' area. The Air Task Message requested an attack on troops and 35-mm flak gun positions on the small peninsula just to the east of Goose Green settlement. After a desperate day's fighting 2 Para had got all remaining enemy forces bottled up in this area, where they were offering fierce resistance. As usual the Argies had plenty of ammunition and their flak guns in particular were causing havoc with 2 Para, who were by now critically short of ammunition. I watched Pete Harris and Tony planning the attack, noting with approval their straight run-in from an excellent coastal Initial Point in the north-west, leaving the setting sun behind them. Their two aircraft, both armed with cluster bombs, were the only two remaining serviceable aircraft; however, just before Pete Harris and Tony walked out to fly I got the message that one more GR3 had come up, armed with rockets. I asked the Boss if I could join in on the back of the sortie – on the understanding that I wouldn't delay their launch in any way. Initially the Boss wasn't keen, but I persuaded him to let me go. Within a couple of minutes I had thrown a line on the 1:50,000 map and spent no more than thirty seconds of briefing time with Pete Harris about the attack. The brief went something like this: 'Standard squadron Escort Attack with you as No. 3 on the left. Any questions WIN?'[21]

There was no time for any more. We raced upstairs and I realised that I didn't even know our call sign! Brian Mason met me with a worried look as I said I was about to climb into aircraft No. 32.

'You can't sir, it's been overstressed,' was his reply.

He had just discovered that the previous pilot had pulled more than 7 G, and the troops were just about to start the essential overstress checks to make sure that nothing important had been broken.

'Come on Brian, don't be silly,' I replied only half in jest, 'I'll probably get shot down anyway – that'll solve the paperwork problem!'

With a grin he let me go, saying that the paperwork would take care of itself. What a player. By Sod's Law I was parked near the bow. It was already only half an hour before sunset and the Navy managed for once to get a real ripple on and launch us with minimum delay.

Pete Harris was on the radio to *Fearless* long before we reached the islands. We heard nothing until finally we were almost directly overhead Ajax Bay, where the ship lay. (This was a fairly routine situation as far as radio communications went.) Now we could just hear a faint voice telling us that we were clear to attack as briefed. Fortunately this was Category 3 Forward Air Control, where the controller merely confirmed that target details were as briefed, after they had already been passed by Air Task Message. From then on the FAC acted merely as a veto, if necessary cancelling the attack if it was no longer needed. Immediately Pete Harris set off south-east in a dive towards the Initial Point near the entrance to Brenton Loch. Fortunately for us large gaps had appeared by now in the stratus layer, and we only had to do a minimum of dodging about to achieve a visual letdown. By now, I had begun to have a few misgivings about this mission, for which I had so rashly volunteered. The Oerlikon 35-mm flak battery that we were about to attack had the highest success rate of all the enemy AA and SAM units so far, having shot down three aircraft (one of which was an 'own goal'). Additionally, the battery had already given me a bit of a pasting on our Goose Green attack a week ago, and again yesterday. However, there was no time for further demoralising thoughts as we levelled off in the Sound. The sun was disappearing below the horizon behind us as we set off in Attack Formation from the Initial Point. Once again I was back marker, and I was doing a bit of my own map reading just to check up on Pete Harris, whose aircraft was just a mile in front. Several miles ahead we could already see drifting clouds of smoke right across our track, which was going to take us through the middle of the battlefield. I was happy about the smoke: with a bit of luck it would give us some cover. So far there was not a peep on the Radar Warning Receiver. I hoped it stayed that way. Just then we made contact with the local FAC, who gave us final clearance to continue.

'Watch out, there are a couple of Pucaras in the area as well.'

Those were his final words to us. We discovered later that the Pucaras had been shooting them up a bit, and they had shot one down with a Stinger not long before our arrival. This piece of information perked us up, and we all started to scan the horizon in search of the enemy aircraft. However, none were seen and the time for the attack was approaching rapidly as we flew into the pall of smoke. Momentarily losing sight of Pete, I hoped that the smoke did not extend as far as the target, now only a few seconds' flying time away. Suddenly I burst out into clear air. Here it was noticeably darker, but I could see the settlement of Goose Green and the target peninsula laid out directly in front, just like a model. I could also see Pete Harris running straight at them and what followed was a textbook Escort Attack. By our fortuitous approach through the smoke we had escaped detection so far. Now I lost sight of Pete in the gloom. I was already in a shallow dive on to the target, having had to ease up a bit during our transit through the smoke. Suddenly the target burst into life as pinpoint flashes appeared right across the middle. I twitched violently in the cockpit, waiting for the inevitable tracer. But these were Pete's cluster bombs exploding, and with that came the briefest of radio calls, 'COME *RIGHT* 50 YARDS FROM THAT!'

It was an excellent call from Pete in the heat of the moment. As he pulled off target he had seen the gun positions just to the right of his aiming point. With a flash of aileron and a kick on the rudder I changed my aiming point fractionally and tensed up on the firing button as in my peripheral vision I saw Tony's aircraft approaching the spot from the right. I couldn't fire until he was through my aiming point, and for a moment I thought I had cocked it up and got myself too close in for a successful attack. In the gloom the target looked closer than it was. Three things then happened almost simultaneously: Tony passed through the faint green aiming bug in my Head up Display; his cluster bombs exploded in a spectacular cascade of sparks from right to left across my front; then I fired all seventy-two of my rockets in a half-second burst. In the dim light I was momentarily dazzled by the rocket exhaust flashes as they sped towards the target. Within two seconds of Tony's attack my rockets exploded on the target in a violent burst of flame.[22]

No time to hang around. Pete and Tony had already disappeared over the dark sea to the east, racing away down Choiseul Sound at wave-top height as I turned off target to follow. We joined up again about 10 miles to the east of Goose Green, to carry out the final task of the sortie. Just as we walked out, Pete had declared his intention to have a sweep through the area where Bob had gone down. Passing well to the north of the smoke, we set off to the south-west across the open Lafonia plain, flying as low as we could in the rapidly fading light. We were also trying to 'skyline' any Pucaras, but had no luck. After a few minutes I nearly collided head-on with a Navy Wessex, which was flying along with its wheels almost on the ground in a shallow valley. I don't know how I managed to avoid it: it must have given the pilot a pretty big shock as well. Pete made a few radio calls but once again there was no reply from Bob. We gave up the search and returned to the ship. After an exhilarating debrief, in which we all congratulated each other on a damn good effort, we retired to the bar to become even more obnoxious after a few drinks.

The following is an extract from *Air War South Atlantic* by Jeffrey Ethell and Alfred Price:

> ... The attack had come as a complete surprise to the Argentinians, and the pilots saw no return fire.
>
> From his vantage point on Darwin Hill Chris Keeble (now commanding 2 Para after the death in action of Colonel 'H.' Jones) watched the Harriers do his bidding. 'They came streaking in, one behind the other; each dropped bombs, some on the tip of the peninsula and others at the entrance of the isthmus. Then I heard the cluster bomblets going off, their explosions merging together; it looked as if some hit the sea – there was an effect like throwing gravel into water. Then came the rockets, which were most effective; they hit the tip of the peninsula where the 35 mm guns were' he recalled. 'The attack gave a great boost to the morale of our troops. I think some of them thought the Harriers had come a bit too close for comfort, but that is war.'
>
> Harris's attack was a textbook example of a Close Air Support mission: a hard-hitting attack against a target of great importance to the enemy. Launched at a crucial time in the land battle, whose results were clearly seen by the ground troops – thus strengthening the resolve of those on one side and demoralizing those on the other.

Chris Keeble had no doubts about the decisiveness of the Harrier attack; 'After that there was a marked slackening in the fighting, which had gone on very fiercely the whole day. Afterwards I sat down and thought, "Where have we got to now? What is the enemy thinking?" I tried to assess the situation from his point of view. Now he was encircled and we had demonstrated that we could bring in the Harriers to attack his positions surgically. It was then that I began to get the notion that their will had been broken and maybe we could go for a surrender.'

There was little flying for us on the following day. Early in the morning we had been on standby to carry out another attack on the Goose Green positions as 2 Para were almost out of ammo. In a brave display of chutzpa, Chris Keeble, 2IC 2 Para, had advised the Argy defenders that they would receive further air attacks if they did not surrender unconditionally. This did the trick, and we were stood down from that task. At 1700 hours Pete Harris and John Rochfort were launched to attack a supposed enemy 'radar' position in the hills to the north of Port Stanley Airfield. This was the first of several mysterious 'radar site' attack missions, none of which was ever successful as far as we were concerned. Information on these targets was supposed to have been gleaned by Naval ships monitoring radar transmissions from ashore, and also by the SAS, from whom the Air Task Messages usually originated. We never managed to establish whether or not anyone had actually *seen* one of these radars, which were usually described as TPS 43/44 type. After several abortive missions on which nothing was seen at the location given (the TPS 43/44, a modern mobile surveillance radar, is quite a substantial piece of equipment) we came to the depressing conclusion that the tasking agencies were relying solely on radar signal intercepts. What was annoying was the fact that each 'radar' was reported in an exact six-figure grid reference, giving the impression that someone had actually seen it in operation there. After the conflict we found out that the Argies had used quite a few of the Israeli 'Eltar' and 'Rasit' miniature warning radars, which stood just a few feet high. I was certain that people were confusing these with much larger radars. Anyone who knew the first thing about Ground Attack would have known that there was no chance of successfully attacking such a small target as this without good photo coverage of the target area beforehand. In the event, on this particular mission John went U/S on deck with a fuel leak, leaving Pete to go alone on what we knew to be a fairly quiet area. Pete saw nothing at the position given, and returned with his weapons unused. While this was going on Tony Harper and I sat for several hours on Alert 5 without being tasked. Finally, the Boss and Mark were sent off to carry out rocket and gun attacks on dug-in troops in the Mt Kent area. At last, some hard intelligence was starting to come in about what was going on in this area. Mt Kent had been identified as one of the enemy's most heavily fortified strong points on the approaches to Stanley.

That night we received the tremendous news that Bob had been picked up by an Army Gazelle after the fall of Goose Green. After an adventurous couple of days of hiding from the Argies, he was reported to be in good shape and would be rejoining us soon. For the second time we had been lucky and one of us had survived against all the odds. For us, at least the period of uncertainty had been filled with action, and we had been able to make some effort to help. However, I felt the deepest sympathy for Dee and Ronnie, who had to sit helplessly over 8,000 miles away, waiting and hoping for any scrap of news. Our mail had never arrived regularly, and after the sinking of *Atlantic Conveyor* there was a gap of more than a week when we received no mail from home. 1(F) Squadron's itinerant lifestyle had proved too much for the mail system to cope with. Up to now I had not had much time to think about the family, although when things got a bit tedious I was able to relax myself a lot just by thinking about what I was going to do with the garden when (if) I came back. However, the loss of Bob had got me down quite a bit. We had been through quite a lot together since our early days of desert flying with the Day Fighter/ Ground Attack Hunter Wing in Bahrain. Ironically, our primary Operational Task at that time (1970–71), was the defence of Kuwait against Iraqi aggression.

On 30 May 1982 my luck finally ran out. Early in the day the Boss and Mark had been back to the Mt Kent area to attack troop positions when a task came in for Tony Harper and me to attack another of the infamous 'radar' targets, this time on Mt Round, to the north of Port Stanley Airfield. (Much later we discovered that this was the location of a tiny 'Eltar' radar, working with a well-camouflaged 30-mm battery.) The aircraft we were allocated were already armed with two 1,000-lb retard bombs each – not a load that we really wanted for this type of target. However, as it would take ages to rearm I said we would go with what was hung on the jets. The previous day Pete Harris had been given one of these tasks, and the location given (once again a six-figure grid reference), lay at the eastern end of Mt Low. Pete had seen nothing at the location but, as the position was only a few miles east of our target area, I briefed Tony that we would take pictures and attack both. Both targets lay in the very hilly area 6 or 7 miles north of Port Stanley Airfield – hopefully beyond missile range. We had no intelligence on any military activity in this range of hills. We approached Mt Round from the west to take some pictures. The mountain was a featureless dome-shaped hill, on which we could see nothing except a scattering of small boulders. I carried on east and decided to attack the Mt Low position straight away.

At this stage my brain had dropped into low gear, perhaps lacking the spur of adrenalin to sharpen my reactions. I pitched in for a strafe attack, not a very bright idea with the heavy bombs aboard. (I should have got rid of the bombs on this target.) Fortunately, just before I opened fire I realised what I was doing. I opened fire early and made it a shortish burst to give me plenty of room to pull out clear of the substantial hill behind the position. Even so, the recovery was distinctly sluggish, and I cursed myself for my stupidity. As expected, there had been nothing remotely resembling a radar at the position given, and I had merely strafed a lump of rock closest to it. Returning via Mt Round, I decided idly to get rid of my bombs on the map reference given for the radar, as I couldn't take them back aboard. Again, foolishly, I was slow to warn Tony of my intentions, and he was a bit put out by the sudden explosions.

Returning aboard ship, I reflected that this had been a pretty gash performance on my part: I apologised to Tony, promising to try harder next time. Tony took it all in fairly good humour and once again I was thankful that he was such a steady and unflappable character. Like me, he had not jumped forward to volunteer for this business but in the stress of action he had proved to be a steady and reliable leader, never complaining about anything he was asked to do. Later on we took a look at the photos we had taken. Not surprisingly there was absolutely no trace of a radar but I was amused to see a 30-mm RheinMetall flak gun concealed among the rocks near Mt Round. We must have flown twice within a few hundred metres of this gun, and yet they never opened up on us.

The Admiral was still desperate to get some deep-penetration free-fall bombs on the PSA runway and, since it was clear from the fiasco of our unsupported loft bombing attacks that the Navy hierarchy did not have a clue how this could be achieved, desperate measures were now necessary. We would have to solve the problem ourselves within the squadron. I came up with a scheme that could well have worked but was to founder because of duff information received from our supposedly expert Weapons Tactics Headquarters organisation back in the UK.

By now we had finally got some Paveway Laser Guided Bombs (LGBs) aboard *Hermes* and we were about to try them out for the first time. (No Brit Harrier pilot had used them previously.) Unfortunately, at this time no usable Laser Target Markers were available ashore (the batteries were all flat!) and so I suggested to the Boss that we should have a go using our own powerful on-board YAG laser. In March we had been given a briefing by a Weapons Instructor of the RAF's Central Tactics and Trials Organisation (CTTO), in which he had described the recent LGB loft bombing trials in Canada, in which the bombs were released from an aircraft that had pulled up into a shallow climb from Low Level. (The weapon was still very new to the RAF.) At the end of the briefing I had asked a question and been told that in emergency *we could use our own on-board laser for target designation*. This turned out to have been complete duff gen, but we were not to find this out for a couple of days yet. I had been Trials Pilot for the definitive Harrier VIFF trials just a few years before and I knew what could and could not be achieved using VIFF. My idea was for two aircraft, the first one a

Bomber and the second one a Designator, to pitch in at very low speed, one behind the other from above 30,000 feet in a near-vertical dive attack, both aircraft using maximum nozzle braking to keep airspeed low. The Designator behind would merely aim his laser at the middle of the runway while the Bomber released his bombs in the vertical, hopefully to home on the laser reflection (this would give the LGB seeker the best possible chance of homing on the laser spot).[23] The Weapon Instructors gave me the bomb flight times and from my knowledge of VIFF I was pretty sure that both pilots could get the attack over and pull out early enough to stay reasonably clear of the defences.

And so it proved. Mark and Tony Harper were the next pair off, and they tried my idea out overhead Port Stanley Airfield. Unfortunately, they saw no bomb impacts anywhere on the airfield. We didn't know at this stage whether it was the attack profile or the bomb fusing that was at fault. (We were also having to use a new type of bomb fuse.) This was our first attempt to get some operational value out of this potentially excellent weapon. Scandalously, our commanders did not seem to appreciate the urgency of putting together the essential package required to achieve successful LGB missions, i.e. a serviceable Laser Target Marker with charged battery, an FAC with a good radio and, of course, the bomb itself. In addition, a crucial error of judgement by the Navy hierarchy would further delay our use of the bombs. These problems would prevent us from achieving any worthwhile results from the LGB until the war was almost over. Until then we had no choice but to continue to use the traditional Low Level Ground Attack Tactics that had cost the Americans so dearly in Vietnam, where hundreds of Ground Attack aircraft were shot down or severely damaged by ground fire.

CHAPTER SIXTEEN

My Luck Runs Out

As usual there had been no useful information about enemy troop dispositions at the morning briefing. In 2006 from *Razor's Edge*, Hugh Bicheno's amazing account of the war, I discovered what was actually going on in the Wall Mountain/ Mt Harriet area at this time. Units of the Argy 3 Infantry brigade had dug in 120-mm heavy mortars in excellently constructed sangars on Wall Mountain (which we were to attack). This was an excellent position to dominate the south-western approaches to Stanley. On 30 May these weapons and supporting troops were in the process of being lifted by helicopter to Mt Harriet, just 2 km to the east. All of this was to remain unknown to us because of the lack of intelligence back-up and the appallingly bad Harrier radios, which meant we could get no useful information from the FAC on the spot.

John Rochfort and I had been sitting on Alert 20 in the pilots' briefing room and our Air Task came through about an hour after the Boss and Mark landed back on. I had already spoken to the Boss about his mission and he had some useful 'gen' for me: their FAC had given them the position of an enemy artillery battery on the saddle of Wall Mt, just to the south of Mt Kent. They had been unable to attack this target, having expended all their weapons. John and I plotted this target, along with a suitable Initial Point run, as a back-up in case of the all-too-common FAC shambles on the primary target. Soon after this an Air Task Message came through for John and me. We were to attack helicopters under FAC control at a Landing Zone on Mt Harriet. I glanced at the planned Time on Target in gloom; as usual there was precious little time to plan anything. We threw a line on the map and raced upstairs for the jets after a hasty brief on the target area. Our launch and departure were uneventful. We were each armed with rockets and during the high level transit to the islands, some 180 miles to the west, my problems began. The Standard Harrier Radio Problem began to manifest itself. Within a few minutes I was unable to transmit or receive on either Main or Standby radio. By means of hand signals I handed over the lead to John, as briefed. On letdown from high level, I began to pick up the FAC on my radio and so I took over the lead again as my radio appeared to work normally. (Normal, that is, for a Harrier radio.)

We passed the Initial Point at the coast at very Low Level, but soon had to ease up as the mountains rose steeply in front of us. I concentrated on the map reading and soon picked out the target area. About 4 km short of the target things began to happen very fast. I could see the target area clearly (the saddle of Mt Harriet) and realised that it was unoccupied, i.e. no helicopters were visible on the ground. At the same moment we crossed a dirt road on which several military vehicles were stopped. Within a couple of seconds I felt a significant 'thump' in the airframe somewhere behind me. I knew I had been hit: having seen no tracer or SAMs, I assumed it was small-calibre stuff. John had seen the vehicles and observed the hit on me. He transmitted straight away: 'Jerry, you're leaking fuel!' This was a considerable understatement, as I immediately began to generate a substantial 'contrail' of fuel which, of course, I could not see.

A quick glance in the cockpit showed nothing amiss and a glance ahead confirmed that our planned target area was bare of activity. All of the above happened within the space of about ten seconds. Before reaching the Landing Zone, I decided to turn hard left immediately and try an opportunity attack on the artillery position, which lay only a few seconds' flying time to the west, before setting course for home with my punctured jet. I crossed over John in the turn, calling my intentions on the radio. (John did not hear this as my radio was packing up again.) I rolled out on a south-westerly heading and looked right to the saddle of Wall Mountain, where the artillery position was located. Within a few seconds I heard a garbled call from John, who I picked up about a mile to my right heading towards me in dive on to the target, which I now saw clearly. Instinctively, I hauled around to the right at full power on to the target, simultaneously calling John to break out left after my attack, which was almost head-on to his. By chance we had achieved the perfect co-ordinated attack. I dimly remember John flashing past me as I rolled out and fired my rockets from close range, aiming low to allow for the reduced gravity drop. (Naturally, peacetime firing ranges were only of academic interest with targets that shot back.) The first rockets were exploding amongst the gun positions before the last had left the pod.[24] After the attack, a hard right turn left me running out at maximum speed to the south-east. I could no longer see John, who was almost back in position on my right, strafing the road as we passed to keep heads down.

Barely two minutes had elapsed since I had been hit, and now I settled down to check a few things. By now one of my two hydraulic systems had failed and, as I pulled up into the climb, several unanswered calls to John demonstrated that my radios had packed up for good. The final twenty minutes of my sortie were flown in silence. In the climb through cloud I checked my fuel again; before the hit I had over 4,500 lb of fuel and, as previous small calibre hits had caused leaks from one side only, I was still confident that I could get back to the ship.

Still in cloud at 10,000 feet I noticed that most of the lights on my Radar Warning Receiver were on. Hastily I switched on the audio (it was off for FAC work because of severe interference with radio reception) to hear the chilling sound of the acquisition radars of the Roland and Skyguard installations at Port Stanley Airfield. With horror I looked down to my left through a small gap in the cloud to see that I had unwittingly strayed inside the missile engagement envelope of the Sapper Hill Roland site. At this height and speed there was no point in turning away – it was impossible to outrun the missile – so I just froze on the stick and searched frantically for any SAMs that might be heading towards me out of the cloud. Painfully slowly, the altimeter crept up to a height at which I knew I was safe.

The next shock was more traumatic. As I levelled at about 30,000 feet, I saw the fuel gauges dropping through 3,000 lb total. I watched in horror as the fuel contents continued to drop symmetrically, as if I was in full afterburner. Experience of previous leaks and simulator training had conditioned me to expect leaks from one side only. (Afterwards, the Engineers calculated that I had received a very unlucky hit in the short length of fuel feed pipe to the engine, at the only point where the two separate halves of the system combine.) By now, I had jettisoned all external stores and, for a moment, considered turning back over the islands. Although Port San Carlos strip was not yet built, at least I could eject over land or even try to get aboard a ship in the landing area of Falkland Sound. *No chance*. There was no *Lame Duck* procedure to penetrate our trigger-happy missile defences without radio, and I knew they would blow me away without a second thought. By now I was already 30 miles east of Port Stanley Airfield and I estimated that with the strong westerly wind behind me, my best chance was to press on east, into the cold wastes of the South Atlantic, to try to make it back to the carrier. Within a few minutes I realised that my aircraft was doomed anyway. As the fuel gauges ran down together I could see that I wasn't going to make it. From 30,000 feet I could see the angry white tops of the waves, and I knew I would need some luck to survive. Because of the lousy radio installation, I could tell no one of my predicament. At the same time I had little confidence in my IFF, which had long been switched to the Emergency setting.

Suddenly, my spirits leapt as John appeared alongside. I had been flying almost flat out (standard procedure with a major fuel leak), and he had only just caught me up. Unbeknown to me, he had already alerted the Task Group and two helicopters were already on their way towards me. I signalled frantically that I was running out of fuel. After a few more minutes both fuel gauges read zero, and I gave the hand signal for my ejection. As if in a dream I watched the engine slowly wind down; I waved goodbye to John, my old buddy, and settled into a steep glide at 250 kt. For the last fifteen minutes or so the adrenalin had been pumping at full throttle, and there was to be no let up. In a silent, cosy glide down to 10,000 feet (the cockpit suddenly became very warm), I had to force myself to accept the inevitability of ejection into the freezing air outside. I was concerned that my hands would freeze up, leaving me incapable of getting into my life raft – my one and only chance of survival.

At 10,000 feet I pulled the handle. My first Harrier ejection was extremely violent, and I clearly remember my head being forced down between my knees by the 3,000-lb thrust of the rocket seat. After this the relief of hanging in the harness was overwhelming. My first reaction was to switch on my Personal Locater Beacon so that my distress signal would be heard at maximum range. I had only the vaguest idea of how close I was to the Task Group. (I must have been only about 50 miles away when I flamed out: with the glide and the strong wind I landed barely 40 miles from them.) The sea below was dotted with large cumulus and there was no sign of a ship in any direction. As I approached the top of a cloud, I felt that I was as prepared as possible for water entry; as expected, I was having to hold my heavy Personal Survival Pack (PSP) between my knees to prevent violent oscillations of the parachute. Suddenly, in the hostile stillness of the cloud I heard the sweetest sound imaginable – the distinct 'chop' of rotor blades. *Thank God for the Navy!* Below the cloud I still couldn't see the helicopter and I concentrated hard on the landing. I dropped the PSP at what I estimated to be about 200 feet and immediately smashed into a large piece of the South Atlantic which rose to meet me.

Now the panic really started. I was unable to release my parachute and straight away I was off, being dragged by the strong wind on a wild roller coaster ride from wave to wave. Luckily I was dragged on my back or I would have drowned very quickly. However, try as I could I was unable to get enough purchase to release my parachute with my rapidly freezing fingers. I could not see what I was doing because of the bulk of my life jacket and the Browning pistol stowed underneath. At last my 'chute collapsed, allowing me to pull in my life raft pack and inflate it, although I was still unable to release the parachute harness. A Lynx was already hovering overhead, but I realised that I had to get into the life raft first in order to get rid of my parachute. Although I should have waited for the life raft to harden up a bit, the urge to get out of the water was too strong. With all my remaining strength I managed to haul myself aboard, helped by the fact that the life raft was travelling steeply downhill as I entered. Temporarily safe in the wildly rocking life raft, I sprawled face down for several minutes, not daring to move in case I fell out. I knew that I would never be able to climb back in again should I capsize. Eventually I slowly turned over, to see that the Lynx had been replaced by a Sea King, which was already dangling a single-lift strop in my general direction. I was going to have to do everything for myself and there was no room for error. Very carefully I finally removed my harness and began to untangle the myriad of parachute rigging lines that were still wrapped around me. I realised that if just one line was still left attached, the winch could severely injure me as it tried to separate me from my sunken parachute. Only when I was 100 per cent certain that I was completely untangled did I start to reach for the strop, which had whistled past my ear a few times already.

This was going to be interesting: the strop alternately dangled in the water and then, within a couple of seconds, hung 15 feet above it. I had no strength left for any fancy gymnastics, so it had to work first time. The next time the strop stabilised beside me for a brief period I grabbed at it and looped it over my shoulders. Although my right arm was well in I had only just got a purchase with an inch of my left elbow in the strop when the South Atlantic fell away beneath me. For a second I thought of letting go and trying again, but the urge to get out of the hostile sea was too great. I clung on grimly and was winched aboard, just retaining the presence of mind to reach down and release my life raft lanyard before it came taut. (This was the first single-lift winching I had experienced: RAF rescue helicopters invariably sent a crewman down on the wire to make sure everything was attached properly.)

After collapsing on the cold metal floor of the cabin I felt safe at last, the screaming engines and thundering transmission seeming to shout back defiance at the anonymous piece of sea that had so very nearly done for me. This was an Anti-Submarine Sea King, its crew more accustomed to the desperate cat-and-mouse game of finding and killing submarines with powerful depth charges. For them, the ridiculously young-looking Pilot and the much older Lieutenant Commander Observer who had operated the winch, the challenge of a live rescue was probably a welcome diversion from their routine task.

With my small remaining strength I grabbed the rather surprised Observer in a joyful hug: I would have kissed him if our helmets had not got in the way. Within ten minutes we had landed back aboard *Hermes*. After walking straight up to Flyco I met John who was taken aback by my blood-spattered face, a result of the usual superficial injuries caused by the explosion of the canopy Miniature Detonating Cord (MDC). John had arrived in Flyco only minutes before me and was debriefing with Wings and the Captain about the mission. I went below to the pilots' briefing room and ran straight into Bob, who had just been brought aboard. We shook hands warmly and the conversation went something like this:

'Jerry, you're all wet – been for a swim?'

'Something like that. I understand you've been taking a few days off in the country – you lazy sod!'

The Sea King carrying Bob from the islands had picked up J.R.'s Mayday call on my behalf when I ejected, and initially the pilot had started to home on to my Personal Locater Beacon. Eventually, he was told that he was not needed, there being enough helicopters involved already. That would have been an interesting little reunion for Bob and me if his crew had picked me up. Within minutes of my arriving in the pilots' briefing room, the alert klaxon sounded and the Task Group came under Exocet and bomb attack from a formation of Skyhawks and Super Etendards. We heard a few bangs as we cowered below decks in our anti-flash gear and later we learned that the Navy had shot down two of the Skyhawks. An Exocet was fired, the last known air-launched missile possessed by the Argies. It missed. This seemed a fitting end to an eventful day as far as I was concerned. Working 24/7 we had no concept of what day of the week it was. Several days passed before I realised that I had been shot down on a Sunday – very appropriate for an atheist, I thought. The MDC 'splatter' injuries were a minor problem, but I suffered an extremely sore neck as a result of the ejection.

The air attack was soon over and I wandered down to the Sick Bay to be checked out by the surgeon. I felt OK, but they insisted on going through the whole business, cutting my immersion suit off and checking me all over for signs of broken bones. After all that the Surgeon Commander dismissed me saying, 'You can go ahead and fly when your neck feels better'. There was no opportunity for the customary post-ejection X-rays: they didn't have the right equipment aboard. (Also, in peacetime the RAF would not allow any ejectee to fly again for some time.)

Bob told us the story of being shot down and landing heavily, hurting his back. He suffered some temporary eye injury and couldn't see straight, making some effort to evade what he thought were enemy troops but which turned out to be sheep! He found a deserted farm-house and hid for several days, existing on some cold baked beans he found. Laid-back as always, Bob gave the impression that this thin diet was the greatest hardship he had endured (understandable for a man of his stature)! He didn't complain, but soon we were to find out just how bad his back injury was.

As I wandered back to the pilots' briefing room I had to keep kicking myself to realise how lucky I had been. I am not a 'smiler' under normal circumstances, but I found myself grinning idiotically at every-one as they asked what had happened. (There were scabs from the MDC 'splatter' all over my face.) I strolled into the ground crew room to tell the lads what had happened before stacking to the bar for a few drinks. By now my neck had stiffened up a lot and after a few horse's necks and a hot shower I crashed out to sleep like a log.

In the morning I found my neck was almost rigid. I told the Boss that I felt OK to fly, but I wouldn't be much use at lookout. He said I should stay on the ground for a day and be DCF, so we got on with it again. First of all, we sent three aircraft to Port Stanley Airfield where Pete Harris, John and Tony Harper carried out some more high tech 'gardening' with LGBs. Once again, there was total frustration. Not a single bomb impact was observed. We were persisting with this at this stage because as far as we were concerned this was the only way of getting a free-fall bomb on the runway, and hence causing some permanent damage. The pilots concerned were in effect carrying out an 'ad hoc' weapons trial over a target that was actively trying to shoot them down! By now it was apparent to us that the 35-mm flak batteries could get rounds up as high as 20,000 feet, where they were self-detonating in spectacular fashion at the end of their trajectory. At the start of this business we had signalled our detailed intentions to carry out the self-designated LGB attacks. Later in the day we received a reply from Northwood who told us to give up trying, as our laser was 'not compatible' with the LGBs we were using. *Bloody marvellous!* After the ballsache of being shot down and the frustration resulting from our failed LGB attacks, I was in no mood to put up with further nonsense at the hands of the Navy. However, over the next few days we were to receive further demonstrations of the Navy's incompetence which would try our patience to the limits.

CHAPTER SEVENTEEN

More Navy Cockups

A bit later on the Boss and Mark were sitting at Alert 5 on deck when they were suddenly scrambled by Flyco. I immediately asked what was going on, to be told that they were being sent to attack a couple of 'Etendards', which had been seen on the ground at Port Stanley Airfield. This sounded pretty suspicious to me, and straight away I tried to find out where this task had come from. There had been no mention of the task to me as DCF before they were scrambled, hence I had been unable to get any kind of map out to them on deck. By the sheerest luck the Boss had been on a Port Stanley Airfield Low Level attack seven days ago, and was thus able to remember the details of a suitable attack run. Sending an attack on Port Stanley Airfield without any maps, planning or briefing was a great risk, which would possibly have been justified had there been accurate intelligence about the supposed target; however, this mission was a result of one of the biggest Air Intelligence cockups made by the Navy. Basically, the problem resulted once again from the Navy's inability to interpret and assess vital intelligence and distribute it to the people who needed it. We were already used to this on *Hermes*: while the Master Tacticians of The Flag worked on their own little planet we had built up our own intelligence situation maps using whatever scraps of information we could pick up. Pilots' reports and debriefs from our hard-working Photographic Interpreters were our main sources of information. However, we could not ensure that this information was passed on to other agencies beyond *Hermes* – *Invincible*, for example. We discovered later that her pilots were given even less information than us. This example shows what they were up against.

Flight Lieutenant Ian 'Morts' Mortimer, (ex-3 Squadron RAF), was serving on exchange duty as Air Weapons Instructor with 801 Naval Air Squadron on *Invincible*. He told me that on 2 May he had been tasked by the Ship's Air Ops to carry out a Radar Recce at night, to a point some 150 miles north-west of the ship's position. During the brief by the Operations Officer he was told nothing about what he was expected to find, about what enemy surface units might be in the area, or what air opposition he might encounter. Being an RAF pilot he had a healthy interest in these things, but was told to shut up and fly the mission exactly as he had been briefed. This was a typical Naval Air Task. Reaching the radar switch-on point in pitch dark at about 20,000 feet, he made a couple of scans with his radar and immediately picked up a lot of surface returns, indicating ships close by. Up to now his Radar Warning Receiver had been silent, but with his radar transmissions it burst into life to show that he was locked-up by a Sea Dart fire control radar. Realising that he was well within their launch envelope, he broke away violently and ran for his life in the realisation that he had stumbled across an Argy Type 42 destroyer, almost certainly in company with their only carrier, *The 25th May*. On return to the ship he reported immediately to Air Ops to tell his story. No one there was particularly surprised by what he said, and he was still intrigued to know why none of the ships he had found were showing on the large situation map in Air Ops (which he had studied before the mission). On an impulse, he walked through into the Ship's Ops, which was not usually visited by aircrew. In there on another situation map he saw an Ops officer casually moving a large pin marked *25 MAY* a few miles to one side. They had known all along what they were sending him into: in typically arrogant Naval fashion they did not consider that a mere pilot should be made privy to such information – even if he was going to be shot down as a result.

There was hardly any cross-flow of intelligence information between the two ships, at least as far as the pilots were concerned. Fairly early on in the war the Admiral had decided to give most of the attack tasks to *Hermes'* aircraft and leave *Invincible* to concentrate on Air Defence. However, their Sea Harriers were tasked for some attack missions, the vast majority of which were 'Area Bombing', carried out from 20,000 feet plus, often above cloud, using their rather inaccurate NAVHARS computers for bomb release. Morts told me with a certain amount of pride that they were able to achieve an accuracy of plus or minus 400 yards with this kit! Come back 'Bomber' Harris – all is forgiven!

To return to the 'Etendard' sighting, an 801 Naval Air Squadron pilot, Lieutenant Charlie Cantan, had taken high level photos of Port Stanley Airfield in the morning as he returned from a routine Combat Air Patrol mission. He had seen what he described as two 'strange' aircraft parked near the end of the runway. According to Morts, Charlie did not describe them as Etendards at the time. The film was processed and the staff aboard *Invincible* agreed that they were Etendards. They passed a message to the Admiral to this effect, hence the panic-stricken order to scramble our aircraft. However, as soon as our Photographic Interpreters on *Hermes* heard about the message they searched through our library of recent high-level Port Stanley Airfield photos. As they suspected, there were indeed two 'strange'-looking aircraft close to the threshold of the runway – *and they had been there for several weeks.* We had known all about these aircraft since our arrival on board *Hermes*: they were a couple of damaged Macchi 339s, which had been parked on some oddly shaped bits of steel planking, giving them the appearance of larger swept-wing aircraft. We had seen this for ourselves on our frequent overflights of Port Stanley Airfield, and had thought no more of it. The thought never crossed our minds that this kind of information would not have been passed on to *Invincible*. However, sure enough, because of the almost complete lack of intelligence liaison between the two carriers, the pilots and Photographic Interpreters of *Invincible* knew nothing of this.

As a direct result of this intelligence balls-up, the Boss and Mark were off on their desperate wild goose chase to attack Port Stanley Airfield. Flyco had somehow managed to organise two Sea Harriers to toss some airburst bombs as defence suppression before our guys arrived. However, once again the effect of this was merely to stir up the defences and by the time that Mark and the Boss arrived, all hell had broken loose. They were armed with rockets and they attacked from a very low height. Because of the lack of planning they both had difficulty in getting properly lined up with the target, hence they both attacked from too close in, picking up some ricochet damage from the hard runway. Later on I had a look at Mark's attack film. It was pretty horrific, and it was obvious that they had fired while they were still turning on to the target. As well as the ricochet damage, Mark also collected a defender's bullet, which half-penetrated the toughened windscreen at eye level. This was repaired later with a steel plate glued on with Araldite. Finally, after landing, it was discovered that one aircraft had so much engine damage that it had to have an engine change, which was to take it out of service for five days. As a direct result of yet another avoidable intelligence cockup by the Navy, we were now left with only *one* serviceable aircraft to continue operations. Flying the last of our sorties that day, Pete Harris took that aircraft for a rocket attack on troops in the hills to the west of Stanley. By now the Boss was understandably furious. We had been in action for just eleven days and we had lost or severely damaged five out of our six aircraft. This looked like the end of the road for our Ground Attack operations. However, we already knew of the bold plan to ferry more GR3s *direct* from Ascension as replacements for us. Plans were well in hand for this, and in the evening the Boss visited the Captain to see if the plan could be expedited, now that we were so critically short of aircraft. The Boss returned in a black mood, to tell us that the Captain was trying to veto the operation! The Captain's exact words had been: 'No, I think it's a waste of time: it's just the RAF trying to lay on a publicity stunt!'

How the Boss managed to keep his temper I shall never know. To me, this was just one more example of the Navy's childish attempts to deny the RAF any credit for participation in the war. Very fortunately for us, 'The Flag' were forced by higher authority to accept the reinforcement plan, which was to begin tomorrow.

Tuesday, 1 June 1982

After poor weather in the morning the weather cleared sufficiently later on for the Boss to take our last remaining GR3 on one of the pointless 'radar' tasks. Acknowledging our obvious shortage of GR3s, the Captain graciously agreed to send along a Sea Harrier as wingman, piloted by Ted Ball, an RAF Flight Lieutenant. This was a laugh, we thought grimly. Perhaps now that the Navy realised that they were going to have to start risking their precious Sea Harriers in Low Level mud-moving again, then we would see a little more enthusiasm for the GR3 reinforcement plan. The Boss's mission was even more ludicrous than the usual 'radar' task. The Air Task Message described a Porta-kabin at the location given, about 1 mile away from the 'radar' itself. The usual six-figure grid references showed the target to lie some 15 miles *behind* our own most forward troops! Quite why the enemy was prepared to leave an operating radar unit in such a position was not explained on the Air Task Message. Naturally, there was no point in querying the task, so the Boss and Ted went off as planned. The Boss fired his rockets at the grid reference given and neither pilot saw anything resembling a radar or Portakabin at either position, as expected. Still, we thought, this was one way of passing the time. Presumably the Master Tacticians of The Flag thought that this kind of mission was contributing to the war effort. Later in the afternoon a message filtered through that a Sea Harrier from *Invincible* had been shot down over the sea near Stanley. A little later a further message came in that the pilot – Morts – had probably survived, but that he had not yet been picked up. We felt for him.

By now I had been agitating for Ops to change our call sign procedures in order to make our attack sorties a bit less conspicuous to the enemy. After the sinking of *Atlantic Conveyor* we had instituted complicated 'Gate' procedures for departure and recovery to the ship, in order to conceal the position of the Task Group from the enemy. The procedures cost us quite a bit of time and fuel, involving a low-level transit after launch to a point some 40 miles away from the ship, from where we could begin our climb towards the islands. A similar arrangement was set up for recovering aircraft, with a low-level arrival 'Gate', from which you transitted at low-level to the ship. However, the Navy still had us using the same old colour call signs: Green and Red for GR3 formations, and Silver, Gold, Black and White for Sea Harriers. To me, it was obvious that after two weeks of joint operations even the dimmest Argy could work out that an attack mission was inbound merely by listening to the call signs. I suggested to Wings that we should from now on allocate call signs at random to GR3s and Sea Harriers, so that the Argies could not tell if an incoming formation was an attack task or a pair of Sea Harriers going on Combat Air Patrol. My suggestion was reluctantly accepted and we began to use the new system straight away.

At about 1730 hours the first two reinforcement GR3s landed on after a nine-hour flog down from Ascension. They carried empty 100-gallon combat tanks outboard and the big 330-gallon ferry tanks inboard, the latter being jettisoned before landing. By now, we had lost touch with exactly who was at Ascension out of the pilots we had trained during our frantic work-up in UK. After the GR3s had landed I walked up on deck to meet them. To our surprise the two pilots were not from 1(F) Squadron. They were Mike Beech and Murdo McLeod of 3(F) Squadron.

On this day we were finally cleared to commence operations into the Port San Carlos forward strip, which had just been completed. The plan was to send Syd Morris plus two of our pilots ashore to the strip straight away by sea transport. Syd was to be the 'Airport Manager' from now on, controlling all operations from the strip. The two pilots were to wait ashore until the first two GR3s arrived, when they could take over the aircraft and fly an Air Task that they had already planned, before returning to *Hermes* to rearm. (There were no weapons available at the strip.) The pilots who had brought the aircraft in would climb out and be available to plan the next Air Task that came in, staying overnight if necessary. As we were not short of pilots this plan offered the most efficient use of our resources and gave us back a measure of control over our own flying operations. By having two pilots ready to plan a task as it came in, we would avoid some of the worst features of the shambolic tasking aboard *Hermes*.

Naively, we also believed that we would enjoy much better communications with *Fearless*, anchored just a few miles away in Falkland Sound. In this we had not reckoned with the incompetence of the planners who, demonstrating the kind of foresight shown at Gallipoli, had failed to anticipate the need for adequate Ground-to-Ground communications between the strip and other agencies. We discovered, to our horror, that we had only an old-fashioned High Frequency radio available. Because of its insecurity, all messages had to be laboriously coded and decoded, adding considerable delays to our response time. Line-of-sight communications direct to *Fearless* were impossible because of intervening high ground. During our peacetime Harrier operations over the last decade we were used to having fully secure and reliable communications with other formations, with back-up systems in the event of failures. Even so, we were often critical of the facilities available, and were for ever striving to gain improvements on what we had. The thought that anyone would plan to operate from the strip without reliable, secure communications was incomprehensible to us.

The choice of who would be the first to go ashore presented some problems. John Rochfort was keen to go: by now he was fed up with the shipborne environment and more than willing to get on to dry land for a while, no matter how bleak the location. The problem was that there was no guarantee that the two guys ashore would not have to remain for several days, sitting around waiting for GR3s to come in. There was no other volunteer, and so we decided that Pete Harris would have to go.

In the afternoon 'Sharky' Ward of 801 Naval Air Squadron shot down an Argy Hercules over the sea. Several days later Sharky told me the story. He was almost out of Combat Air Patrol fuel and about to return to the strip when the LAAWC vectored him towards a 'slow-moving' target north of the islands. Apparently, the Argies had been using this Hercules as an Airborne Command Post for their raids. Having been lurking in a safe area well out to the west, the Hercules pilot decided to go closer in to the islands at Low Level. Although they were warned that this was not safe they pressed on in, to be picked up by the LAAWC as they strayed briefly above the radar horizon. Underestimating the range to this large target, Sharky fired his first Sidewinder out of range and was disgusted to see it fall into the sea. Ignoring his fuel gauges, he pressed in closer and fired a second missile, which hit one of the Hercules engines with no immediate effect. Furious at his apparent lack of success, Sharky got in even closer and sprayed it with cannon fire. After backing off the smoking target, he was relieved to see it slowly drop a wing and then cartwheel violently into the sea. The crew had no chance – they knew they were dead meat as soon as Sharky saw them ...

CHAPTER EIGHTEEN

Bad Weather Sets In

On 2 June the weather looked pretty poor from the start of the day. The forecast was appalling for the islands, although it wasn't too bad at our location. After a lot of messing about from Flyco I was finally teamed up with McLeod to go and attack yet another of the phantom 'radar' targets, this time in the far north of East Falkland. I thought this would be a suitable 'milk run' to introduce him to the operating procedures, although I thought we had little chance of getting to the target area in the prevailing weather. I briefed him carefully on all the usual details, emphasising the important stuff I had covered the day before. Finally, during the Escape and Evasion part of the brief I said: 'If you get yourself shot down, don't get smart with your pistol. People out there are going to shoot first and ask questions later: our side and theirs. Just use it for shooting geese.'

Just after start up McLeod called me to say that he had no Head up Display. This was not one of our briefed 'no-go' items. 'It's OK, we'll go anyway,' was my reply.

After launch and the protracted low-level departure procedures McLeod joined up on me in close formation and we set off on a long climb through 20,000 feet of cloud. We broke out briefly on top but then we were back in it again up to the letdown point. I had a good final steer from 'D', giving me confidence that we were on track as we plunged back into the thick stuff for the descent to Low Level well offshore. I realised that we had only about a 20 per cent chance of getting visual below. The big unknown factor was the accuracy of the forecast pressure setting I was using as an altimeter datum. For all I knew, the cloud could be right down to sea level, and I had already decided to go no lower than 200 feet indicated in cloud. Just a 3-millibar error in the Met man's forecast could put me 100 feet closer to the sea than I wanted to be. I knew that I would have to fly the last part of the descent very carefully if I wasn't to throw McLeod off my wing in an attempt to avoid the sea. With no Head up Display he would be poorly placed to recover from such a situation.

At 500 feet indicated the cloud was as thick as I had ever seen it, menacingly dark and clammy and typical of an active frontal cloud system. The 'clag' seemed to penetrate right into the tiny, comforting haven of the cockpit with impunity, coating the instrument panel and consoles with a thin layer of dew, a chilling reminder of the fragility of the thin metal and Perspex shield between me and the hostile elements all round. Starting at about 2,000 feet I had progressively and smoothly reduced my rate of descent so that there would be no last-minute jerk to make a final level-off. I had always found it depressing how many supposedly experienced pilots couldn't be bothered to practise this kind of thing properly when leading others in formation. Unfortunately, within the Harrier Force we suffered from quite a few 'Good Weather Cowboys' who regarded careful instrument flying as fit only for 'weeny' Flying Instructors and suchlike. You could not get it through their thick skulls that good instrument flying habits at all times would see them right when the chips were down and their flying was under pressure. In these circumstances all pilots reverted to their habitual style of flying.

By 300 feet I had reduced the rate of descent almost to zero, and we were still in the thick of it. I edged a bit lower. After a short while we entered a patch of thinner cloud, and for a moment I caught a glimpse of the sea, just a few grey crests hinting at the treacherous, shifting boundary between air and water. Having established that my altimeter was not far out I descended further. By now, McLeod was hanging on as if his life depended on it. I sensed the tension in his cockpit, almost close enough to touch alongside. I knew exactly how he felt, having been there myself many times. Now he could do nothing but trust me absolutely: he would know by instinct just how low we were. I hoped that he had sufficient trust in my flying to cope with what might happen next. If I screwed up we would both be shark bait. I flew on for a while at about 100 feet, half on instruments, but it was no good. The cloud occasionally thinned to give us a clear view of the sea immediately below us, but then it closed in again to plunge us into solid instrument conditions. I knew that the target was at least 200 feet above sea level, and it would be foolhardy to try to make a landfall in these conditions. Even if we found temporary low flying weather, there was a very high probability that we would run into low cloud again, forcing an Emergency Pull Up. This was an individual manoeuvre, and McLeod would be poorly placed to carry it out safely with no Head up Display. I broke radio silence to say we were going home – I could hear the relief in his acknowledgement. Still in tight formation, we climbed smoothly back into the murk for the long trek home, most of which was flown in cloud.

This was the only mission flown that day. Later on there was a bit of excitement with another Stand To for an air raid, but it all came to nothing and no enemy appeared. We were also much relieved and amused to hear of the rescue of Morts, who had been shot down the previous afternoon near Stanley. Flying on Combat Air Patrol from *Invincible*, he had cruised idly within range of the Sapper Hill Roland site at about 14,000 feet, promptly being shot down for his pains. He had imagined that he was just out of range, but was rather put out to see the flash and smoke trail of the missile launch. After turning to watch its flight path below him he lost sight of it. The next event was an almighty bang and the undignified shock of his aircraft falling to bits around him. We were not surprised at this: our opinion was that he had been rash to get so close at that altitude. We discovered that on *Invincible* it was a commonly held belief that the maximum engagement altitude of Roland was about 13,000 feet, this information having been gleaned from *International Defence Review*. On *Hermes* we knew of this figure but always added 5,000 feet as a 'wife and kids' factor. Luckily, Morts had survived after an anxious eight hours spent bobbing about in his life raft just a few miles offshore. The Argies had attempted to get him using a helicopter, but had eventually been driven off by some Sea Harriers. He was picked up by an RN Sea King after dark.

In the evening I had a talk with the Boss in which he confided some of his worries. He told me that he was very hacked off indeed that we had had three aircraft shot down and two badly damaged. I guessed that he was thinking ahead to what kind of squadron he was going to have left when the war was over – at this rate a very small one.

Mail from home was still pretty slow in coming. Some of the touching items we did receive were anonymous cards from school-children, usually illustrated with scenes of war and addressed to all of us. One in particular I found comforting. This child said 'I hope you won't be killed'. Yes. We hoped that too.

Next day it was apparent that the weather situation was going to get even worse. At the morning briefing the Met man showed us huge low-pressure systems – the infamous 'Zebra's arseholes' – moving rapidly across from the Pacific. We were in fog and low stratus for most of the day and no fixed-wing sorties were flown. However, Mark and I had been 'fingered' to fly a photo recce mission, searching along a line from Fitzroy cove to Hooker Point, just south-east of Port Stanley Airfield. We were to search for a *land-launched Exocet*, the first time any of us had heard of such a beast. Having run out of air-launched missiles, the resourceful Argies had adapted some of their ship-launched Exocets to be fired from a lashed-up launch tube mounted on the back of a truck.

For some time now the Navy had planned to have two warships shelling Port Stanley Airfield and the surrounding area each night from the 'gun line' south of Stanley. A land-based Exocet would be a serious threat to these ships. Having been let off the hook for the Port Stanley Airfield pre-attack recce on 24 May, I was finally going to have to stick my neck out on my own at Low Level over Stanley. The line-search route ran right through all the well-defended areas and I would have to do some careful planning. The Air Task Message called for the sortie to be flown 'minimum risk' – whatever that meant. I had asked for and been given a second GR3 to act as a decoy.

Friday, 4 June 1982

Once again we had fog and low cloud all day long. Conditions were no better ashore, and so no flying was carried out at all. By now, a distinct sense of boredom had begun to set in after the hectic flying of the past few weeks. I took some time off to wander around the ship and meet some of the characters. I found a NAAFI shop hidden in the bowels of the ship, and I was delighted to discover that they sold 8-mm cine film, my stocks having almost run out. While we floated in relative comfort some 200 miles east of the islands, the troops ashore were already moving up into their start positions for the final assault on the Stanley area. In the freezing rain and the mud they were suffering unbelievable privations as they hiked across the hostile terrain. Very fortunately for Britain, the tough and realistic peacetime training of our marines and foot soldiers paid handsome dividends under operational conditions. However, both our Naval and Air Forces had been severely hampered by an unrealistic approach to peacetime training. Both services had many bitter lessons to learn before the war was over. We knew that the final assault would commence soon; however, winter was approaching rapidly and there was now a real danger that the weather was going to place severe constraints on all of our operations.

CHAPTER NINETEEN

Yet More Navy Cockups

By the afternoon of 5 June the appalling weather conditions had improved sufficiently for Flyco to think about launching some missions. The first pair off comprised Bob and Tony Harper, who were to land at the strip and relieve the long-suffering Pete Harris and J.R., who had been kicking their heels ashore since 1 June. When Bob and Tony were on deck we already knew that weather conditions at the strip were poor, and forecast to get even worse. At the same time the conditions over the deck were still atrocious. There was a lot of very low stratus and sea fog floating around and the ship was drifting in and out of the worst parts, more often in it than out of it. None of us believed that Bob and Tony would be launched for the strip in these conditions, bearing in mind that there were no approach aids available to help them find it. Additionally, once committed to vertical land at the strip, they would not have enough fuel to return to the ship – there was nowhere else to go and they would have to eject. They had been sitting on Alert 5 for a while when Flyco suddenly said that they were to launch and transit to the strip anyway. There was no associated Air Task with the launch order. Bob mentioned the weather and suggested a delay. The reply was the usual: 'Standby'.

After about fifteen minutes the only thing that had happened was that the weather over the deck had deteriorated markedly. This was plain to see from my position lurking nervously by the door to the island. By now they were already lined up and suddenly the order came from Flyco to launch anyway. There was no argument: the order had been given and off they went. Bob went into cloud at the top of the ramp. Just at that moment his Head up Display failed, leaving him on standby instruments. *Later he described this experience as being closer to death than he had ever been.* Already a bit disorientated, he had great difficulty in achieving a safe climb away in cloud on the head-down instruments. Bob and Tony managed somehow to join up and set course for the strip. At high level Syd Morris advised them that the strip weather was not too hot, and about to get much worse. They made a hasty approach from the west as the conditions deteriorated and had great difficulty in finding the landing area. Within five minutes of their landing the weather had clamped in completely. Because of basic stupidity on the part of Flyco, we had come within a hairsbreadth of losing two more aircraft. There was no need to launch these aircraft at this time. There were no operations in progress that required urgent Air Support over the islands.

Later on the weather did improve a bit and Mark and I launched to fly the Exocet recce mission. During the last couple of minutes of this linesearch I would be well within range of all the weapon systems in the Stanley and Port Stanley Airfield area, and I had planned a diversionary attack from the south-east by Mark, to take some attention away from me on my approach from the west. My plan was to let down to Low Level at the southern tip of Lafonia and then fly at Low Level up to Fitzroy ridge, a 10-mile long humpback feature ending some 15 miles south-west of Stanley. (Fitzroy settlement had been occupied by elements of 2 Para since 3 June. As usual, no one had told us – I would have stayed well away from it had I known.) Behind the cover of the ridge we would split and Mark would run out at high speed over the sea to the east, to turn back towards Port Stanley Airfield and approach from the south-east while I remained hidden behind the ridge for a while. He was to fly high enough to ensure they could see him easily on radar, and then at the last moment drop chaff and break away to the east just before he came within maximum Roland range. Things went OK and I set off on my linesearch after a couple of minutes of lurking in an orbit right on the deck behind the ridge. If the timing worked OK then the defenders would all be looking to the south-east at Mark, just as I crept up on them along the road from Bluff Cove. Soon I was flying along the track towards the town.

Because of the poor coverage of the recce pod I had to spend a lot of time flying along with one wing slightly raised, using opposite rudder to counteract the tendency to turn. This made low flying a bit awkward; however, by the time I passed below Sapper Hill I was hugging the ground as if my life depended on it. Up to then I had seen nothing resembling an Exocet launcher. The only vehicle I had seen was a fuel bowser on the road. I was now approaching the southern edge of Stanley town. There was a rain shower, which was cutting down forward visibility. I was already pretty tensed up and expecting a lot of flak at any moment. I was happy about the rain – hopefully it would give me a bit of cover. I was going pretty fast by now, searching and filming alternately right and left as I noted areas of possible interest. The wretched cameras in the pod kept on stopping; this was indicated on a system of green 'run' lights in the cockpit, and I was having to keep on releasing the film button and repressing it to get the cameras to work. (This was a pretty normal operating problem with our crummy recce pod.) I had been looking left into the back gardens of the nearest houses when I looked forward into a seemingly huge array of radio masts, which I was about to miss by an unpleasantly small margin. These were actually marked on the map, with no height given; I had not intended to be quite so close to them. They looked over 200 feet high as I flew past. This near miss gave me a bit of a fright and as I was now approaching potentially the most dangerous area, Port Stanley Airfield itself, I found myself flying lower and lower until I passed Hooker point almost at wave-top height. After the point I scuttled away to the east over the sea as low as I possibly could. Once again I found myself literally 'cringing' in the cockpit, at any second expecting the sky to light up around me. Eventually I drew out of range and joined up with Mark for an uneventful return. I had managed to keep up the search to the end, and had seen nothing remotely resembling an Exocet launcher. More interesting was the fact that I had seen not a trace of enemy fire throughout. What had happened to the flak? Maybe the diversionary tactics had distracted their attention.

After landing, I hovered around the film processing office, anxiously waiting to debrief the film with our Photographic Interpreters. When at last it was ready I was disappointed in the results. The Admiral particularly wanted good photos of Hooker point; in my undignified dash across this last part of the linesearch I had failed to raise the wing sufficiently to give adequate coverage. The point itself was right at the top of the picture, and you could see only a few hundred metres behind it. The rest of the coverage was fairly good (where the cameras had worked) and I had managed to get quite a good coverage of the dug-in defences around the town area despite my height and speed. Some of these pictures were the lowest recce photos we had seen. There were blurred shots of astonished troops looking horizontally straight into the lens over the top of their slit trench revetments, just a few feet away from me. However, the coverage of Hooker point wasn't good enough, and I cursed myself for my lack of professionalism in not lifting the wing enough at the most critical part of the linesearch. As soon as the Admiral realised that the photo coverage was not complete he ordered an *immediate* refly of the sortie, to get better pictures of Hooker point, not trusting my visual report that no Exocets were visible on the ground. I had taken over as DCF by then and I wearily reminded the fools in Flyco that it was now barely half an hour before sunset. There was no chance of any more successful photography that day.

Sunday, 6 June 1982

The morning was reasonably clear and McLeod and I sat around for several hours of Alert 5 on deck without being launched. The Boss and Beech launched at 1310 hours for a repeat of the Exocet recce, once again with zero results.[25] They also encountered no flak, and we began to wonder what exactly was going on at Port Stanley Airfield – perhaps they had all gone home. Having heard my warning of the radio masts at Stanley, the Boss successfully avoided them, only narrowly to escape collision with another unplotted set of masts! He actually flew *between* a pair of masts, giving himself a bit of a fright: he was lucky not to collect the bracing wires. The Boss had also taken along a brace of cluster bombs, which he unloaded on troop positions shown on my photos of the previous day.

Monday, 7 June 1982

This was to be yet another typically shambolic day in the life of an RAF Harrier pilot working for Her Majesty's Royal Navy. I was lead of the first pair to brief, with McLeod as wingman. This was the first episode of the saga of the 'Sapper Hill 155-mil guns'. The Air Task Message gave two grid references on either side of Sapper Hill where the guns were supposed to be, and we started to plan a suitable run-in to have at them with 2-inch rockets. (We were still saving our cluster bomb stocks for the final assault on Stanley.) Just as I was about to draw a line on the map, the word came down from Flyco, 'All change: you're now going to do an FAC task and then land at PSC strip – and get a move on while you're at it!'

'Crisis management setting in rather earlier than usual today' I thought as I rebriefed McLeod on the new task. As we walked out I noticed Pete Harris and John Rochfort also busy planning a rather familiar-looking task – none other than the Sapper Hill guns!

'Ours not to reason why,' I said as we climbed into the jets in the early morning gloom. Within a short time Pete and John climbed in alongside us on a deck that was rapidly turning into an ocean-going shambles. Several Sea Harriers were supposed to be launching at the same time as us, just to add to the fun. Our pair should have launched first, but McLeod went U/S after I had started, to the consternation of Flyco. Almost straight away Pete also went U/S, requesting Flyco for a delay on his launch so that he could go as planned with John. By now

the Captain was shouting at Wings to 'Get 'em airborne' as usual, and in the usual panic aircraft were launched off the deck at random. This was a classic situation where Flyco should have paused for thought and consulted with our DCF about the best course of action with the aircraft available, before committing them to a launch. Without any decision from Flyco as to which tasks were to be flown and which cancelled, I found myself airborne. On deck I had already suggested to Flyco that I should take John (not a mission leader) along with me on my FAC mission.

'Stand by,' was the standard response from Flyco.

After five minutes without a decision I repeated the suggestion.

'Stand by,' was the response again.

By now, I had been marshalled to the launch point and I asked finally, 'What do you want me to do, continue my original task as a singleton or join up with John for another task?'[26]

'Stand by.'

After another period of silence from Flyco, I was launched without warning. John was to follow, after asking the same questions and receiving the familiar reply.

'Well, fuck this. I'll just carry on as a singleton on my original task,' I thought.

About 60 miles out from the ship 'D' called me up and said that I was to join up with John (who had just launched) *who would lead me on* **his** original task! After all the milling about on deck where the problem should have been squared away, they had managed to get us 60 miles apart before telling us to join up and continue on task. This was priceless.

'Okay, you get us joined up then,' was my weary response.

Together again with John I said to him, 'Uh, John I know where you're going – and I just happen to have a run-in planned'.

'Fine by me,' said John 'I'll follow you.'

And so after a quick brief on the radio we set off for our letdown point. The attack went well in the early morning gloom, the rockets exploding in fine style all round the target area. There wasn't enough light to identify anything positively (later on we were to discover that the guns weren't in this position anyway). An interesting postscript to this attack came from Rod Frederikson, who happened to be passing not far from Sapper Hill at 20,000 feet, en route to his Combat Air Patrol station over West Falkland. In his words: 'Looking down into the darkness around Stanley I suddenly saw a rippling line of flashes on the ground near Sapper Hill – gave me a bit of a fright as I thought it might be some kind of secret weapon that the Argies were firing!'

Rod added that he next saw a SAM launched from the Sapper Hill area. The missile flew quite a long way out to sea to the south before falling in the water. John and I were very interested to hear this. Although we had seen no gunfire or SAMs during our run-out to the south, the missile was obviously chasing us. Additionally, the engineers found a bullet hole in my aircraft after landing, so someone had been awake in the target area.

Pete Harris and McLeod flew the next sortie, and they launched at 1430 hours to position at the strip without an Air Task. Tony Harper was then sent off as a singleton to take some pictures of the Port Stanley Airfield area from high level. The last sortie of the day was Mark and Bob returning from the strip where Pete's pair had relieved them.

After landing, Bob walked in very stiffly, his face grey with pain. We found that he had been doing a lot of Ground Alert in the cockpit at the strip and his back was giving him a lot of pain. As *Hermes* was not equipped with the right sort of X-ray gear, neither Bob nor I had been X-rayed for back injuries after our ejections. (Normal peacetime procedures invariably called for a period of grounding of all ejectees – in the situation we were in these rules went by the board.) After some discussion with Bob about his back, it was obvious to all of us that the pain was too much for him to go on. Against strong protest from Bob, we finally managed to persuade him to go to the surgeon. The Boss and I argued that while the war would be over in a matter of weeks, he could end up permanently crippled if he persisted in flying with an injured back. This was a desperate moment for Bob. I could see in his eyes that he realised that he couldn't go on flying, and that we were giving good advice. But he found it an almost unbearable decision to make – he wanted to stay in the fight. He knew that the end result would be a casevac home, taking no further part in operations. He was to spend the next four or five days lying miserably on his back in the Sick Bay, where we visited him to try and keep his spirits up. Eventually he was transferred to another ship to be sent back to Ascension.

CHAPTER TWENTY

A Crash on the Strip

For the Task Force, 8 June was to be a fateful day, a day on which all of the gains of the previous weeks were nearly thrown away because of major tactical errors in moving the Welsh Guards forward to Bluff Cove. It was to be a memorable day for 1(F) Squadron too.

The previous evening the Boss, Bob, Tony Harper and I had argued at length about the problems of using the strip. The weather factor, still very uncertain, was a major hazard area but the biggest problem was with communication with *Fearless*. Although the strip lay just a couple of miles away from the ship, the intervening hills prevented direct communications by UHF or VHF voice radio. No thought had been given to providing any kind of secure communications link between the two. As a planning blunder this took the biscuit. After all the blood and sweat that had gone into getting the strip across 8,000 miles of sea and set up ashore with its associated fuel dump, nobody had given any serious thought to the problem of tasking the Harriers for which the strip existed. Fortunately this proved to be of little consequence to the Sea Harriers, who were already using the strip as a forward diversion and occasional launch base for Combat Air Patrols. Their aircraft holding on the ground were often as not 'scrambled' by a relayed radio call 'in clear' from a Combat Air Patrol already airborne. However, for Ground Attack and recce tasks it was vital to have rapid, clear and secure communications between the Tasking Agency and the pilot on the ground. The only tasking link available was the good old-fashioned insecure High Frequency radio, incontinently blasting its messages around the whole of the South Atlantic. Air Task messages were en-coded aboard *Fearless* and had to be decoded again at the strip. This was a tedious waste of time, often taking up to thirty minutes for a long Air Task Message.

The whole *raison d'être* of the strip was to make aircraft available at *short notice*, to give a more rapid response than was possible from shipboard aircraft based some 200 miles away. The communications problems threatened to negate this advantage. An additional problem was the extreme vulnerability of the strip to damage from Harriers hovering too low. Already, Syd was spending a lot of time with his engineers repairing damage due to careless low hovering. Extreme high hovers before Vertical Landing were mandatory; this in itself was a fairly hazardous manoeuvre. In principle, you never hovered higher than was absolutely necessary to avoid damage, or you risked losing control of the aircraft because of your distance from ground reference points.

Before the morning briefing I brought up all these points again with the Boss. My argument was that the combination of difficulties of using the strip, its poor weather factor and the insoluble communications problems meant that we should try to avoid use of the strip except as an absolute last resort; after all, an aircraft lost in an accident at the strip was just the same as an aircraft lost due to enemy action. As I expected, the Boss disagreed forcibly, arguing that it was the classic use of CAS assets etc. This was all ironic, bearing in mind what was to happen to the Boss later in the day. At 1130 hours Beech and I got airborne for a transit to the strip. Straight after launch Beech's radio packed up completely, and I had no option but to send him home. About 100 miles out my radio also began to play up, and by now I also had problems with my IFF, so I decided to return to the ship rather than take a U/S aircraft into the strip. The Boss and Mark were immediately tasked to go to the strip in our place in the two remaining aircraft. Later that day I got the story of events from Mark, also confirmed later by Syd Morris. We all knew that we had to hover very high at the strip before the pad Vertical Landing. Mark saw the Boss go in first and hover 'too low' (Mark's words). Mark saw parts of the aluminium strip blow up towards the Boss's aircraft, which promptly crash-landed right across the strip as a write-off. Back aboard, having just taken over as DCF, I got the message from Flyco: 'One of your aircraft has crashed on the strip: you'd better come up.'

Wings passed on the details of the accident, with no news of the Boss's condition. Having heard this my first slightly chilling thought was, 'Jesus Christ, I'm now Acting Squadron Commander'. A bit later the message came through that he was uninjured, though badly shaken up.

The Boss described it thus: 'In the hover I suddenly saw these pieces of the strip flying up all round me and I tried to transition away, but the aircraft just fell out of the sky.'

With a large part of the strip torn up, Mark was now short of places to land. With very little fuel remaining, he managed eventually to carry out a very skilful 'Creeping VL' on the undamaged portion of the strip.

Two incoming Sea Jets also had insufficient fuel to go back to their ship and had to make the first ever Harrier VLs aboard HMS *Fearless* and *Intrepid* in Falkland Sound. (There was just enough room for one Harrier on each ship.)

With both carriers far to the east (*Hermes* was busy with boiler cleaning), having the strip out of action was to make a significant dent in the available Combat Air Patrol cover over the islands for the rest of the day. Unfortunately, by chance the Argies decided to make a big air attack 'push', launching no fewer than five separate formations to the islands before sundown. Their most significant success was the Skyhawk attack on the LSLs (Landing Ships Logistics) *Sir Galahad* and *Sir Tristram* at Bluff Cove, a near-disaster for the Land Forces. Mike Blisset was first to pass on the news of this attack to us, reporting two 'very smoky' ships at Bluff Cove when he returned from a Combat Air Patrol. Later that night Mark was able to return for a night landing aboard. At the same time I heard that the Boss was unhurt and would remain aboard *Fearless* overnight. I was glad about this as I hoped that he would be able to talk some sense into them about the lack of pure recce tasking from *Fearless* recently. Everyone knew that the final push on Stanley was imminent, and we knew that we were urgently in need of good photo coverage of the enemy defensive positions on the main lines of advance into the town. Up to now we had been given not a single such task which was flyable. There had been some wild Air Task Messages requesting photo coverage of vast areas, which could only have been carried out from High Level (HL). However, the recent poor weather had precluded HL photography. Without tasking we were quite prepared just to go and do it on our own at Low Level: we already had a pretty good idea of the most important areas. Of course, we weren't allowed to do anything of the sort, even though we had demonstrated that we could accurately hit just about any target if we had Low Level photo coverage. Unfortunately, no one above us in the tasking chain had yet hoisted this aboard.

Late in the afternoon Ross Boyens and Nick Gilchrist landed on after another heroic ferry mission direct from Ascension. They both made excellent first-ever carrier landings and once again I was to spend some time giving them the 'arrival brief'. After the bad news of the Boss's crash all of us were delighted to see a couple of well-known squadron 'shags' aboard.

An amusing little footnote to the attack by John and me on Sapper Hill the previous day ... By now the Captain had given up his impractical demand that leaders of all formations should debrief with him immediately on landing (we now had to debrief with the ship's Education Officer). I went to see the ship's Operations Officer, in order to pass the MISREP (Mission Report) for the attack. This character didn't seem to know much about Ground Attack operations. I had a hilarious debrief with him after the shambolic sortie, taking pains to point out the totally incompetent way in which the Navy were running things. I told him that I was amazed that we managed to get any effective missions flown at all, the way that Flyco operated. When we got to the part of the MISREP where we had to describe what we did at the target area I said, 'Well, we fired at the grid references – at the positions given – so write down "TARGET POSITION ATTACKED" okay?' 'Oh, I can't put that down,' he said. 'This Air Task Message says DESTROY the target, not just attack it!'

He was perfectly serious, and couldn't understand why I fell about laughing. I said that even if we had had a good attack photo, in that dawn light it would have been impossible to identify a camouflaged gun position: anyway, how the hell were we supposed to know whether or not the target was destroyed? He was still not happy about this: 'But you didn't carry out what was requested on the task form,' he bleated, looking even more worried. After some more slightly hysterical laughter on my part I walked out, leaving him muttering about what he was going to put on the MISREP.

The following day was frustrating: we flew quite a few missions but seemed to achieve very little. First off were Tony Harper and Ross Boyens, who flew to the strip to await a task. Next, Pete Harris and McLeod were tasked once again to attack the Sapper Hill guns. They fired rockets at the positions but saw nothing resembling a camouflaged gun. This mission was flown later in the day than my sortie of the previous day, and Pete and McLeod managed to attract quite a bit of flak over the target. McLeod didn't notice any hits on his aircraft, but on his return to the ship he had to blow his landing gear down on the emergency nitrogen bottle as it wouldn't work on the normal system. After landing, the ground crew found his aircraft to be fairly well peppered with small holes from flak fragments. The undercarriage hydraulic system was shot through, and this was the reason for the gear problem.

That morning I was DCF and spent some of the time hanging around in the corridor between Flyco and the bridge. At one stage I overheard the Captain having one of his periodic 'rants' against the RAF. He had just heard of Pete's MISREP in which he claimed to have seen nothing at the position given after firing rockets. The Captain's response to this news was, 'The bloody RAF haven't done their weapons effects home-work! They're using the wrong bloody weapons. They ought to use 1,000-lb bombs to turn the guns over!'

The thought of lobbing a retard bomb exactly between the wheels of a gun to turn it over brought a smile to my face. The man was living in dream world: even with fully operational inertial weapon aiming there would be little chance of getting a level-delivery retard bomb any-where within 20 or 30 yards of a pinpoint target (see Appendix 4 – Bombing Techniques). For a dug-in field gun you would literally need to place the bomb in the gunpit to do any worthwhile damage. Because of the shortage of cluster bombs and the Navy's problems of arming us with 1,000-lb bombs, we had little choice but to use rockets on this type of target anyway. By now, I was quite happy with the 2-inch rocket level delivery and I felt it was perfectly adequate for the kind of extreme Low Level attack we were doing. I had been firing them from about 50 feet agl with no major problems.[27] For retard bomb delivery we would need to climb to at least 150 feet: this was not calculated to enhance life-expectancy in this kind of target area. Later on I spoke to Wings about these comments by the Captain. I told him once again that we might as well throw popcorn at the target area for all the good we could do. Without photo coverage we had little chance of identify-ing any half-reasonably camouflaged target on a hillside scattered with outcrops of rock. I was wasting my time, as expected. He merely shrugged his shoulders to indicate that his hands were tied. It appeared to us that the Captain's scorn for the RAF was such a power-ful influence that no one on the Naval side was prepared to back up any of our suggestions for fear of antagonising him.

The Boss and Ross Boyens now teamed up at the strip with the two armed aircraft (there had been no task for Tony Harper and Ross Boyens), and went to attack troop positions on Mt Longden, sub-sequently to land back aboard. I had little time for discussion with the Boss before I was sent off with Beech to the strip after a period of Alert 5 on deck. This was my first visit to the strip and both Beech and I were careful to carry out extremely high hovers (300 feet plus) before the VL. The weather was pretty good at the strip and I was rather taken aback to see how open and exposed it was to any overflying aircraft. It lay parallel to the rocky coastline on bare ground without so much as a bush for cover. Just off the eastern end was a depression in the ground, and this was where the 'choppers' had a refuelling point, sharing the Harriers' fuel hydrants. Syd had set up quite a comfortable dug-in camp for himself just off the edge of the strip, his HQ being well-provided with slit trenches. There was also an Army Rapier battery just off the western end of the strip, so we all had to be extremely careful to follow the recognised Safe Passage Procedures to get in without being shot at.

Ironically, a Harrier approaching at low speed with landing lights on and gear down was about the only target the Rapier batteries could guarantee to hit. In spite of wildly exaggerated claims of successful Rapier 'kills' during the conflict, Alfred Price and Jeff Ethell discovered only *one* confirmed kill *solely attributed to Rapier* in their post-war researches with the Argentine pilots who took part. One confirmed kill – after seventy-plus missiles fired! Their meticulously researched book *Air War South Atlantic*, recorded this highly embarrassing fact, which was predictably ignored by the Senior RAF and British Aerospace establishment as being too uncomfortable to admit in public. For years, RAF airfield defence doctrine had been based entirely on the grossly overestimated capabilities of this British weapon system, a so-called 'hittile', which couldn't produce the goods when tried under active service conditions. I recalled Ritchie Profit's comments on the exceptional overconfidence of the RAF's Rapier battery crews whom he had encountered on Trial 'STRAND', one of the first comprehensive Rapier trials against 'realistic' low-level targets. In Ritchie's words, 'The average Rapier crew's level of bullshit makes the old-fashioned fighter pilot sound like quite a shy and retiring character in comparison!'

There were other targets that the Task Force SAM operators could hit easily: unfortunately, not all of these were enemy. At about this time we heard of a Navy 'own goal' that was to be hushed up for a long time. One evening we heard that the Army had lost a chopper: it had disappeared without trace. A little later we saw an intelligence report from HMS *Cardiff* saying that she had engaged a Low Level target at maximum range with Sea Dart. A kill was claimed, although it was too far away to be seen visually. Some bright spark of an Intelligence Officer put two and two together and realised that this engagement took place at about the same time that the chopper disappeared. We strongly suspected that the two events were linked, although both the Army and the Navy were to deny this for some years after the conflict, before finally admitting that the Navy had shot down one of our own aircraft.

Personally, I could not understand how the Argies failed to pinpoint the strip and lay on an attack on what was obviously a number one target. A few tanks of napalm scattered around would have put an entirely different light on our strip operations. As it was, the strip was at Air Raid Warning Red as Beech and I climbed out, to be ushered into the vicinity of a slit trench by Sid. He was pretty cool about things and said we needn't actually get into the trench until we heard gunfire signalling aircraft attacking in the Sound! So we stood in the weak winter sunshine and chatted about this and that until the warning was cancelled, no enemy aircraft having appeared this time. Just over the strip we saw the dark, choppy waters of Falkland Sound and beyond that the brooding grey peaks of West Falkland, darkening rapidly in the fading light. The smell of 'cam' nets, spilled fuel and hot aluminium reminded me of the glorious days of the Field Deployments of the RAF Germany Harrier Force in the early 1970s. Syd and I had been on many enjoyable exercises together; he on 4 Squadron, me on 20 and Bob on 3. In those days we would put thirty-six Harriers into the field, on six dispersed sites, pilots flying up to six sorties per day with Cockpit Tasking. We would 'Surge Fly' up to fifty sorties per site per day. They were great days.

It was good to feel solid ground under my feet again – I had been at sea for over four weeks. After a couple of hours cooling our heels with no task, Beech and I set off back to the carrier, to land at last light. Back aboard, I discovered that there had been yet another task on the now-famous Sapper Hill guns. On the Air Task Message it actually said that 'the guns are put there at last light and taken away again at dawn'! In other words, it was now confirmed that we had been wasting our time and risking our necks attacking something that the Tasking Agency knew wasn't there. The mission was cancelled anyway because it was too late in the day. Later on it was confirmed what we had suspected all along, that the Argies moved all high-value targets back into the built-up area of the town during daylight hours on the not-unreasonable assumption that we were not going to put the civilian population at risk.

CHAPTER TWENTY-ONE

SAM Kill

Much later we found out how the Argies used their Learjets as High Altitude Command Posts and Recce aircraft, making frequent overflights at very high level over the islands. None of these aircraft was successfully intercepted by Sea Harriers. Because of their extreme altitude they were not always tracked on radar. Eventually, the Navy got their act together and had a chance of a shot at them with a Sea Dart. (Fired from HMS *Exeter*, lurking nearby in the Sound.) Bob and Tony Harper had witnessed this engagement on 7 June from the safety of a slit trench at PSC strip during an air raid. As Bob described it:

> Initially I thought they were Sea Jets returning from Combat Air Patrol – we could see two contrails approaching from the West at very high level. The Navy were in a bit of a rush to get them: instead of waiting until both aircraft were well within range, they fired too early in my opinion. The first Sea Dart went wild and disappeared stage left completely out of control. We watched the second one climb all the way up to a hit, straight as a dart. It was pretty sobering to see what looked like a straight-winged jet spinning all the way down. We thought it was an Argy Canberra at this stage. There were no parachutes. (The wreck was found later on Pebble Island.) As soon as the hit happened the other aircraft turned tail and cleared off at Warp Snot, so they had no chance of getting them both.

10 June began as a good weather day, and things appeared to be hotting up. However, the Air Tasking was no better organised. After all our efforts we were finally tasked with a recce mission on Sapper Hill! The Air Task Message referred to M109 Self-Propelled guns, which was a revelation to us as we didn't know the Argies were using them. First off were Pete Harris and Nick Gilchrist, who launched to the strip, to sit around for a couple of hours before being recalled to the ship with no task. We had finally got a task in for a photo recce of troop

positions of the Mt Longden area and the Boss and Mark were sent to do this. They took cluster bombs as well, dropping them in the target area as well as getting some excellent photo coverage. It was from this sortie that Mark brought back the famous photo of an Argy troop wrestling with a Blowpipe launcher in an attempt to point it at the fleeting target, which had obviously completely surprised him. A little further away stood another troop with a SAM 7B launcher, also looking in the wrong direction. On a later mission the Boss and Mark were pursued off target by a missile, which exploded harmlessly between them.

In the afternoon Tony and J.R. were planned to launch to a safe area of Lafonia to carry out a mini-LGB/LTM trial to prove that the system worked. Over the last few days more LGB kits had arrived aboard *Hermes* and there had been a lot of liaison with SAS troops ashore about finding suitable targets to designate with their LTMs (Laser Target Markers). Although the troops ashore had LTMs with them, there had been problems with the batteries, which were as often as not flat when they had to use the kit in anger. I had spent a fair bit of time that morning as DCF organising our end of the trial; it was essential that things should go smoothly so that we would be able to use the LGBs operationally in support of the ground forces as soon as possible. I had told Flyco that we needed priority on arming up the LGBs for this reason. In order to give everyone plenty of time to get into position, the TOT for the trial was fixed at 1800 hours. Unfortunately, the Admiral found out after lunch that the TOT wasn't until 1800 hours. Seeing that there were several hours still to go before the planned TOT he then said, 'I want this TOT brought forward, then we can get in two trial sorties before dusk!'

The Ops Officer rang me up with the news and I argued in desperation that the slowness of the communications chain would mean that the SAS wouldn't know about the changed TOT. All to no avail. The Navy would not budge and when Tony called up the FAC at 1700 hours (the new TOT) there was no reply. As I had predicted, the SAS hadn't received the message. Tony returned to the ship and had to jettison two valuable LGBs into the sea before landing. As a result of yet more basic stupidity and arrogance we had lost another vital opportunity to prove the new weapon delivery profile.

Next, Ross Boyens and I were tasked with the Sapper Hill recce, which promised to be a fairly 'hot' mission. After planning a similar profile to the Exocet recce mission, only this time approaching from the north (I felt that I had used the south-western run-in enough by now), the task was cancelled. We were now given another task, to support Special Forces using a FAC in the Port Howard area. This sounded very strange to me. *What the hell was going on at Port Howard that was so important at this stage of the war?* We all knew the basic strategy that once Stanley had fallen things would be just about wrapped up. The other major problem was that the TOT given on the Air Task Message was only forty minutes away when we received it! This was an impossible task and I knew there was no point in requesting a delay – the communications were just too slow. The only thing to do was to 'go for it' as fast as possible. So, in true Harrier Force fashion Ross and I scribbled a couple of lines on the map and raced out to the jets. After a forty-minute transit there was no contact with the FAC – as expected. As briefed, I led Ross in battle formation on a Low-Level run through the general target area given, to see if we could find anything going on. Having seen nothing we had to set course immediately for the ship, at this time over 200 miles east of the islands.[28]

During the climb to high level in the fading sunshine we listened to a lot of chatter on the LAAWC frequency about a big incoming air raid. We could hear several sections of Sea Harriers getting in on the act as they were vectored towards the raiders. While this was going on I noticed that both my fuel 'BINGO' lights had come on. This meant trouble. According to the gauges I had over 3,000 lb of fuel left; however, when in doubt we always took the BINGO light indication as being more accurate than the gauge. This meant that I could only rely on 1,500 lb of usable fuel – not nearly enough for the long flight back to the ship. Suspecting a fuel leak, I dispatched Ross Boyens back to the ship and got clearance into PSC strip for a check up and refuel, landing just behind a couple of Sea Harriers scrambling for the raid. Being totally unaware of the desperate situation at Port Howard (see note 28), my thoughts were uncharitable. Once again I envied the Sea Harrier pilots' cushy number. Here I was being messed about by their totally inept tasking system, risking my ass to attack targets that weren't there half the time, while they were enjoying a good old-fashioned Turkey Shoot. To add insult to injury, instead of being safely on my way home I was going to have to land in the thick of an air raid: as likely as not the strip would be one of their targets. Taxying-in in great haste I jumped out and headed for the nearest slit trench. I was getting used to the routine by now. In the event no enemy aircraft appeared, and I hastily shoved in enough fuel to guarantee a safe return to *Hermes* before scuttling off into the gathering darkness. A brief external inspection had shown no battle damage that I could see.

After landing I discovered that the Boss and McLeod had been off to attack troops in the Moody Brook area. This was a response to the discovery of a large number of vehicles on some of our recce film taken earlier in the day. Because of the cumbersome task system, the attack mission did not arrive over the target until some six hours later, by which time the vehicles had vanished, naturally enough. There was another cockup on the Air Task Message, which specified the use of 'delayed action retard bombs'. A delayed action retard bomb was a contradiction in terms, as the bomb would bounce away over the countryside after impact, coming to rest thousands of yards from the initial aiming point. Ironically, when the bombs were released the retard tails failed to deploy anyway (they were probably incorrectly armed), and they bounced even further after impact, one unexploded bomb finishing up in a barrack building at Moody Brook. The pair took some hits from flak, a round passing through the Boss's cockpit close to his feet, causing severe damage to the weapon system wiring and putting the jet out of action for several days.

At intervals, to add to our frustration at being confined to the Ground Attack task, we were regular witnesses of 'hot' debriefs from the Navy and attached RAF Sea Jet pilots returning from successful air engagements. I can remember Andy Auld landing with both outer pylons clean, indicating both missiles used, with two confirmed kills. After each successful sortie all available pilots would sit and watch the developed Head up Display film in the pilots' briefing room. Andy's film was particularly spectacular, showing two missiles in flight to two separate Mirages, both of which were clearly hit on film. However, the reader should not imagine that this kind of thing was the norm for all the Sea Harrier pilots. During the war hundreds of Combat Air Patrol missions were flown and on the vast majority of these nothing was seen and no enemy aircraft engaged. For each successful kill, the average Sea Jet pilot had to fly some fifty Combat Air Patrol sorties. By the end of the war boredom was their main enemy.

By now we had also realised that, from the Ground Attack point of view, our sorties were about to become much tougher. As the perimeter around Stanley closed relentlessly upon the remaining Argy forces, their resources of flak guns, SAMs and small arms were concentrated in an ever-decreasing area. While this indicated an abundance of worthwhile targets for us, it also meant a lot more holes in our aircraft over the target area.

We had yet another good weather day on 11 June, and I hoped that we would at last be able to achieve a successful LGB/LTM trial. The Boss decided to make Ross Boyens a mission leader with immediate effect. He was a punchy and reliable character, and we were sure he would do a good job. In the first mission of the day Tony Harper and Nick Gilchrist were to carry out an LGB drop in Port Stanley town. The FAC was an SAS man who had been 'staked out' for some days on the peninsula just across the bay from the town: according to the Air Task

Message he would be able to designate the Army HQ on the waterfront as a target. (This lay inside the town police HQ building.) This FAC was obviously a pretty courageous character, but he didn't know much about LGBs because his first comment to Tony was, 'I'm sorry, my battery's flat, but could you make an attack on the target anyway?'

Without laser guidance, an LGB could end up just about anywhere in the town, so Tony very wisely turned him down and tossed both bombs unguided in the general direction of Wireless ridge. So, another two guided bombs were wasted, and we had yet to prove the LGB/LTM system in action. My first sortie of the day was with Beech again, and we were unable to proceed to the target area because of IFF failure. On landing, I was met by the Boss who said rather pointedly that he thought I could have continued with the sortie, even without IFF. My reply was, 'Well I'm sorry Boss, but we did agree that IFF was a no-go item, except for life-or-death missions. As far as I'm concerned this mission wasn't in that category. Are we now going to change the policy?'

His response was affirmative: from now on IFF was optional. After a quick turnround with a new IFF box fitted, Beech and I were off again on the same task. The following, now unclassified, Combat Mission Report was submitted after this fairly run-of-the-mill task:

****
RESTRICTED

NO. 1(F) Squadron – COMBAT MISSION REPORT

DATE:	11 Jun 82	MISSION NO: TARTAN 3/4
PILOTS:	Squadron Ldr J.J. Pook	
	Flt Lt M. Beech (No. 3(F) Squadron)	
BASE:	HMS HERMES	
LAUNCH:	1450	LAND: 1600
WEATHER:	Good	
WEAPONS:	4 cluster bombs	
MISSION:	Mission tasked against artillery and mortar position on Mt Harriet (VC3070)	
COMMENT:	Ingress was from the South. No AAA or SAM UTMs were attacked and Beech saw SSV (poss Land Rover) at his tgt position. No radar lock-up but I-Band search radar heard on Radar Warning Receiver during run-in	

****

During the run-out to the south off target I fired off some infrared decoy flares from the launcher that we had just had fitted in the rear fuselage. (It had taken this long to get us equipped to defend against missiles.) Although I hadn't seen any SAM launches I wanted to see how they looked to my wingman and how they performed if fired at extreme Low Level. The effect was spectacular. Beech said in the debrief that he thought I had taken a major flak hit, the flares shooting straight into the ground and exploding in a brilliant white flash right under my tail. So much for decoying infrared missiles. However, I thought that this might be a reasonable diversionary tactic to use on a regular basis during run-out from the target when the defences were already alerted. With a bit of luck they might think you had been shot down and stop shooting at you. I passed this idea on to the rest of the squadron, for what it was worth. During the debrief Beech seemed a bit disappointed that he hadn't seen any flak! I explained gently that just because you couldn't see it, it didn't mean that they weren't firing at you. (In bright daylight it was difficult to see tracer anyway.) I told him the story of the SAM seen by Rod Frederikson. After the war I fell into conversation with some Scots Guards NCOs who had observed quite a few Harrier attacks from close quarters. They commented that on several occasions they saw SAMs fired after the retreating Harriers, though none was seen to hit. They also said that, since the Bluff Cove disaster, all their troops fired automatically at any fast jet which came near them; later they changed this to firing only at aircraft releasing weapons, and this was to have repercussions for our coming LGB attacks.

At 1425 hours Ross Boyens and John Rochfort launched to the Sapper Hill area armed with cluster bombs. John's launch nearly turned into a disaster, due in part to my own carelessness. J.R. was flying the dreaded '03', a known 'heap' that we hoped would never arrive in the South Atlantic. For some reason it had been sent to us on Nick Gilchrist and Ross Boyens's ferry flight, and now we were stuck with it. The main problem with this rogue aircraft (a rebuilt 'wreck'), was its lousy VSTOL performance, which was the worst of any of our aircraft by far. Afterwards I calculated that I had failed to make sufficient allowance for degraded take-off performance in working out the deck launch distance – one of the important tasks of the DCF. However, there was another much more important factor involved. For some reason I was standing on deck for the launch and I observed John's take-off. Just before launch the ship was still manoeuvring into wind, and as we steadied up on the launch heading I noticed straight away that there was an ominous lack of wind over deck. I had seen any number of launches by now and it was obvious to me that there wasn't anything like the usual wind over deck this time. Before I could do anything, the Flight Deck Officer's flag went down and John slammed to full power. I watched in horror as his aircraft flopped over the end of the ramp like an overweight albatross. As J.R. described it, 'Things didn't feel too good as I left the ramp. The jet started sinking straight away and showed no sign of accelerating.'

Instinctively, John hit the 'Clear Aircraft' bar, dumping his cluster bombs and two full fuel tanks into the sea. After this he was able to make a very dodgy transition away just clear of the water, having pushed the throttle through the 'gate' to override the engine limiters. What had gone wrong? I went immediately to Flyco, to be met by a wall of silence about the incident, leading me to suspect a cockup. They weren't going to admit it under any circumstances in case the Captain got to hear. Needless to say, the ship had put on a lot more speed before the next jet was launched.

John continued anyway on task, to return safely with Ross Boyens after 1 hour 10 mins, well short of fuel. Pete Harris and Nick Gilchrist took some cluster bombs to the Mt Longden area, and the last sortie of the day was flown by the Boss and Mark who went to the same area with retard bombs. This had been quite a busy day for us, with no losses or significant damage. We were still not sending aircraft to the strip, which was still under repair after the Boss's crash.

That afternoon I overheard yet another of the Captain's 'rants', this time directed at the long-suffering Ship's Operations Officer. The final land assault on the Port Stanley area was imminent and we had at long last put together a reasonable portfolio of prints of our Low Level F95 photos of major enemy troop dispositions in the area. Apparently the Captain had insisted, not unreasonably, that the Ops Officer should take them ashore *personally* by helicopter, in order to ensure that they reached the right people. I overheard him shouting: 'Jim, I TOLD you to take those fucking photos PERSONALLY: now they've gone and lost the fucking things! Why didn't you do as I said?'

After grovelling apologies, Jim (the Operations Officer) agreed that they would have to get the whole lot reprinted and sent ashore again in case the lost items didn't turn up. I had to smile: after all our efforts to get the photos the Navy had lost the prints at the most crucial moment.

After weeks of unceasing effort, all of our ground forces were now in position for the final assault on the main Argy defences around Stanley, most of which was planned to take place at night. The helicopter lift had gone on day and night to bring forward troops, guns, ammunition and food. That which could not be flown had been humped across the excruciating terrain on the backs of the long-suffering infantry. Sleeping bags, blankets and all except the most vital rations had been left behind to allow each man to carry the maximum amount of ammunition across the sodden tussock grass and rocky hills, a total distance of some 40 miles from the landings at Ajax Bay. The strains on the walking troops had been immense: by now the damp conditions and regular night frosts had made conditions miserable in their hastily dug trenches and revetments as they awaited the final order for the attack. Although hungry, cold and weary, officers and men alike tried to go about their business and daily routines as if this was just one more slightly-more-arduous-than-average exercise. They knew full well that they could not afford to stop and think the unthinkable: that the assault might fail; that the Argy positions might be far stronger than expected; that they might fight with far more determination than expected; ultimately, that they themselves might be killed or maimed in the bloody and sordid confusion of the night battles to come. This fear of death or mutilation was the only bond they shared with us GR3 Harrier pilots who spent most of our time floating in relative comfort far to the east, enjoying many of the comforts of home.

The next day started in good weather, beginning with several tasks in the Sapper Hill area. During the morning brief we were told that HMS *Glamorgan* had been hit by a land-launched Exocet while on the 'Gun Line' during the night. Once again, many sailors had died in the fires that followed the impact. Ross Boyens and Mike Beech were off at 1250 hours with cluster bombs, to be followed by Pete Harris and McLeod. McLeod took a hit through the reaction control ducts in the rear fuselage, which only carry hot air when decelerating to land. Again, McLeod noticed nothing untoward in flight, but on reaching the hover over the deck the back end of his jet caught fire. Having been warned by Flyco, he then carried out a pretty nifty Vertical Landing and shut down as soon as he touched the deck. Unfortunately, the fire had caused severe damage to the electronics compartment, and this aircraft was to be out of action for several days. The electricians had their hands full already trying to repair a severed cable loom in the Boss's aircraft, which had taken a hit through the cockpit. It would be many days before this aircraft flew again, as hundreds of individual wires had to be identified and reconnected before the aircraft could once again release weapons. With two aircraft now severely damaged, the Boss went to Wings and said that if we continued at this rate we would be out of aircraft yet again within a very short time. The final assault had only just begun, and we needed to conserve our resources for emergency assistance to the ground battle. A signal to this effect was sent to *Fearless*, and there were no more tasks for us in the afternoon.

In recognition of his achievements, Murdo McLeod was appointed 'Duty Flak Sponge' in place of Mark, who had held the title up to now.

CHAPTER TWENTY-TWO

LGBS on Target

Sunday, 13 June 1982

The day started off with an intelligence report of yet another major push on Stanley that had taken place overnight. John Rochfort and I were hit with a very dodgy task long before the morning briefing. Air Ops told me that there was an Argy Hercules on the ground at Port Stanley Airfield. Our task was to attack it with rockets just before dawn. John and I were on our own and I didn't like the sound of this task one bit. We had long ago run out of fresh tactical approaches to the Port Stanley Airfield area, so I decided on an Initial Point in Berkeley Sound to the north of Stanley and hoped that the early morning poor light would mask our approach. We planned and briefed the mission, to sit around nervously awaiting a night launch. After about an hour we were told the mission was cancelled – the Sea Harriers would see to the task and shoot down the offending Hercules as soon as it took off. Unfortunately, the Navy managed to make a cock of this. Having got one pair of Sea Harriers in the area, waiting for the Hercules to move, they had to scramble a second pair as the first pair ran short of fuel. This second pair arrived late, and the Hercules got away unscathed. I wished them luck. Much later we found out that no fewer than eight Hercules had been into Port Stanley Airfield that night and many of the flights were being used to evacuate the wounded. We should have been able to work this out for ourselves; however, by this stage a defensive weariness had overtaken us as a result of the weeks of mistakes and lack of understanding by the Navy. We just weren't thinking straight any longer.

After a couple more cancelled missions we were finally tasked to use our LGBs in conjunction with an LTM. We received word that (at last) an FAC was in position with a serviceable LTM, fully charged battery and working radio. The Boss was tasked to attack a Company HQ position. He took off with Mark, reaching the Initial Point without incident. The first attack was cocked up by the FAC, who fired his laser too early, causing the bomb to land well short. (We had specifically warned the FACs against this.) The Boss frightened himself a bit on the recovery from the first attack. He made the error of breaking *away* from the released bomb for his recovery manoeuvre (a hard break down to Low Level). When he attempted a rolling pullout from the steep dive the 1,200-lb dead weight on the lower wing made it extremely difficult to level the wings. During the second attack everything went like clock-work, and the bomb was a direct hit. Beech and I eagerly debriefed with the Boss on landing, and I resolved not to make the same mistake on the recovery.

Our LGB task came in shortly and, much to Beech's disgust, I took the bombs on my aircraft. Beech (a Weapons Instructor) had done a hurried LGB trial back in the UK and was hoping that we would use him for the first attacks. However, the whole procedure sounded very straightforward and so I took the LGBs, with Beech acting as 'SAM Lookout' during the attack. My Air Task Message gave a switchback Initial Point run through the hills to attack an artillery position at the base of Mt Tumbledown. I didn't particularly like the run, but I drew it up anyway. On arrival the FAC told me that he was now using a completely different Initial Point run, coming in from the Bluff Cove area. Now I had to trust the FAC completely, there being no oppor-tunity to check out his calculations in the air. During the Initial Point run, for a short period I ran parallel to a road on which I could see quite a few vehicles. With no accurate FLOT I couldn't be sure if they were theirs or ours, and it was somewhat disconcerting to see a lot of troops jumping out of the vehicles and pointing weapons. (Much later I discovered that they were *our* troops, and they *were* firing at me.) I couldn't take evasive action anyway, or the attack would have failed. I pulled up on time into a shallow climb, stabilised for a moment and called 'Bomb gone!' as the aircraft rolled away from the thump of the Explosive Release Cartridge. For a moment I paused and flew in close formation with the evil-looking bomb, its seeker head nodding menacingly in the airflow as it waited hungrily for the coded laser reflection from the target. *Let's get out of here!* Breaking over the top of the bomb, I dived behind the nearest hill and ran out to the west. As briefed, Beech was flying line abreast and turned with me to cover my 'six' as I broke away. There were no SAM launches.

'Green Lead, that was right on the barrel!' was the message from the FAC.

'Money for old rope,'I thought as we repositioned for another attack on a new target. I repeated the run and the next bomb fell a bit short. The FAC this time was Major Mike Howes of the Royal Regiment of Wales, using the call sign RED DRAGON.

A sequel to this sortie came many months later at the London barracks of the Honourable Artillery Company. Representatives of all three services were there for the Victory Marchpast. I fell into conversation with a few NCOs of the Scots Guards, over whom I had pulled up for the LGB attacks. 'Oh yes, we all fired at you, Sir – both times round!' said one. 'It was standard practice in the battalion. If any aircraft released a weapon then we could shoot at it!' The fact that the bomb was heading some miles into the distance made no difference to this lot. After Bluff Cove they were taking no chances with attacking aircraft.

There were no more tasks for us that day, Beech and I having landed at 2000 hours. That evening the mood was upbeat amongst the 1(F) Squadron team. We had a substantial stock of LGBs (*if only we could have started using them earlier*) and the future of Ground Attack operations looked rosy. From now on, anything the FACs could mark, we could hit with devastating accuracy. After weeks of scrabbling about trying to use unsuitable weapons on unseen targets, we could at last do the job properly, at relatively small risk to ourselves.

CHAPTER TWENTY-THREE

ENDEX – 14 June

At briefing we heard that the attacks on the Stanley area had continued unabated during the night, and we anticipated more LGB sorties during the day. We heard that there was heavy fighting in progress at Wireless Ridge, and that the Argies were now using their heavy flak guns against our troops on the ground. They were not short of ammunition at any time, and I was able to see this for myself when I checked out a 35-mm Oerlikon installation near Port Stanley Airfield a couple of weeks later. The gun was surrounded by piles of unused ammunition.

Ross Boyens and McLeod were the first away, to land forward at PSC strip, after receiving no in-flight task. Pete Harris and Nick Gilchrist were off next with LGBs, to attack a target on Sapper Hill. I was DCF and, suddenly, while Pete and Nick Gilchrist were airborne, we heard the electrifying news that they had been told not to attack the target because a surrender was in progress. Pete was just about to commence his target run when the FAC said, 'Hold it! I can see white flags in the target area. Yes, they're surrendering – we'd better call this one off.'

Pete returned, still armed with 2,400 lb of LGBs. Before launch we had gone very carefully through the VSTOL calculations and worked out that with the prevailing temperature and pressure it was just possible to land back on with the bombs still aboard. We had wasted so many already that I wanted to hang on to as many as possible. Watching from Flyco, I saw Pete make an immaculate heavyweight VL with the bombs still aboard. I had left the final decision to him and he did a grand job. Pete had always been a good flyer. As expected, no more tasks came in for us, and Ross and McLeod returned uneventfully from the strip.

This was it: no more flak for the boys; no more SAMs to dodge – for the moment. News was coming in by the minute of the scale of the surrender, leaving us in no doubt that it was finished. Feelings were mixed amongst our small band of GR3 and Sea Harrier pilots. Some were visibly relieved, but others would take some time finally to wind down to a peacetime attitude of mind. We had all taken a lot of risks and there was an intense feeling of frustration that we could have achieved so much more – flown more missions, hit more targets – if only the Navy had let us do it our way. For now, the emphasis on our flying was to be switched from the Ground Attack to the easy Air Defence role, the one for which we had done most of the extra training back in the UK. That night there was a mini-celebration in the bar. We still weren't sure that we wouldn't be tasked for more Ground Attack missions on West Falkland in the morning. However, as an omen that night the wind blew up and the sea became extremely rough, the ship pitching and rolling in an increasing swell.

All next day the wind blew continuously at Storm force, reaching Force 11 at times. From the safety of Flyco we could see gigantic foaming rollers advancing from windward, the face of each wave the size of a football pitch, crest upon broken crest flying to pieces under the screaming air. The superstructure of the 26,000-ton ship hummed and vibrated like a sailboat, the hammering of the gusts clearly audible through the thick, toughened glass. All flight deck movement was suspended, except for a few hardy Flight Deck crew sent out to check on aircraft lashings. Conditions were lethal on deck, with green rollers crashing at random over the ski-jump, to sweep the length of the flight deck with foam. Our trusty Type 22 'Goalkeeper', a faithful sheepdog regardless of weather, stayed with us through it all, the pretty 3,500-ton frigate flying from wave to wave with at times a third of her keel visible and green water over the bridge. What price a small boat in a big sea?

All we could do was sit back and listen to the intelligence reports coming in. There was a film show in the pilots' briefing room, a bit of welcome relaxation for the team. By the end of the day it was confirmed that all enemy forces in the Falklands had surrendered, and therefore there would be no more Ground Attack sorties for us. Now the operational aim was to defend the whole area against any kind of revenge air attack from the mainland. Our aircraft had already been rearmed with Sidewinders in anticipation of this.

We settled into a period of winding down from the extreme tension of the last eight weeks. The Task Force was buffeted by storms for a couple of days, and when flying did resume eventually we joined the Sea Harriers practising Air Defence routines and Practice Interceptions with the occasional burst of practice Air Combat thrown in. We were joined by more characters who had trained up with us back in the UK in April: Tim Smith, Clive Loader, Roger Robertshaw and Dave Haward. Settling into a peacetime flying routine was not easy for those of us who had been aboard longest: we had to make a conscious effort each day to readjust to the normal constraints and safety precautions of peacetime flying. This had to be done or we would have lost more aircraft and pilots. However, the Navy still seemed to be 'Going for it' as if the war was still on.

One day the Admiral organised a 'Sail Past' of all the ships in the Task Group for some reason or other. This promised to be the usual pantomime so, not being involved in the flying, I stood idly at the back of the bridge while the various ships were marshalled into line, the Admiral shouting orders into a microphone via a ship-to-ship radio link. One particular frigate incurred an extra dose of the Admiral's wrath, being a little too slow to move into position. The Admiral became quite heated and was shouting more and more in his frustration as the ship concerned did not appear to respond to his instructions. After a while the problem was solved when a grovelling minion quietly pointed out that the Admiral was using the wrong call sign and shouting at the wrong ship! This was all good entertainment for us RAF 'goofers', chuckling quietly in the background; however, yet more pantomime was to follow. Part of this display was to be a flypast of Sea Harriers. As Dave Morgan (call sign Green Two) taxied forward to the launch point, he declared on radio that he was unserviceable, with the Head up Display not working at all. In fine weather this would have been no snag, but the weather was distinctly unfriendly, with sheets of low stratus scudding across the deck. Then followed the customary dick dance in Flyco. After a couple of minutes delay while Wings waited nervously to see if the problem would go away, the Captain came storming in and shouted, 'Come on Wings! Get 'em airborne!'

At least Wings had the decency to explain to Dave what was going on this time. As if in a dream I heard him say, 'You may not think this is very sensible, Green Two; but we're going to launch you anyway!' And they did. By now Dave knew the Navy routine, and dared not query the order.

On 2 July there was a Victory flypast over Stanley. I led the five flyable GR3s behind eleven Sea Harriers plus lots of helicopters over the town and surrounding area. (The Boss was busy ashore.) The Harrier launch from *Hermes* (at anchor outside Port Stanley) was an epic display of the efficiency of the Flight Deck crews. There being insufficient space for all the Harriers on deck, some aircraft were ranged below in the hangar and were brought up on the lift with engines winding up in readiness for immediate launch. The whole deck movement went like clockwork, which was fortunate as we were packed in with wings interlocked and the slightest hiccup would have brought everything to a grinding halt. The recovery was equally impressive, with many Harriers stacked up in the hover (all short of fuel) waiting to land on. At last our time on the Rat Infested Rust Bucket was drawing to a close.

CHAPTER TWENTY-FOUR

Dry Land at Last

On 4 July we were to fly all our remaining jets ashore to operate permanently from Port Stanley Airfield. Leaving the ship left me with mixed emotions. During four weeks of wartime operations we had been too preoccupied with our own survival to consider the prospect of peace; however, the last two weeks of 'peacetime' training had brought home to us once again the relative comfort and convenience of having your own ready-made floating airfield. The RN Senior Officers who had given us such a hard time during the war were less prepared to risk our lives at the push of a button. At the same time we realised from reports from Port Stanley Airfield just how bad the living and operating conditions were ashore. Despite my contempt for RN Senior Officers, I was in no hurry to go ashore. We knew that we would be going home by Hercules in a week or two, once the damaged runway had been repaired sufficiently and the Navy was able to organise a fuel supply for the transiting Hercules and for us. This fuel supply was to come from a 'Dracone', a huge floating condom that the Navy was trying to tow inshore and set up just off Port Stanley Airfield to connect with fuel hydrants ashore. Unfortunately, there were a lot of difficulties with this, caused by the winter gales which had already wrecked one attempt to set up the system. I remember a conversation at this time with the 'Commander' of *Hermes*, in which he stated rather grumpily that the sooner he could get rid of us (GR3 Harriers) from the ship, the sooner *Hermes* could sail home. I said that there was no way we were going ashore until we had an assured fuel supply – and that was a Navy problem to set up. I don't think he appreciated my intentionally take-it-or-leave-it attitude, especially when I added that we were quite happy aboard ship now that the war was winding down.

On the day of departure we were suffering intense snow showers which swept horizontally across the deck, driven by a freezing gale. After the long-delayed launch we joined up into a loose tactical formation and headed west for the last time towards the islands that had so nearly claimed our lives. En route we weaved through majestic halls of towering cumulus, which spewed dirty grey snow showers into a sea glistening blue-black in the winter sunshine. From the air our erstwhile target, Port Stanley Airfield, looked serene and virginal under a light dusting of the first winter snow, the hand of Nature trying to atone for the violence done to it and its defenders. After landing and taxying to the steel-planked parking area, I shut down and looked round on a scene of devastation. At ground level the weak winter sunshine and light snow cover could no longer disguise the wrecked aircraft and cratered landscape. As well as bullet-riddled Pucaras and Macchis, there were quite a few civilian aircraft lying about in various stages of disassembly, depending on whether they had suffered the blast of a 1,000-lb bomb or been shredded by cluster bombs. We were shown to our commandeered Squadron Ops truck and small tented camp area, which lay right in the middle of the airfield. Everything was heavily sandbagged and dispersed in case of Argy air attack. We were immediately briefed on the dangers of booby traps and mines, which had been scattered indiscriminately around – quite a few Army personnel had already been injured. Some evil booby traps had been left behind, an example of which was a pair of seemingly serviceable boots which had been discovered lying on the ground waiting for someone to pick them up. The laces were attached to an underground explosive charge. Apart from these delights the airfield was littered with unexploded ordnance, including cluster bombs, rockets and 1,000-lb bombs. I noticed that some of our 1,000-lb bomb casings lay about on the surface and were split open like a banana, with no obvious bomb crater nearby – yet more evidence of the inadequacy of the weapons we had used.

1(F) Squadron soon settled into the customary field lifestyle in the tents and ops caravans we had used so often in peacetime exercises. Just outside our ops caravan lay the tail of an Argy 250-kg bomb. Safe paths were marked out between living and working areas; everywhere else was a no-go area until the Army had swept for mines and booby traps. Our stalwart ops clerks had built a luxurious 'bomb-proof crapper' the appropriate distance downwind. Fortunately for us the RAF Mobile Catering Support Unit had followed us up into action and was producing excellent grub from mostly 24-hour 'compo' ration packs. I did a bit of touring around the local area to see what weapons had been left behind by the Argies. On the road from the town to the airfield were several of the latest flak guns, including a 35-mm twin Oerlikon, the type which had so nearly done for me on two occasions over Goose Green. The gun was surrounded by dozens of boxes of ready-use ammunition and I checked over the configuration of the belts which were still cocked into the breeches. I could see that every third round was tracer, which accounted for the pretty firework displays over the targets. I was sorely tempted to climb into the gunner's seat and fire off a burst – something I'd always wanted to do. In the town itself I found a Tigercat launcher still loaded with missiles, plus a mobile Roland launch truck, obviously withdrawn from the Sapper Hill site. There was also a TPS43 surveillance radar, which looked brand new. Just before we had flown ashore Gavin Mackay had found an empty Exocet container/launcher, which had been used by the squadron to improvise a temporary bridge over a ditch across the track leading to the squadron's operating area. Soon, various Army wheels were snooping around looking for examples of all the weapons the Argies had been using. Gavin kept mum about 'Exocet Bridge': he didn't want the Army taking his bridge away.

Our immediate task at Port Stanley Airfield was to continue Ground Standby Alert in the Air Defence role to counter possible revenge air attacks. Armed with Sidewinders and cannon, we took turns to sit out in the 'QRA Hut', a draughty, bullet-riddled cabin beside the QRA jets parked next to the runway (QRA = Quick Reaction Alert). There were a few real 'scrambles' to make life interesting, usually caused by our local Air Defence radar misidentifying a Sea Harrier or GR3 coming back from a training sortie in the west of the islands. The routine for Alert was to get out to your aircraft, thoroughly check it and then leave it 'cocked', i.e. with all switches and levers set up for the fastest possible getaway. After that the two QRA pilots would have to sit in the cabin next to the dispersal and wait for the call to scramble. Pretty boring stuff really, and very straightforward once you got airborne and under radar control. The last time I had done it was on Hunters in the Gulf. With a ripple on we could be airborne within a couple of minutes of the alarm.

A cherished memory of the war was an impromptu tri-service party we gatecrashed aboard an RFA in snow-covered PSA harbour shortly before we went home. Just about everyone was there, including faces we had not seen since Ascension, some of whom we feared had not survived. We had little idea of who had become a casualty. Booze flowed freely as Navy, Army and Air Force swapped yarns and war stories deep into the night. Through portholes we could see the silent, gentle snowfall as it cleansed and muffled everything on deck and on the deserted quayside. In the warmth and cheer of the Wardroom it felt like Christmas and New Year rolled into one. As the party warmed up, latent fears and tensions drained away and an intense feeling of pride and comradeship took over. Slowly we realised the enormity of what had been achieved against the odds – and at what sacrifice. We had been privileged to take part in a unique feat of arms, which would probably never be repeated by British forces acting alone. Having survived, now we had the same chance as everyone else back home of walking down the years to retirement and old age. For most of us, the chance of ever again becoming involved in such a desperate military adventure seemed remote.

We were now in the grip of the South Atlantic midwinter and temperatures dropped way below freezing at nights, leaving us shivering in our inadequately heated tents. The Argies refused to admit defeat and accept that the islands were once again British possessions. We therefore had to provide a standing force of GR3 Harriers for many months until Port Stanley Airfield could be improved sufficiently to allow Phantoms to operate and provide Air Defence. Much to our relief, after about a week ashore a bunch of 3(F) Squadron pilots arrived on one of the first RAF Hercules to land at Port Stanley Airfield, and the remainder of the 1(F) Squadron contingent (except the Boss) embarked for the fourteen-hour marathon slog back to Ascension. There had been some doubt as to whether the Hercules would be able to land, but one of our 3(F) Squadron pilots kindly volunteered to hover-taxy up and down the runway to clear the snow! My happiest memory of the flight was of standing at the back of the Hercules flight deck looking out at a brilliant starlit night and getting quietly drunk on coffee laced heavily with rum, in company with a Colonel of the Royal Engineers. For me, the endless thunder of the engines in the night was a catharsis, a soothing balm which I needed to suppress some of the chaotic memories of the months of hectic action. It was to be a long time before I could get myself back into a settled frame of mind. At Ascension we had been looking forward to a good meal and a few hours' rest, but a super-keen Air Mover told us that the RAF had other plans. As the first returning RAF Harrier pilots, we were in line for a VIP reception in the UK. Within a short time we had transferred to a VC10 and were on our way to the UK and the assembled media. I was dragged in for an ITN interview, the content of which remained hazy. Eventually, we were released and allowed to go on to Wittering.

On arrival we were given a splendidly emotional reception and a welcome party before returning wearily to our families. After the unrelieved tension of the last three months I was badly in need of a rest and was looking forward to the two weeks' leave promised by Pat King. Some hopes! Within a few hours of arriving home the phone started to ring. First of all I had see Pat who showed me a signal – fully 3 feet long – which contained just the *titles* of the subjects on which I was to comment for the 1(F) Squadron report on the operation that he told me to write. Pat commiserated with me and hoped it wouldn't spoil my leave! As usual, HQ Strike Command wanted the final report by yesterday, so I just had to sit down and get on with it at home. The Boss was still in the Falklands helping the 3(F) Squadron guys settle in, so I was on my own. At the same time the phone was busy most of the day. Everyone and his uncle wanted to ring up and congratulate me on surviving and doing a good job down there. It was heart-warming to hear from so many old chums from near and far away. Not so welcome were calls from Wittering, asking for a hundred and one different bits of information and telling me that they hoped I didn't mind but they'd agreed that I would be guest of honour at this or that function, or that I would be required to give a talk to this or that organisation.

As the commitments built up I found myself starting to wish that I had never become involved in a shooting war. The last straw came when a Corporal from Sick Quarters rang up to say that I had to go immediately to RAF Ely for a spinal X-ray. The medical establishment was furious that I hadn't had one so far. At this I cracked and gave the unfortunate Corporal an earful, telling him that I was on leave and how dare he ring me up with such a trivial item when I was already up to here with paperwork. This childish outburst made me feel better, but writing the report took me about the whole of the two weeks 'leave'. I reserved my greatest criticism for the vital IFF, stating categorically that it was unfit for use in either peace or war. (During the work-up to the Gulf War of 1991, the RAF still did not possess a usable IFF, having to borrow sets from the Americans in order to be able to participate in operations.) Eventually I did go to RAF Hospital Ely to be examined by a rather supercilious Group Captain, who was quite scathing about my flying again without a post-ejection X-ray. I pointed out that there was a war on at the time. He seemed concerned at my attitude and asked me if I had heard of Post-Traumatic Stress Syndrome. This was the first time I had heard the expression. I wrapped up the interview pretty smartly and got out of there before I said something I would regret. I had no intention of being 'interviewed' about that kind of thing. Unfortunately, the medics wouldn't give up easily and I was visited by several of them at Wittering, trying to use me as a guinea pig for their pet theories. At the time I was far too busy to be concerned about possible long-term psychological problems. One bloke in particular was quite interesting. Claiming to be some kind of civil servant, I worked out that he was almost certainly a 'trick cyclist' working for the MoD.

Later I saw the final version of the report on Operation *Corporate* as produced by HQ Strike Command. In a fifty-page report detailing the exploits of the Staff Officers and the Tanker, Nimrod, Hercules and Vulcan forces (only the last of which actually exposed themselves to danger from enemy action), the efforts of our GR3 Harriers occupied barely two pages. More galling at the time was the apparent wall of silence we met from the rest of the RAF Ground Attack aircrew. Although I was commissioned to give talks about the war to Round Table groups, ladies' luncheon clubs, schools, universities, factory workers etc., *not one* RAF Ground Attack station or squadron invited me or any other 1(F) Squadron pilot to talk about our experiences. To be fair, there was one short 'Post Operation *Corporate*' conference held at Wittering, attended by some Staff Officers and representatives from other stations, but to my knowledge no formal notes were taken. Later on the Boss was invited to some exotic locations overseas with the MoD Briefing team, and I went to HQ RAFG and Gibraltar with a Strike Command Briefing team, on the strict understanding that I was there only to answer questions – after the 'Official' Strike Command report had been read out (by non-participants). This apparent lack of interest from other operators puzzled me for a while: I was not particularly bothered as I was already fed up with the briefing commitments. I had no particular wish to blow my own trumpet but I thought, naively, that these other operators would have liked to hear details of tactics and problems under fire direct from pilots who had just done it for real, bearing in mind that this was the first time that any RAF mud-moving or Tactical Recce had been carried out in the face of modern defensive weapons. It was also the first time that the RAF had used cluster bombs, LGBs, retard bombs and a recce pod in action. Eventually, I came to the reluctant conclusion that we were facing a case of good old-fashioned Professional Jealousy. I felt that the non-participant Harrier, Jaguar, Buccaneer and Tornado forces just did not want to have anything to do with us – in case our experiences challenged their established ways of doing things. If this was indeed the case, then the Falklands war was more or less a wasted experience for the Fighter Ground Attack and Tactical Recce elements of the RAF.

CHAPTER TWENTY-FIVE

Jeff Comes Back

After a short while at home we all turned up at Wittering again to welcome Jeff home, when he returned from captivity in Argentina. Jeff seemed to be in relatively good form, as we had expected. Of all the 1(F) Squadron pilots he was the most easy-going and capable of enduring what was a deeply frustrating and tedious experience. This was Jeff Glover's story.

On reaching the Falkland Sound area, Jeff eventually got in contact with HMS *Antrim* on the radio who gave him details (including a map reference) of an Armed Recce task in the Port Howard area. (Later on, no Navy agency would admit to having spoken to Jeff on the radio.) From here on Jeff played things very sensibly. Having made one fast and low recce pass through the Port Howard area – during which he saw no sign of enemy activity – he climbed to about 12,000 feet and got in contact with *Antrim* again, suggesting he carry out a recce pass, to take some photos of the area. *Antrim* agreed to this plan. Jeff now ran into Port Howard from a different direction. Unfortunately, his luck didn't hold and as he ran out down the sea loch to the south-west, he felt three bangs in quick succession. Flying at more than 500 knots and very low, Jeff saw no sign of tracer or a missile until he was hit. The Argy forces in the area were firing at him with everything they had, but told Jeff that a Blowpipe missile brought him down.[29] Jeff was immediately in desperate straits: rolling out of control, he remembered being inverted just above the wave tops and delaying pulling the handle until he was starting to roll upright again. In the event he ejected with over 90 degree of bank, after which his next recollection is of struggling for his life deep underwater. He suffered severe shoulder injuries and was extremely lucky to be picked up by enemy troops in a rowing boat. He then spent a miserable couple of months as a prisoner-of-war. Some eighteen months later Jeff was back in the Falklands on duty and visited Port Howard, where some locals described seeing him being hit and 'a large piece of wing coming off'. No wonder he rolled.

Amongst the huge piles of paperwork, the rest of us were given a long and detailed questionnaire in which we had to describe what it felt like to be at war. I noted that this survey was being carried out by the RN medical branch, and I took some satisfaction in describing the main effect on our morale as a result of the appalling attitude of the average Senior Naval Officer.

To add to my disillusionment with the aftermath of the war, I was pretty unimpressed with the inaccurate books on the subject which had been rushed into print in order to cash in on the immediate post-war euphoria. Obviously, these people had been given access to our Flight Authorisation Sheets. Unfortunately they had no idea how to interpret them, sometimes fabricating events that happened on missions that appeared in the sheets but were cancelled before launch and never flown. The experience of reading this kind of military 'history' soon helped me decide to write my own account of what happened to us. There are many unsatisfactory aspects of the war that have never been publicly aired, and probably never will be if the Navy has anything to do with it. In particular, I discovered in conversation with a pilot of Wessex Naval Air Squadron, that the experiences of the helicopter crews at the mercy of the RN Helicopter Tasking Cell were even more tedious than our own. This character had been a shipmate of ours during the initial voyage south aboard *Norland*, and I was not to see him again until 30 June, at the party aboard the RFA in Port Stanley harbour. We had quite a few war stories to tell each other, and I was not greatly surprised to hear of the lousy way he had been treated by the Navy.[30]

CHAPTER TWENTY-SIX

1(F) Squadron Returns to the Falklands

T o our disgust, we soon learned that we were all to be sent back to the Falklands again in late August, after less than two months at Wittering. This was because the RAF Germany Harrier squadrons were whining about having spent so much time away from their families already this year! They had three times the number of pilots that we had, and we were disgusted that they had managed to 'swing' this on HQ Strike Command, dropping 1(F) Squadron in it once again after we had done all the dirty work during the shooting war. Hence, in early September 1982 we were once again camped out in the familiar tents and ops vans parked in the middle of Port Stanley Airfield. Our immediate Boss was Wing Commander Gerry Honey, ex-OC Operations Wing at Wittering and also an ex-Flight Commander on 20(AC) Squadron at Wildenrath when I was there in the 1970s. Gerry was good value and more or less left me to do as I wanted. As Operations Officer and general dogsbody we had a young Flying Officer called Dave Haigh, who was awaiting a Harrier course at Wittering. Unfortunately, within a few months he was to die with John Leeming in a mid-air collision during the Air Combat phase of his course.

Since June the Royal Engineers had worked like Trojans to improve the airfield facilities, although the constant movement of vehicles had turned the whole area into a Passchendaele of early spring mud. At last we had a few professionals on the intelligence side and various Army intelligence officers briefed us that the threat of attack from the mainland had faded almost to insignificance. Our few GR3 Harriers were committed mostly to the Air Defence role and we continued to keep a pair on QRA throughout the daylight hours. Unfortunately for the

173

peace of the South Atlantic, the Air Defence of the islands was still in the hands of the Navy, with HMS *Illustrious* having replaced *Invincible*. The new Admiral aboard her seemed determined to restart the war by goading the Argies into action, or so it seemed to us. On one occasion we were tasked by the Navy to put up all our aircraft in company with Sea Jets on a High Level 'Sweep' out almost as far as the Argentine coast, 'to see how the Argies would react'. This was all good old Second World War stuff and we suspected that the Admiral – peeved at having missed the war – had been reading too many *Battler Britain* comics. As Acting Squadron Commander on the planned date of this ludicrous operation I took great pleasure in cancelling our participation – on the excuse of poor weather at Port Stanley Airfield. I had discovered to my delight that although the Admiral had operational control of our aircraft, he could not actually *order* us into the air in peacetime.

Port Stanley Airfield was still the stinking mudpit we knew and loved, and we kept our pilots' interest with hard-working training sorties around the islands. We had been joined by some of our new Junior Pilots (JPs) who had joined us since April 1982 and had done hardly any Combat Ready work-up training in the intervening months. One of the more interesting sorties for these guys was the routine 'Laundry Run' to *Illustrious* for an overnight stop and a few beers in the air-conditioned comfort of their Wardroom bar. Despite the generally primitive conditions ashore, the Sea Harrier pilots were quite keen to bring an aircraft ashore to Port Stanley Airfield for a few nights and enjoy some return hospitality (i.e. get drunk with us). They seemed happy to live in tents and put up with a bit of personal discomfort in order to get away from the rigidly controlled and generally uninteresting peacetime flying aboard ship. They turned a hand to stints of QRA with us, and we also arranged some quite punchy 'bounced' sorties where we would go off after a simulated target, to be attacked by Sea Harriers en route. Unlike the Argies we always had plenty of fuel available for a good 'punch-up' with the bounce – this being the main aim of the game. A highlight of our social life was the occasional drive into town along the muddy, potholed track for the luxury of a hot bath with water heated over a peat fire. We had made private arrangements with some of the long-suffering locals to make use of their houses while they were away in the 'camp' (out in the islands) for this purpose, and we were eternally grateful for the privilege, there being no running water on the airfield.

After a few weeks I left the Falklands for the last time to organise the training of our remaining non-operational pilots at Wittering. Within a short time I heard news of a particularly dodgy incident at Port Stanley

Airfield, which nearly led to the loss of young Roger Robertshaw, one of our newest pilots. In common with standard RAF operational practice, all of our parked aircraft at Port Stanley Airfield had to be ready for immediate operational scramble to keep them safe from air attack. As soon as the air attack warning sounded, all available pilots were to run to the nearest aircraft and get airborne as soon as possible. This was to be done without paperwork and, if necessary, without assistance from ground crew. This had been done a few times already without major problems. With a ripple on we could get everything airborne in less than five minutes.

During this scramble Roger jumped into a jet that had a 'Red Ink Entry' (Limiting Technical Defect) recorded in the aircraft Technical Log, which of course Roger did not see. The problem was that the Flight Instrument Master Switch did not automatically switch on as it should when the pilot hit the 'Quick Start' gangbar. This meant that the 'Woolworth's' Artificial Horizon would not start up, leaving the pilot with no instrument references at all after take-off. (There was no time to align the Inertial system, hence there was no Head up Display.) Unfortunately, the weather was also very poor (this scramble was for real). Roger was 'going for it' in the best traditions of the Harrier Force, and in his innocence did not notice the lack of Artificial Horizon until after he had entered some very thick cloud. After a series of death-defying gyrations he plunged out of cloud out of control and just managed to pull out of the dive a few feet above the distinctly unfriendly-looking sea. By the merest fluke he had avoided becoming yet another Harrier Loss of Control in Cloud statistic.

Before the squadron returned to the UK, we had yet another ejection in the Falklands, when the Boss had to abandon his aircraft near Port Stanley Airfield after an engine failure. He landed in the sea and was quickly picked up by a passing Navy Sea King.

The squadron's return to Wittering in late October 1982 was the end of an eventful year for 1(F) Squadron. Years of training in the hard and unforgiving school of the RAF Harrier Force had enabled us to do our job in war and survive against all the odds. It had been a close-run thing. After the first eleven days of our war operations 50 per cent of our aircraft had been shot down, two of our pilots surviving only by the skin of their teeth. Until the last two days of action we had no 'smart' weapons available to carry out stand-off attacks and had to rely mostly on the traditional RAF Low Level tactics, which had proved so costly to the Americans in Vietnam. At the end of that war the Americans decided that Low Level overflight of targets was far too risky and put a lot of money into 'smart' stand-off weapons that could be delivered accurately and in relative safety for the attacker. At the same time they increased their already substantial investment in Electronic Warfare equipment. Just as the Americans made this decision, in the early 1970s, the RAF was about to commit itself irrevocably to the Tornado/JP233 combination as its only effective means of airfield attack. At the time those of us in front-line mud-moving agreed that this was a mistaken policy, the results of which were to be seen in the Falklands and when some chickens came home to roost nine years later in the Gulf War. In my view this was yet another example of the RAF's seemingly never-ending short-sightedness and parsimony when it came to weapons procurement. The provision of maximum numbers of airframes regardless seemed to be the primary consideration of our Senior Officers – no matter that those aircraft were poorly equipped and had an inferior range of weapons.

CHAPTER TWENTY-SEVEN

Afterthoughts

Acynic would say that in the Falklands our 1(F) Squadron pilots were the victims of the success of RAF propaganda and self-delusion on the likely effectiveness of Low Level Ground Attack operations in war. In early 1982 the most recent RAF experience of Ground Attack operations (albeit against a primitive and poorly equipped enemy) had taken place in Dhofar in the early 1970s, mostly using the slow and poorly armed Strikemaster (an upgraded version of the Jet Provost basic trainer). Since then, apart from the introduction of the cluster bomb and the LTM, we had hardly improved on our aircraft weapons and aiming systems. In spite of this our Senior Officers would still rant on about the 'devastating effectiveness of Air Power' as illustrated by various Firepower Demonstrations designed to impress the other services and visiting foreign customers for British weapon systems. During such demonstrations an easy target like a tank hulk or suchlike would be set up on some Army range and then a few aircraft would attack it with live weapons, having had plenty of time to study the target area and plan a suitable profile. (If there was a lot of money in the contract for British industry then there would also be a couple of full-scale practices with weapons to make sure the pilots couldn't miss on the day.) This kind of thing bears about as much relation to real wartime Ground Attack as village cricket does to a Test Match. To get a more accurate impression of our true capability the Army or Navy should have asked a few searching questions of those same Air Marshals (not many of whom had flown a Fast-Jet Ground Attack Air-craft operationally). In particular, they should have asked the following:

'How often do your squadron pilots practise trying to hit a realistic (i.e. camouflaged), target with a realistic weapon load (i.e the maximum you would carry in war)?'

'Honest answer: 'Never.'

'All right then, when you *do* practise realistic attacks with what-ever weapon load, live or dummy, then how often do your pilots achieve a first-pass damaging hit on the target?'

Honest answer: 'Er, not very often.'

'So what chance do you give of your pilots being able to destroy their targets in wartime?'

Honest answer: 'Er, not much.'

'Then why don't you do something about it?'

'Er, let's talk about something else.'

In the end the Falklands war was won because of the availability of reliable, high-technology American weapons. In the AIM9L Sidewinder the Air Defence forces possessed an Idiot's Weapon, which was almost foolproof in operation, demonstrating a better than 90 per cent Kill Probability in action. This was an unprecedented performance for a missile system when used in anger. In the Paveway Laser Guided Bomb we had a devastatingly accurate weapon which could have revolutionised Ground Attack operations throughout, had its potential been recognised earlier by our senior commanders. By the same token, the war was almost lost because of the British use of unreliable, low-technology British weapons to defend against air attack. As the Admiral admitted to us when it was all over: 'It was a damned close-run thing: if we had lost the use of one of the carriers we would all have had to go home.'

Very fortunately for us the Argentinians had made an irrecoverable strategic balls-up in starting the war when they did. If only they had waited a few more weeks until they had bought a few dozen more Exocets from France – and given their pilots more time to train in the use of them – then they would have made mincemeat of our shipping from Day One.

For us landlubbers from Wittering the whole operation had been the most unlikely adventure from start to finish. Although used to regular deployments and exercises around Europe, we had no inkling that we would ever be required for such a distant seaborne operation. We had no squadron contingency plans to operate from Navy carriers. At regular intervals during the whole business I had to kick myself to realise that this was actually happening. My greatest regret was that our 1(F) Squadron element was not allowed to take part in any of the relaxed Air Superiority operations during the shooting war. Most of us would have given our right arm for a shot at an Argy Skyhawk or Mirage, but this was not to be, the Navy hogging it all for themselves. We knew that we were the only pilots in theatre properly trained to carry out the difficult and dangerous Low Level Ground Attack and Recce tasks and this meant that we had to leave the fun flying to them. This caused no friction between us and the Sea Harrier guys at the time, but there was a strong feeling among our pilots that *we took most of the hits – they took most of the glory.*

The way we were tasked was shambolic and wasteful almost from the first day of our operations. Many of our Ground Attack sorties were completely wasted and should never have been tasked. By contrast, the types of Ground Attack mission that did promise effective results, such as the toss attacks in company with Sea Harriers and the attacks on pre-recced targets, were not exploited. Their value was not appreciated by The Flag, despite our energetic endorsement of them. Additionally, we should have been tasked on far more *pure photo recce* sorties, in order to *find* the targets that proved so elusive during pure attack missions. As an example, just one well-planned recce pass through the middle of the Stanley/PSA area could have solved a number of intelligence problems at a stroke: the location of the 155-mm artillery, the land-launched Exocet and the TPS 43/44 radar. All of these and many more high-value targets were hidden among the houses.

We (1(F) Squadron pilots) were the only Ground Attack and Recce professionals in theatre – and the Navy refused to listen to us.

Timely Low Level photo recce in good light could have been the key to several other operations – the Goose Green battle, for example. Once the Port San Carlos strip was in operation it would have been easy for us to fly several recce sorties a day out of that location, with just the capability to reload cameras ashore. The recce GR3s involved could also have been armed with Sidewinders as a short-notice reinforcement for the local Combat Air Patrols, the missiles having no effect on recce capability. Finally – and conclusively in my view – the Navy demonstrated their almost total ignorance of the potential of photo recce by their cavalier treatment of the Photographic Interpreters and their essential equipment aboard *Hermes*. With just a little forethought they could have allowed them far better facilities, in a location where they could process and disseminate their essential intelligence with the minimum of delay. But it was not to be. The Naval hierarchy aboard *Hermes* – who appeared to know next to nothing about recce – couldn't even trust the Photographic Interpreters to interpret accurately what they found on film, a specialist task for which they had been superbly trained. On the occasions when there *was* clear photographic evidence of a suitable target, the Navy seemed incapable of appreciating the urgency of attacking that target as soon as possible. An independent opinion of the meagre photo recce effort comes from Brigadier Julian Thompson, Commander Landing Force Task Group (from *NO PICNIC*):

Not until the very end of the campaign were there any photo-graphs showing enemy dispositions, defensive positions, strong points, gun positions and so forth. Even they arrived so late and were so poor that they had no influence on planning.

This is a *scandalous* indictment of the Navy's incompetent utilisation of the considerable recce assets in theatre (both GR3s and Sea Harriers carried recce cameras at all times).

It is not enough for the Navy to claim that the shambolic Tasking System – supposedly controlled from *Fearless* – was to blame for all this. For a lot of the time the Admiral held back some of our aircraft for his own personal Naval Air Tasks, regardless of the requirements of the land battle. Thus our tiny resources were diminished even further at the hands of those who had the least idea of how to use them effectively. At least the Admiral could have shown some appreciation of the flexibility of Air Power by leaving some of our aircraft armed with Sidewinders at times. On occasions the Air Defences were almost overwhelmed by enemy attacks, and it would have been a piece of cake for some of our GR3s to accompany Sea Harriers on Combat Air Patrol.

Back in the UK I was nauseated to see the extent to which the RN Public Relations machine had been used to claim exclusive credit for almost all aspects of the operation. There were wild claims as to the number of Low Level Ground Attack sorties flown by Sea Harriers, giving additional credence to media misreporting of Sea Harriers carrying out attacks that 1(F) Squadron GR3s had made. (Interestingly, there were no erroneous media reports of GR3s shooting down Argy aircraft.) The Post-war RAE Farnborough analysis of all Operation *Corporate* attack sorties lists just nineteen Low Level Ground Attack sorties flown by Sea Harriers over land, whereas our GR3 pilots flew over 130 sorties with just a handful of aircraft. (These statistics ignore Sea Harrier attacks on unarmed shipping.) RN pettiness extended even to the post-war celebrations, when *Hermes* sailed back into the English Channel and prepared to fly off her complement of Sea Harriers to Yeovilton for a huge welcome bonanza. On the instructions of the Naval hierarchy, only one RAF Sea Harrier pilot (who had no Air-to-Air kills) was allowed to fly his aircraft back into Yeovilton on this day. Even Flight Lieutenant Dave Morgan – the top-scoring Air Defender – was not allowed to fly ashore.

As for the Navy's attempts to run Offensive Air Support operations, I can only quote the Official RAF history of Operation *Corporate*:

It is a remarkable achievement of extemporisation (by pilots of 1(F) Squadron) that, with neither control agency (TACC, SACC) properly organised, with the failure of the HF communications, and with HMS *Hermes'* lack of OAS support facilities, effective OAS (Offensive Air Support, i.e. Ground Attack) missions were still mounted successfully.

This brief summary is far too kind to RN Senior Officers. In my view, their effect on our operations was mostly negative. They made little attempt to conceal their open contempt and hostility towards the RAF, and it appeared that we were little more than expendable ordnance as far as they were concerned. For us GR3 pilots this created feelings of anger, uncertainty and bitter frustration at not being able to carry out difficult Air Tasks as efficiently as we could. For most of us the constant nagging worry was, 'What are these clowns going to make us do next?'

In retrospect, if our advice had been even half listened to, we could have flown far more sorties and hit more targets with much greater precision to assist the ground forces in their difficult and dangerous task.

From Squadron Leader J. J. Pook DFC RAF

Stds Sqn TOCU
RAF Cottesmore
OAKHAM
Rutland
Leics.
LE15 7BL

tel. Oakham 812241 ext. 581

Wing Commander Neal   19 Oct 88
RAF Staff College

Dear Wing Commander,

I am sorry to have to give notice that I feel unable to give the lecture 'Morale in Battle' at Camberley on 22 Nov. I have already spoken to Colonel Cross to explain my reasons. Basically I cannot see how I can talk about RAF Harrier Pilots' morale in the Falklands without being extremely rude to the RN. Over the last few weeks I have been carrying out some research, including a visit to the AHB and going through my taped diaries of our experiences in the war. (I am also in the process of putting my diary on paper.) The overwhelming emotion which I have rediscovered is one of *sheer cold anger* at the incompetent and arrogant way in which the RN did their level best to foil our efforts to carry out effective air operations.

For me – a mere Specialist Aircrew Squadron Leader – to stand up and say as much in front of an audience including RN senior officers is a task which is beyond my capabilities. I have a short fuse about the whole business, and I do not want even to discuss the matter with Naval officers, for many of whom I have the utmost contempt. I do not include the RN aviators alongside whom we flew in battle, and who gave us full assistance and co-operation at all times.

Once again I am sorry to have left you in the lurch, but I am afraid I have no option.

Yours Aye,

J.J. POOK Sqn Ldr

Conclusions

As the months and years went by after the war I asked myself what it was all about as far as I was concerned. I was surprised to discover that I wanted to know some reasons why we had done what we did, at such cost. I was no career officer and certainly no blimpish patriot, eager to defend the Empire wherever it was threatened. As a life-long cynic I took a fairly jaundiced view of the whole business: surely it was just a part of the RAF job about which you had no choice? I did not even feel any particular attachment to the Falkland Islanders themselves. The few I had met during the war seemed typical bluff farming types, grateful yet slightly embarrassed that all this trouble and sacrifice had been made on their behalf. This was no reason to fight a war, was it? And yet …

Some months after the war, on BBC radio I heard the wife of a Falklands farmer describing her experiences when the invasion took place. Her husband had been 'arrested' and dragged outside into the garden by some hot-headed Argy soldiers who forced him to his knees and put a rifle to his head. She felt sure he would be shot. She opened the windows and put on her record of *Land of Hope and Glory*, so that it would be the last thing her husband heard before he died. In the event he was released unharmed. This story seemed almost unbearably poignant and my reaction to it gave me the solution to many unanswered questions. Maybe I am less cynical now. Who knows? In the military, too much self-analysis can be counterproductive. After all, the main task is to enjoy the flying and survive to pick up your pension.

> Speak for the air, your element, you hunters
> Who range across the ribbed and shifting sky:
> Speak for whatever gives you mastery –
> Wings that bear out your purpose, quick-responsive
> Fingers, a fighting heart, a kestrel's eye.

Speak of the rough and tumble in the blue,
The mast-high run, the flak, the battering gales:
You that, until the life you love prevails,
Must follow death's impersonal vocation –
Speak from the air, and tell your hunter's tales.

(Anon.)

APPENDIX 1

Harrier GR3 Technical Details

Max speed at Low Level: Approx. 570–580 kt

Maximum Radius of Action: Approx. 200 nm (High Low High Profile with 2,100-gallon drop tanks)

Normal Weapon Load in Falklands (Ground Attack or Recce):
Outboard   2 × cluster bombs
or, 2 × 1,000-lb free-fall bombs
or, 2 × 2-inch rocket pods
or, 2 × Laser Guided Bombs
or, 2 × 1,000-lb retard bombs
or, 2 × AIM9 Sidewinder
or, 2 × SHRIKE ARM
Inboard   2 × 100-gallon fuel tanks (usually)

Plus: 2 × 120 rounds cannon for fuselage-mounted Aden guns (high explosive/incendiary shells). Combined rate of fire: forty rounds per second.

NOTE: An extra cluster bomb or 1,000-lb bomb could be loaded on the centreline pylon in place of the Reconnaissance Pod. Often this pylon was unused: being so close to the deck it was the most awkward one to load in a hurry.

Single-seat Low Flying

The Technique

From the pilot's point of view, Low Flying over friendly territory was not particularly difficult or dangerous – just great fun! All you had to do was get down as close to Mother Earth as possible, and avoid flying into any user-hostile obstacles. The odd thin telephone wire or leafy tree top wouldn't do you much harm, but an encounter with overhead power lines or solid ground was usually fairly terminal. Naturally, Low Flying in unpopulated and uncivilised terrain (such as the Falklands) meant not having to worry about any man-made obstacles, which were usually the most difficult to see. Hence, we could really 'go for it' where necessary and get right down as low as we could.

A lot of bullshit has been spoken and written about how low it is possible to fly an aircraft such as the Harrier, and this is a favourite bar topic for the more 'macho' pilots. The facts are that even the most competent (or foolhardy) pilot cannot get the aircraft much below about 10 feet above ground – and that over pretty flat and well-defined terrain. At these heights and at speeds of 420 kt plus, it feels as if the aircraft is skimming the grass. Old films of the Red Arrows show that genuine aces such as Ray Hanna could get the Gnat down consistently to just a few feet *over an airfield*, but this was exceptional and not so easy in a larger and faster aircraft over normal terrain. (The tiny GNAT T1 was the RAF's Advanced Trainer of the 1960s and 1970s, and it was an aeroplane custom-built for hooliganism. Unlike its replacement, the Hawk, the Gnat was a genuine Fast Jet, capable of 600 kt at Low Level, combining high performance and, for its day, a very high-tech cockpit.)

When flying at such low heights, all of the ground up to some 200–300 metres in front of the aircraft appears as a blur, and the pilot can only take avoiding action on obstacles he can see and identify beyond this distance. As speed is increased, so proportionally does this

186

blurred area, and there is an overwhelming instinct to fly higher in order to be able to identify small obstacles in time to avoid them. The pilot's eyes are locked to the straight ahead position while this is going on; only the most experienced and practised will have any capacity left to look at a map or briefly look to one side to check for 'Bandits' (hostile aircraft). The problem is much worse in a turn, when as much as 80 degrees of bank angle must be used to get around corners. This puts the wingtip some 15 feet closer to the ground at a stroke, and must be compensated for by an increase in height as the bank comes on. Consistent failure to do this leads to digging-in of the wingtip, followed by instant oblivion. Less experienced pilots tend to over-compensate for bank angle and will fly higher and higher above ground the more they are forced to manoeuvre, thus making themselves easy targets for the opposition.

Low Level Navigation

The Falklands war was the last to be fought by the RAF in which Ground Attack aircraft relied on the traditional 'map-and-stopwatch' style of navigation, a method almost as old as flight itself. In the absence of reliable modern navigation aids such as the inertially driven moving map and GPS, this was the only available technique, and demanded considerable pilot ability to achieve success. The technique is simple in principle and involves plotting the desired track on a 1:500,000 or 1:250,000 scale map, measuring required headings and putting in timing marks to show distance covered every minute. After some map study before take-off, all the pilot has to do is to fly the planned headings, allowing for drift, and start his stopwatch at the beginning of each leg of the route. In flight, he will follow the features shown on the map while using the time elapsed on the stopwatch to give him an indication as to how far he has progressed along track. If drift can be accurately measured in flight (impossible in the Harrier) and if ground speed and heading are both flown with total accuracy (also impossible with the unreliable and inaccurate instrumentation available) then pilots would never get lost! As an additional problem, Ground Attack pilots are rarely afforded the luxury of being allowed to follow the planned track throughout the sortie – especially in wartime. Deviations to avoid bad weather or hostile aircraft are an obvious problem. As a result, a large part of peacetime RAF Low Level training used to be devoted to free navigation off track, where the pilot reads from ground to map and identifies the features as he passes them in order to keep tabs on his position. Even at normal peacetime Low Flying heights (250 feet) this can be a bit of a lottery as many areas are relatively featureless or, alternatively, crammed with too many similar features for consistent map reading. In such circumstances the pilot can only 'Seaman's Eye' the approximate vector and hope to pick up an accurate position check later on when he finds a more identifiable feature. Bear in mind that every minute spent on the wrong track will take the pilot 7 miles away from where he thought he was.

As a result of all this uncertainty it will not surprise the reader to learn that all Single-Seat Ground Attack and Recce pilots held Honorary Membership of the 'Fukawi' tribe.

'Operational' Low Flying

At the 'operational' heights mentioned above, navigation becomes much more difficult. For a start, time available to look at the map is strictly limited. Additionally, at such heights the horizon is much closer, thus allowing far less time to see and identify features. The reader must bear in mind that throughout all this the pilot will also have to monitor his position within a formation of aircraft and keep a lookout for enemy aircraft and likely targets on the ground, to say nothing of monitoring aircraft systems, fuel state and the warnings on his Radar Warning system.

Attack Navigation

If Low Level en-route navigation was so difficult, how then was the pilot able to find a small, camouflaged target? The answer lay in the 1:50,000 (tourist) map on which the target was plotted. Basically, the pilot would select an Initial Point (IP), which was a large, easily identifiable feature on the 1:500,000 scale map, and which lay within a couple of minutes' flying time of the target. This feature would then be plotted on the 1:50,000 map and a line drawn direct to the target position. An accurate heading would be measured, and he would plot timing marks every ten seconds of distance on the Initial Point map. On reaching the Initial Point the pilot drops the half mil map and switches navigation to the 1:50,000 map, setting off from the Initial Point exactly on heading and 'hacking' (starting) his stopwatch when exactly overhead the point. He is now map reading on the equivalent of an OS Landranger map at a speed of 7 or 8 miles per minute. This takes years of training to get consistently right. During planning, after selecting a good Initial Point the pilot makes a careful map study of the route in order to pick out a limited number of easily identifiable check points such as buildings or woods that are on or close to track. Close to the target it is essential to have a final check feature to guarantee line up for the last few miles of the run-in.

This method was good enough to attack a target such as a SAM site or group of uncamouflaged vehicles. However, for a 'difficult' target – such as a single camouflaged vehicle at the edge of a wood – it was highly desirable to see a recce photo of the target and its surrounding area before taking off for the attack. This could make all the difference between a hit and a miss.

In my experience, sensible selection of Initial Points and attack directions marked out the difference between the successful and the merely adequate fighter-bomber or recce pilot. (All of these navigation problems are the same if not worse in the recce role.) Far too often pilots would select Initial Points that would only be visible from 500 feet agl because they were hidden behind folds in the terrain. Similarly, the final run-in would often be a shambles because the pilot had not taken sufficient account of the terrain and features immediately surrounding the target. The secret to success lay in the ability to *interpret* the 1:50,000 map accurately and visualise how the terrain was going to look from Low Level. Some pilots could do this instinctively, some learnt how to do it with experience and the rest never really got the idea.

The RAF had always set a high standard of Low Level pilot navigation and we were merely following in the footsteps of our distinguished predecessors on the Hunter, the Swift, the Venom etc. As an illustration of the standards that had been reached there could be few better examples than a typical advanced 'chased' sortie on the old Fighter Reconnaissance course at RAF Chivenor. In the Hunter FR10 this would consist of up to five difficult targets spread over England and Wales, the planning for which had to be completed at breakneck speed (a maximum of twenty minutes per target). After this the chase pilot (a member of staff who would follow the student throughout), would as likely as not *take away ALL the student's maps before he got airborne*. This was a test of how well the student had memorised the details of the 1:500,000 and Initial Point to target maps while he was planning – an essential part of sortie preparation. *He was still expected to find all of the targets.* A typical In Flight Task would also be given on the radio by the chase pilot, e.g. 'I want you to follow the A5 from here to Bethesda and find all the AA phone boxes'. The student would be expected to find *and photograph* the lot, plot them accurately on his 1:50,000 map, and then give an In Flight Radio Report of the positions to his chase pilot, all the while continuing to fly at an authorised 50 feet above ground level. Sadly, these skills were already disappearing from the front line with the introduction of ever more accurate navigation systems and the ubiquitous moving map display.

APPENDIX 3

Fighter Ground Attack Weapons

General

At the time of the Falklands war, RAF Fighter Ground Attack weapons were (with the exception of the cluster bomb and the Laser Guided Bomb) very much outdated and in many cases unreliable. In spite of a constant stream of criticism from the squadrons, little had been done over the years to remedy these deficiencies, the standard Staff reply being 'Ah, but just wait for the new, improved Mark 2 version, which we should get next year'. Unfortunately, 'next year' never seemed to arrive. Even when a new weapon was finally cleared for use with a particular aircraft then we were constrained by so many operating limitations that it was more or less useless. A typical example was the 1,000-lb live retard bomb as cleared for use by the Harrier. We were limited to a Minimum Interval of 320 milliseconds between bombs in a stick, giving a distance between impacts of some 80 yards on the ground. This was far too much for an effective attack.

We had only one type of bomb, the 1,000-lb High Explosive Medium Capacity, fondly described within RAF Ground Attack circles as the *Standard British Terror Weapon* or *Cracker*. This bomb, a slightly upgraded version of a Second World War weapon, could be fitted with either a free-fall or a parachute retard tail, the latter for Low Level (150 feet minimum) delivery. In both cases the fusing of the bomb was often unreliable, especially when carried by the Harrier. The other problem with this bomb was the surprisingly small amount of damage it would do to dug-in targets, notwithstanding the spectacular bang on the occasions when it actually detonated correctly. As far as rockets were concerned, we did have the 1960s' vintage SNEB 68-mm anti-armour rocket, carried in pods of nineteen rounds, but these were not available on *Hermes*. Instead, the Navy used the 1950s' vintage 2-inch calibre high-explosive rockets, carried thirty-six to a pod. The main problem

190

with all of these weapons was their old design, combined with an excess of safety devices designed to stop them from going bang at the wrong time. The RAF was obsessed with weapon safety in peacetime: while this may have prevented some accidents, we had ended up with weapons that all too often would not go bang when you used them in anger. The cluster bomb was a classic example, containing no fewer than seven safety devices. In the Falklands our armourers disabled the first two of these in order to improve weapon reliability.

Comment on ACM Harris's Despatch on Wartime Operations (1945)

ACM Harris reserved much of his criticism for the armament design staffs of the Air Ministry and MAP, whom he charges with incompetence … The depressing regularity in the Appendix of phrases such as 'no improved design (of weapon) was received in the Command before the end of the war' suggests that there was much substance to Harris' complaints.

Sebastian Cox (Head of the RAF Air Historical Branch)
Plus ça change.

APPENDIX 4

Bombing Techniques

Retard Bombing

The basic problem is to get the bomb on the target, which is (usually) stationary, from an aircraft moving through the sky at approximately 800 feet per second. To achieve this, the pilot has an aiming index in the Head up Display which indicates where the bomb will fall – providing several other vital parameters are correct. The bomb takes several seconds to fall to earth, during which time it will also travel a considerable distance forward through the air, e.g. about 1800 feet for a retarded bomb released from 200 feet. In zero wind – assuming the pilot sees the target in good time – he merely has to line up his flight path with the target, fly at exactly the right height (Pass Distance) above target level and then press the bomb release button on the stick at exactly the right millisecond to achieve a direct hit. Easy, isn't it?

The Harrier GR3 Weapon Aiming System

For bombing, this system (when fully serviceable) would allow for wind, aircraft speed and weight. Pilots still had to estimate correct height or Pass Distance above target, time of bomb release and a suitable attack track upwind of the target. In the Falklands, because of poor Inertial Navigator alignments none of these facilities were available, and we were left with only the Reversionary Weapon Aiming System, which gave a completely fixed aiming index, little better than a chinagraph cross on the windscreen. It might seem a simple solution merely to get as close as possible to the target before releasing the bomb, thus reducing all errors to a minimum – 'Scraping the bomb off on the target' as it was called. However, if you wanted the bomb to go bang and not cause yourself too much damage, this was not an option. For safety (always top priority in the RAF) the bomb would not 'fuse' (become live) until a minimum time after leaving the aircraft. This automatically defined a minimum release range/Pass Distance.

Typical Bombing Errors

Height error: 30 feet of forward throw error per 10 feet of height error.

Release timing: 80 feet forward throw error for every *tenth of a second error* in release timing.

In peacetime training a 140-feet bomb error is the minimum acceptable standard, so pilots have to be capable of estimating the release time to less than a couple of tenths of a second. For real, you have to get a bomb very much closer than that to achieve worthwhile damage, or drop a lot of bombs and hope that one of them will hit. (However, see Stick Spacing Limitations above. We tended to ignore these in wartime.)

Bombing Real Targets

Retard bombing of realistic targets in war is very much more difficult than this, for the following reasons.

Target Acquisition
Real targets are difficult to see. To have any chance of a successful attack you must visually acquire the target at least five (and preferably ten) seconds before bomb release, and you must already be on the correct Attack Track. Simple arithmetic puts this point between 1 and 1½ miles short of the target. Try picking out a camouflaged gun position through the visual clutter of the Head up Display from this range ... Even in good weather it is more a matter of luck than anything else to get lined up correctly in time for accurate bomb release, especially when you are trying to fly as low as possible. This also means that you must judge very carefully the point at which to pop up to release height: too soon and you are immediately vulnerable to the defences; too late and you will miss the target, or your weapons will not explode. There is usually no chance of a re-attack.

Height Judgement
It is difficult to be precise over rough terrain, or if the target is on the side of a hill. In practice, operational bombing is very much a 'Seaman's Eye' exercise. Only as you get close to release range does it become apparent that your height may be wrong – this is too late to

make a height correction. In these circumstances the pilot makes a guesstimate of how long to advance or delay the moment of bomb release in order to get a good bomb. With practice, the best squadron 'bombers' would become quite adept at this, achieving a 50-feet *average* miss distance in peacetime competitions. Bear in mind that the pilot may be trying to compensate for being an estimated 30 feet too low by releasing the bomb a *tenth of a second* early (see Typical Bombing Errors above). Finally, the tactical requirement to stay as low as possible until the last moment makes height judgement even more difficult.

Release Timing
This is a self evident problem (see above).

Wind Effect
The pilot must 'lay off' his ground track on the upwind side of the target. During Reversionary Bombing he must also make an allowance for headwind or tailwind by releasing early or late as appropriate. In this, peacetime practice bombs give useless training: they do not have anything like the 'Cross-Trail' performance of the real cluster bomb bomblets, which drift well downwind.

Airspeed Errors
The pilot must make an allowance for any airspeed errors at bomb release. (Too fast and the bomb can be too long; too slow and the bomb can be short.)

Dive Angle
In principle, more accuracy can be obtained with steep dive angles (viz. the Stuka). However, steep dive angles make you more vulnerable to being shot down, and may result in a 'sporty' pullout off target in hilly terrain.

Distraction
The enemy will probably be making determined efforts to put you off by shooting at you. This is a big problem in poor light at dusk or dawn or at night, when tracer is much more of an attention-getter.

Bombing a Previously Marked Target
If you are fortunate enough to have another aircraft attacking in front of you, then the problem of target acquisition becomes much easier: you merely line up on the smoke of the previous fall of shot – providing that the aircraft was on target. However, the smoke rapidly drifts downwind and you must allow for this. Ground Attack pilots

must always be aware of the local wind for best weapon accuracy. (In the Falklands we always had to guess the wind – there was no readout in the cockpit.)

Free-fall Bombing

All free-fall bombing was carried out from a steep dive angle (30 degrees plus), with a release range some 5,000 feet from the target because of the much longer flight time of the free-fall bomb. With an accurate sighting system this can be almost as accurate as retard bombing, with the additional advantage of deeper penetration of hard targets (the bomb impact velocity was much higher). However, even with a fully serviceable weapon system and with the assistance of Laser Ranging, the Harrier pilot could not drop free-fall bombs as accurately as retard bombs. Reversionary free-fall bombing was a joke: even the best of our 'bombers' had little chance of getting the first bomb within 200 feet of a target – even on a peacetime range with an accurately calculated wind. As an additional disadvantage under operational conditions, although the High Dive profile kept you out of the worst of the small arms fire zone, you were far more vulnerable to radar-laid heavy-calibre guns and SAMs. (We had no effective self-protection jammers.) Finally, High Dive bombing requires a cloud base of at least 8,000–10,000 feet – this was difficult to achieve in the Falklands.

Toss Bombing

For some free-fall bomb deliveries on known targets we used the Toss Bombing Technique. In this, the pilot flies a planned run-in along a line on the map at a constant speed. At the planned Pull Up Point, he pulls up to a specified climb angle and releases the bomb or bombs, which are then 'lobbed' in the general direction of the target. With no toss-bombing computer the attack is very inaccurate unless terminally guided LGBs are used. Bombs were released some 2–3 miles short of the target, keeping us clear of the short-range defences.

Cluster Bombs

Each bomb contained 146 anti-armour/anti-personnel bomblets, which looked and performed rather like a large shuttlecock. The spread of the pattern of bomblets made up for a lot of errors in bomb release! The technique was similar to the retard bomb delivery. This was a very useful weapon against lightly armoured targets and un-protected troops, with considerable demoralisation effect.

Laser Guided Bombs

The Laser Guided Bomb used by the RAF consisted of a standard 1,000-lb Medium Capacity bomb casing with the well-proven American 'Paveway' seeker head and guidance unit bolted on the front end. A set of flip-out stabilising fins was bolted on at the rear of the bomb. The total combination weighed some 1,200 lb, and we normally carried two of them. Basically, the bomb was delivered via the free-fall or toss method, to be guided during the latter part of its flight via laser reflection from an illuminated target. This illumination was provided by a Ground-based Laser Target Marker, a suitcase-sized apparatus containing the laser beam transmitter, which was aimed with a binocular sight by a FAC in sight of the target. The whole was powered by a heavy NiCad battery. Because of this very accurate terminal guidance, there was no requirement for any precision accuracy in the initial delivery of the bomb: however, the system could not cope with gross delivery errors.

RAF Practice Bombs

Because of inertia in procurement and development up to 1982, none of our peacetime practice bombs accurately simulated the characteristics of the 'real' weapons.[31] This meant that you could build up to quite a high standard of accuracy using the practice bombs on peacetime bombing ranges, only to be disappointed when you used the 'real' (usually concrete-filled) bombs. Because of environmental and other considerations, opportunities to drop real bombs were pathetically few for the average squadron pilot in peacetime. Practice drops of live cluster bombs were unheard of, mainly because of cost and the big problem of unexploded bomblets.

APPENDIX 5

Rocket-firing Techniques

General

Rockets were used as anti-armour and anti-personnel weapons, and were fired in pods of nineteen (SNEB) or thirty-six (2 inch), discharged in a half-second burst. The GR3 could carry up to six pods, but in the Falklands we never carried more than two. If accurate, rockets were a very effective weapon. To fire, the pilot aims the whole aircraft accurately at the target, allowing for wind (for Reversionary rocket-firing we had only a fixed firing index), and then lets go of the whole lot with one push of the rocket button on the stick. For peacetime practice, we usually fired only one rocket at a time.

Firing Techniques

The planned firing range in peacetime practice was at about 2,500 feet from the target. As with bombing, this demanded good Target Acquisition by at least 1½ miles from the target to have a chance of a good attack. It was not possible to take a 'snap shot'. The pilot had to 'track' (aim steadily at) the correct aiming point for some seconds before firing, using the fixed aiming index in the Head up Display. The wind has a big effect on the impact point and for Reversionary rocket-firing the pilot must make an accurate estimation of a suitable aim-off distance – especially with a crosswind. In these conditions, the pilot has to fly the attack with the correct bank angle to hold the aiming index on the calculated upwind aiming point.

Level Rocket Attacks

Most attacks were from a shallow dive; however, in the early 1980s 1(F) Squadron was given clearance to carry out rocket attacks from level

197

flight at about 100 feet agl. This technique had been shown in trials to give a far better chance of hitting targets that stood up above the surrounding terrain[32] (i.e. tanks), and we had been practising it with good results both on academic ranges and on the more realistic Otterburn range in Northumberland. I had been fortunate to be the first to use this new technique on the newly built Level Rocket target on Holbeach range. Foolishly, the range personnel had built the target (a tank-shaped pile of oil drums) at ground level, and it was completely trashed after I had fired four single rockets. Cunningly, they rebuilt the target on an embankment 6 feet high, which absorbed the impact of level-delivery rockets.

Errors in Rocketry

The biggest error by far is always Aiming Error. This is the overriding factor in all peacetime rocket practice, when pilots are severely penalised for firing too close. There is a small danger of ricochet damage in these circumstances. However, accuracy obviously increases the closer you get to the target, and in the Falklands we didn't worry too much about minimum ranges. Other typical errors were:

Firing Range
If too far away at firing, the rockets will fall short, and vice versa. The GR3 on-board laser could be used for accurate ranging – if it worked.

Speed
Too fast, and the rockets will overshoot the target, and vice versa.

Tracking Error
If the pilot does not track (aim) steadily before firing, the rockets will not be accurate.

Strafing Techniques

General

The 30-mm calibre Aden guns were a direct development of a German Second World War aircraft cannon. The guns were excellent against 'soft' targets and unprotected troops. Although old and firing at low velocity, they were reasonably reliable and – in contrast with more modern high-velocity weapons they could be fired at quite close range to the target, provided you took care to avoid flying into the ground. The advantage of this was that you had much more time for Target Acquisition before firing: additionally, lay-off for wind was much reduced. Apart from this, the aiming and firing technique was very similar to that for rockets, with the difference that the trigger on the stick was used to fire for however long you wanted. In practice, this was rarely longer than about two seconds, i.e. about eighty rounds fired using both guns.

For a long burst in a crosswind, the pilot had to apply a steadily increasing bank angle during the burst in order to keep the rounds on target. Unfortunately, the Harrier's cannon were mounted so that they pointed well above the aircraft's flight path. This meant that in level or shallow dive attacks you would fly into the ground long before you finished firing. In peacetime training this was no problem because we always had to use a steepish dive angle and pull out early in order to avoid the slight possibility of ricochet damage. On my initial conversion to the Harrier, having come from the Hunter (in which you could strafe at a very low dive angle), I suggested to the Weapons Instructors that this was a significant operational limitation. As a mere Flying Instructor my views were scorned and I well remember a Weapon Instructor giving me a detailed and patronising lecture about how the Harrier's gun system was much more effective than the Hunter's!

Unfortunately in my view, many RAF Weapon Instructors at that time seemed to think no further than peacetime training on academic ranges. They were supposed to be the weapon 'experts' and they tended to ridicule anyone who showed signs of lateral thinking about weapon delivery techniques under operational conditions. I remember making myself unpopular at RAF Wildenrath for trying to get the Squadron Simulated Attack Profiles changed to allow for realistic wartime weapon delivery parameters. The Weapon Instructors insisted that we use the unrealistic peacetime self-damage criteria for all attack planning and Simulated Attack training – even when it was obvious that this would expose us far more to the very real hazard of enemy flak and SAMs. As a result, some of us had privately worked out and practised our own level strafe technique (cine only), involving a short pull-up just before firing and then a quick bunt and shoot at the last moment. I used this tactic in the Falklands war.

Air-to-Air

The Aden gun was also a useful back-up Air-to-Air weapon: unfortunately 1(F) Squadron pilots had no opportunity to use it in this way in the Falklands. The Sea Harrier pilots did have some success with the cannon, Flight Lieutenant John Leeming's point-blank Skyhawk kill being the first Air-to-Air gun kill by an RAF pilot since the Korean War. Once again, our RAF peacetime training had given us little preparation for what was likely to happen in war. For decades, the standard cine gun 'kill' parameters in Air Combat training had demanded at least one second's steady tracking of the target with the aiming index – almost impossible to achieve in real combat. I had argued for years that we should allow for 'Fly Through' or 'Snap Shots', which suggestion had been contemptuously dismissed by various Weapon Instructors over the years. As far as the Harrier GR3 was concerned, we had no accurate Air-to-Air gunsight anyway, because of the inefficient way in which the system had been initially approved and introduced into service. What we had ended up with was an aiming system vastly inferior to the Second World War vintage gyro gunsight of the Hunter. Air-to-Air in the Harrier GR3 had been described as 'like trying to stuff wet spaghetti up a mad cat's arse', which was a fair description of the problems involved. Because of this we all knew that our only chance of success in wartime was to get in dangerously close to the target and stir the stick and rudders around to get as much spread as possible from the guns. Naturally enough we couldn't practise this particular kind of attack in peacetime because of the real danger of mid-air collisions – of which there had been many over the years.

Forward Air Control Techniques

General

In 1982 RAF FAC techniques were little changed from those used successfully in the Second World War. The FAC observed likely targets from a front-line position and gave attack details to Ground Attack aircraft orbiting in a safe area within radio range. Having spotted a likely target, the FAC would plot it as a six-figure grid reference and then work out a suitable run-in track and time from a known Initial Point some 10–20 km back from the target. The waiting attack pilots would have a large-scale map (usually 1:250,000 scale) on which were drawn up a large number of Initial Points that had been agreed with the FAC. Having passed all of these details to the pilot, the latter would be cleared to run in from the Initial Point to carry out the attack, usually under the direct control of the FAC.[33] As the FAC observed the aircraft pull up for the attack, he would then begin a rapid commentary, designed to get the pilot's eyes on the required target as soon as possible.

Forward Air Control Problems

Problems with FAC were as follows:

Quality of Current FACs
Traditionally, Primary FACs had been selected from the ranks of ex-Ground Attack pilots. As these became scarcer, other aircrew and many non-aircrew types were brought into the trade, with predictable results on the quality of control.

Radio Communications
The Harrier GR3 radio was of a scandalously poor quality, and it was usually impossible to hear what the FAC was saying unless the pilot

201

got so close to him that he was within range of enemy defences. During peacetime exercises in Germany, some of us would refuse to fly any closer to the FAC than we thought was 'realistic' and therefore fail to carry out the required attacks. This would be reported on the Mission Report after the sortie, invariably without follow-up action from higher echelons. We were trying to make the point that FAC attacks in their current form would be suicidal in wartime, but they just weren't interested.

Choice of Initial Points

The choice of Initial Points was entirely out of the control of the attacking pilots, and was often inept. Because of the average FAC's lack of Low Level navigation experience, they had only the vaguest idea of what kind of feature could easily be found from the air. Initial Points such as minor road junctions hidden in woodland; farmhouses amongst a profusion of the same; and tiny, thin masts visible from only half a mile appeared with depressing regularity on our FAC Initial Point maps. In many cases it was easier to find the target than the Initial Point! The most common error by FACs was failure to take account of terrain in hilly areas. Many attacks would fail simply because the Initial Point or the target was hidden behind a hill until the last moment.

Target Acquisition

At the end of the Initial Point run – assuming that the pilot had flown 100 per cent accurate track and distance, allowing for wind effect – he would pull up and look for the main Reference Point indicated by the FAC. Like the Initial Points, these Reference Points were often poorly chosen. The pilot had at most only a few seconds to correctly identify the Reference Point and then look from there to the target, with the assistance of a commentary from the FAC.

Target Marking

Often, the FAC would offer to 'mark' the target or Reference Point with coloured smoke. In the confusion of battle, this was often difficult to pick up.

Our FAC Techniques

In order to achieve at least some measure of success in our peacetime FAC exercises, we adopted the following measures:

Rear Briefing

If at all possible, we would insist that target details were passed to us as we overflew Ground Forces HQ in a safe rear area. From then on the FAC acted merely as a Veto, cancelling the attack if it was not required.

In-flight Target Study
After Rear Briefing the better pilots would be able to plot the target position on their own 1:50,000 scale map in the cockpit – at the same time flying and navigating at Low Level in battle formation at 420 kt and looking out for hostile aircraft. A little 'target study' carried out before the attack could make the difference between a successful first pass attack and a miss. Often this target study would reveal a useful Reference Point that the FAC had not noticed, which would also help during the attack. In effect, the pilot was doing most of the FAC's job for him.

Straight-in Attacks
The old-fashioned 'turning' tip-in attack was abandoned in the early 1970s, in favour of a Straight-in run at the target, called the 'Iron Spike' technique. The turning attack was always a source of errors: with a straight run at the target it was possible for the better pilots to draw a line on their cockpit maps *in flight* and fly along this line straight to the target. This proved to be a much more reliable method than listening to the FAC's commentary. Another advantage of the Straight-in attack was that now the Laser Target Marker could be used by the FAC and the target designator was visible in the Head up Display all the way into the target.

APPENDIX EIGHT

Air Combat

General

There was very little *Air Combat* in the Falklands war. Air Combat implies *mutual aggressive manoeuvring by two or more antagonists*. If one or other party does not manoeuvre aggressively because they do not have enough fuel, they are untrained in Air Combat techniques, or they are merely seeking to avoid combat, then *that is not Air Combat. It is merely Air Interception* (degenerating occasionally into a Turkey Shoot). While there were a couple of moderately aggressive 'Fighter Sweeps' carried out by Argy Air Defence Mirages on 1 May 1982 (in which they fired a couple of ineffective head-on aspect missiles at Sea Harriers), that was the limit of their aggression in the air. From then on, wisely, they confined their efforts to attacks on our shipping and ground forces while avoiding Sea Harrier Combat Air Patrols. This was an eminently sensible policy. They knew they could not match the weapons technology of the magnificent AIM9L Sidewinder, nor were they well trained enough for Air Combat manoeuvring against the aggressive Fleet Air Arm and RAF pilots. In spite of air refuelling they were also desperately short of fuel at all times over the Falklands, some 300 miles from their nearest bases, and this was the major limiting factor on their manoeuvring over the islands.

History of Air Combat Post Second World War

British Air Forces had not been involved in true Air Combat against comparable adversaries (*i.e. ones who were prepared to fight back*) since the Korean War. In the most notable engagement an FAA Sea Fury shot down a Chinese MiG 15. At Suez, our considerable Air Superiority forces were hard put to catch up with Egyptian pilots fleeing in terror. As far as the Cold War was concerned, even NATO Intelligence told us to expect little in the way of Air Combat from Warsaw Pact forces. Their training was mainly in rigidly controlled interception techniques. For both ideological and security reasons they could not risk allowing

204

the necessarily free and uninhibited manoeuvring of full Air Combat Training (ACT), because their main risk in peace *and* war was in losing aircraft and trained aircrew through defection to Western air bases. Finally, the Gulf War, Kosovo and the Iraq war were non-events as far as true Air Combat was concerned.

Because of this obvious lack of credible opposition in the air, it would have been both sensible and cost-effective for British air forces to abandon ACT altogether over the last twenty years or so and concentrate our training efforts and equipment purchases on the requirements of effective All-Weather and All-Altitude[34] Interception, Ground Attack and Reconnaissance, in order to achieve maximum effectiveness in war with our steadily dwindling forces. However, RAF squadrons I have known have always insisted on carrying out demanding ACT as a major part of all fighter and fighter-bomber training exercises. A pilot joining the squadron could be forgiven for assuming that ACT was the *most important* training exercise by far, so much attention and kudos were attached to it and there was so much of it being done. There were many historical reasons for the perceived importance of skill at Air Combat over all other skills. This had resulted in the continuing 'macho' bullshit culture surrounding Air Combat within the military pilot fraternity, particularly among averagely talented American pilots (see *Top Gun*).

Since the first aggressive air-to-air engagements of the First World War the fighter pilot has been seen both popularly and professionally as the supreme exponent of military flying skill. The gallant deeds of the famous combat aces of both World Wars have always outshone those of the less well-known bomber pilots and other mundane toilers of the air, often unfairly dismissed as mere 'bus drivers' in their unglamorous and unwieldy craft. This attitude continued after the Second World War, the sordid business of Ground Attack being left to more old-fashioned aircraft, while the best pilots wanted to fly the latest and most potent Air Superiority fighters. If such pilots were required to carry out Ground Attack operations then it was done very much as a Secondary Task, a distraction from the more important business of shooting down other aeroplanes. After all, the only way you could become an 'Ace' (and impress the girls) was by shooting down enemy aircraft. Merely clobbering ground troops and tanks was not the true way into the annals of aviation history.

Air Combat Training (ACT) in the RAF

The following points are relevant to training for Air Combat. Under the broad heading ACT I also include Low Level Evasion, in which formations are attacked and have to defend themselves at Low Level. By the RAF definition full ACT is only permitted at higher altitudes. However, the way that we interpreted the rules for Low Level Evasion meant that in practice the exercise was just as demanding as full ACT, albeit with some limitations on vertical manoeuvring. Because Evasion was carried out close to the ground the risk was much higher. This was especially true for the 'Bounce' or attacking pilot, who would attempt to fly very low in order to remain unseen for as long as possible, and at the same time maintain visual contact with the target formation. This could lead to the Bounce flying into the ground because of lack of attention to terrain avoidance. Because of this, RAF squadrons (if sensibly run) would normally allow only the most experienced and skilled of Air Combat pilots to act as the Bounce. There was an almost irresistible temptation to bend the rules in order to achieve a successful 'kill' at Low Level. Successful Bouncing was a fine art, at least as difficult as ACT manoeuvring at higher altitude, and a lot of kudos and competitiveness was involved in this excellent 'sport'.

Medium Altitude ACT was the standard Default flying programme when bad weather prevented Low Level training. There was one overriding reason for this: ACT was *fun*. It was the most challenging and exhilarating of all forms of fighter flying by a long way, and we were drunk with the thrill of it. Air Combat was the ultimate demonstration of the pilot's art: it required him to handle the aircraft instinctively to the far limits of its performance while under severe physical and mental stress, at the same time maintaining a cool chess-like appreciation of three-dimensional positioning involving large numbers of competing aircraft. On most squadrons skill at Air Combat was the most envied and cherished quality in a pilot. The ACT 'kill' ladder (showing which pilots had achieved the highest number of simulated 'kills') was the most important barometer of a squadron's morale and motivation. Jokingly we called it 'the sport of Kings', but this was no exaggeration.

Within the RAF this overriding preference for ACT had a strong influence on the training of all squadrons, both Air Defence and Ground Attack. From the early 1970s there were just two basic types of Fast Jet squadron in the RAF (ignoring the few specialist recce units). Air Defence squadrons practised All-Weather Air Interception and carried out ACT. Fighter-bomber squadrons practised Ground Attack and also carried out *a lot* of ACT (much more than our so-called Air Defence squadrons), much of it at Low Level.

Maps

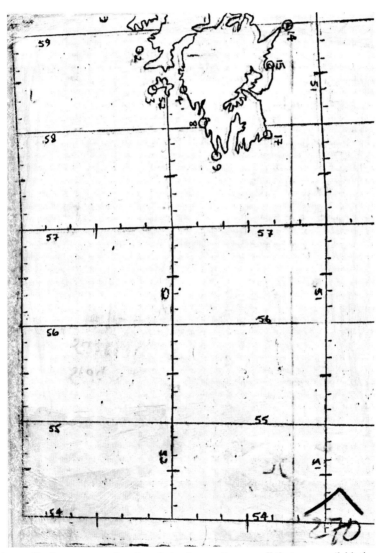

This scruffy sheet was our kneeboard-sized en route map, all that was available for our transits from *Hermes* to the islands.

This is the author's 50,000 scale target map used for the Goose Green dusk attack on 28 May 1982 with the course lines drawn in just three minutes. The leader was Pete Harris with Tony Harper as No. 2. When the author raced for his jet he didn't even know the mission call sign. Nevertheless, quite a bit of damage was done to the enemy.

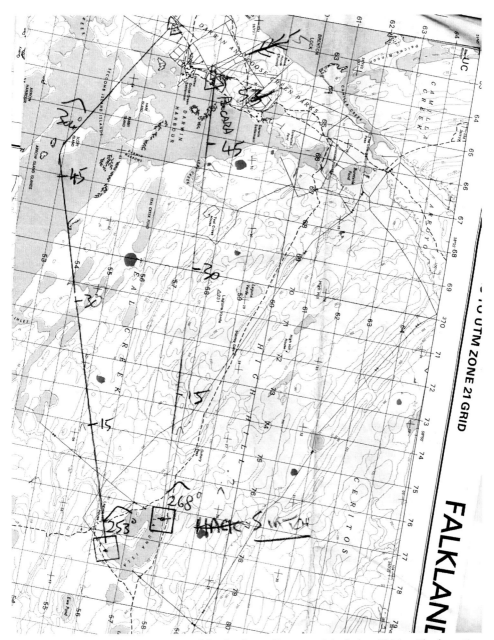

The author's 50,000 scale target map used for the Goose Green attack he led on 22 May. The formation including Bob Iveson, Pete Harris and John Rochfort. They encountered a great deal of flack which nearly downed the author.

This is the author's 250,000 scale Initial Point Map. It shows the Initial points used for ground attack missions. He used this map for missions flown after 30 May when he was shot down. The tracks planned in the Port Stanley area were for his two missions on 13 June. The first was cancelled; the second was an LGB drop, his last operational mission. The circle around Fitzroy (South-west of PSA) indicated the position of a Rapier missile battery a good place to avoid!

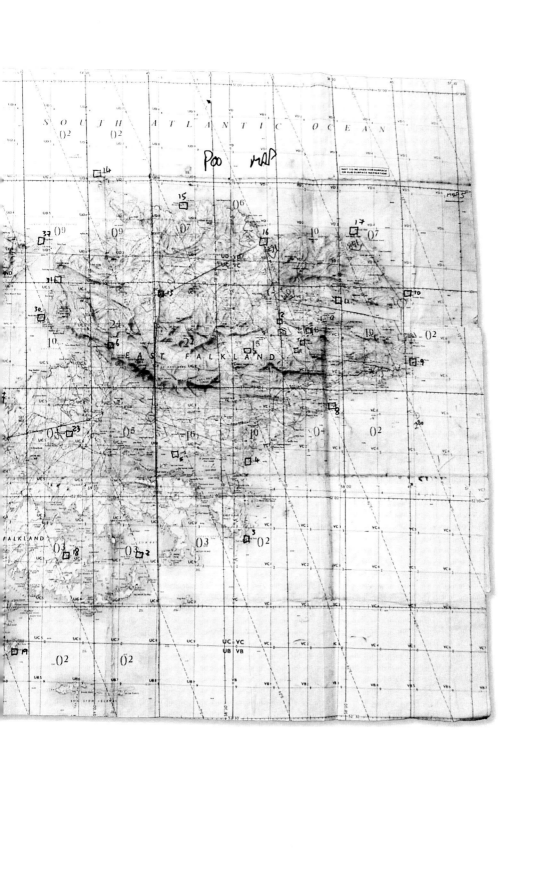

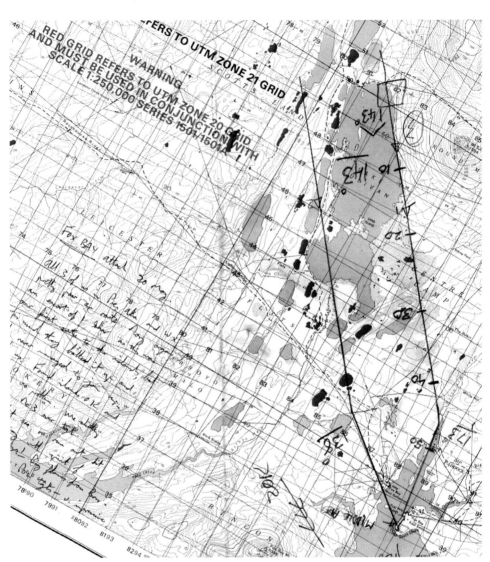

This 50,000 scale target map was used by the author for the Fox Bay POL attack on 20 May 1982, the squadron's first mission over the islands. There were impressive explosions on the target despite the bad weather encountered. The 'Boss' led, followed by Iveson and the author.

Notes

1. Later augmented by two more, plus two pilots of No. 3(F) Squadron.
2. Splash Targets. The Splash Target was a sledge-like device towed behind an RAF launch to throw up a plume of water for us to aim at. We had to drop the cluster bombs in the sea, as any unexploded bomblets were extremely dangerous to the Bomb Disposal team. Within a few days an RAF technician was to be killed by the accidental detonation of a bomblet on a land range. Our Bomb Disposal teams were also getting ready for their war tasks. In spite of the RAF's internationally acknow-ledged expertise, senior officers of the RN did their best to prevent them from participating in the Falklands war. Flt Lt. Al Swann, the leader of the Wittering Bomb Disposal team, told me that his group was twice thrown off South Atlantic convoy ships by unthinking RN officers before they managed to secure a passage. In the event the RAF team did much of the useful work in the war after the Army team was blown up aboard *Ardent*. Al was awarded the Queen's Gallantry Medal, among other things for volunteering to sleep underneath an unexploded 500-lb bomb stuck in the roof of the Ajax Bay hospital.
3. Flight Authorisation Sheets: each RAF flight had to be properly authorised in peacetime. The sheet contained flight details, names of pilots, ac [aircraft] number, permitted exercises to be carried out, etc. During the Falklands war we just put OPERATION CORPORATE – AS REQUIRED for all missions.
4. Under peacetime rules we were only allowed to attack this target with small practice bombs. However, in the current crisis just about anything was possible.
5. VIFF combat. I had been extremely lucky to take part in the definitive Phase 2 VIFF combat trial a few years before.
6. VSTOL handling: The Sea Harrier design had benefited greatly from RAF experience with the early Harriers. I flew a Sea Harrier later on and was much impressed with the ease of VSTOL handling compared with the GR3.
7. Airfield Defence: The RAF showed similar short-sightedness, relying almost exclusively on the grossly overrated Rapier for airfield defence.
8. The Pop-Up was from ingress height (as low as possible) to a minimum of about 100 feet. The cluster bomb pattern was ineffective if delivered from a lower height. See Appendix 3 – Ground Attack.
9. An *Air Request* was a request for Air Support from our troops. These were all vetted by the Task Organisation and only some requests would be approved and turned into *Air Tasks*, depending on the availability of Ground Attack aircraft.
10. Hugh Bichenot emailed me in May 2006:'Your (wonderfully described) attack on CAB 601's helicopter fleet was probably the most decisive air strike of the war, utterly disrupting Argentine plans for airmobile warfare.'
11. GR3 radar signature: Because of the enormous intakes the GR3 had the radar cross-section of a much larger aircraft.

12. Much later we were to be equipped with proper flare and chaff dispensers, but at this early stage we used the standard RN lash-up system of skillets of chaff in the airbrake and between pylon shoes and stores. These would deploy whenever you selected airbrake out in flight or dropped a bomb. Obviously you had to remember not to do this by accident, as the cloud of chaff effectively neutralised all radars in the vicinity for some time. This had happened a few times already (not, I recall, with a GR3), to the considerable displeasure of the Navy. We had already discovered that the Task Group warships adopted an extremely cavalier attitude towards 'locking up'returning friendly aircraft in order to give their trigger-happy SAM operators something to do. This was usually done without warning, when you were already in good radio and IFF contact with *Hermes*. We had agreed that we didn't mind – as long as they warned us first. Of course, this was anathema to the Navy, who treated their own aircraft as expendable ordnance, to be used for whatever purpose they wished without consulting the pilot. We did not trust them one little bit, and on more than one occasion our pilots dissuaded them with a threat to drop airbrake chaff if they did not break lock immediately.

13. Offset: If the target is not visible on radar (and the runway wasn't) then you need a prominent geographical feature or offset which is identifiable on radar and lies a known distance and bearing from the target. While the radar looks at the offset the computer calculates steering information direct to the target.

14. Stand-Off Target Acquisition Photos: These were standard for our pre-planned targets on the Hunter Wing in Bahrain.

15. Training and War Operations: in peacetime, RAF fighter-bombers were carrying out 'training' all the time: only in wartime did 'training' stop and 'operational' flying begin. This was the situation in 1982.

16. Low Level Navigation: In practice this was one of the most difficult things to get right, especially under fire. See Appendix 2 – Single-seat Low Flying.

17. Vertical Landing technique: For many years now I had been a great fan of the 'pad corner' landing technique, as taught unofficially by the legendary Ritchie Profit when he was OC B Squadron at the Harrier OCU at Wittering. This technique for landing on small 'Mexe' pads involved keeping one corner of the pad in view throughout the vertical descent; at the same time the usual pad markers could be safely ignored. Inevitably, this involved a slight sideways movement during the descent, which had to be arrested just before touchdown in order to achieve a smooth landing. This was not at all difficult, and the tremendous advantage of the technique was your independence from the usual pad markers, which could be misplaced or difficult to see in certain light conditions. I had the greatest respect for 'Prof', both as a VSTOL flyer and as a lateral thinker, and I used his technique exclusively from then on. I used to pride myself on the speed with which I could get from the hover on to the ground. This was not due to any unusual skill on my part – the technique itself was almost foolproof, and in my view should have been adopted throughout the Harrier Force. The technique was ideal for the less-demanding task of deck landing.

18. It should have been either *Armed Recce* (in which the aim was to attack any opportunity targets in a designated area), or *Recce* (in which targets were to be *Photographed* and not attacked).

19. Free navigation back to opportunity target. This was a self-taught technique that some of us used to find a target overflown too late for an attack. The method consisted of remembering the major features of the terrain overflown since passing the target so that – lacking any other navigation aids – you could 'eyeball' the return track straight to the spot. For accuracy of final approach the secret was to remember accurately a couple of reference features exactly on the last couple of miles of track

before the target. You had to make your brain work in reverse to achieve this, as you overflew these checkpoints in reverse order with the target behind you.

20. The Air Defenders' job was equally straightforward in the Gulf War. Once again the mud-movers had to take all the risks and got shot to bits for their pains.

21. Pete used my old 20(AC) Squadron nickname WIN, short for Winnie the POO.

22. From *Razor's Edge* (Hugh Bicheno): '2 (GR3s) swept in from the north-west to miss long with cluster bombs, the third near-missing short with rockets from the north-east – although shrapnel from this attack in fact disabled the guns. (Maj) Crosland's men (B Coy, 2 Para), overflown by the first two, were shocked by the experience, and one can well imagine its effect on the 100 Kelpers and the 600 Argentines in Goose Green.'

23. Normally, LGB attacks were carried out from Low Loft attack profiles, and the planning was complex to ensure the bomb ended up in the acquisition 'basket', from which it would home on the laser reflection. If the basket was missed the bomb would not guide to the target. I worked out that in a vertical attack the 'basket' was as big as it could be, thus allowing for quite large bomb-release errors.

24. Comment by Hugh Bicheno in an email to me (2006): 'I think it most likely that you were holed by the machine-guns set up in AA mode on Mt Harriet. The gunners were good, and later gave 42 Commando a hard time despite being under hellishly accurate mortar fire. Your "slashing attack" put the fear of Jesus into the helicopters moving RI 4 from Wall to Two Sisters, and the poor unfortunate little Indians had to complete the move on foot, with the added joy that their sappers had strewn the valley floor with mines and put up flimsy little warning signs, which blew away almost immediately. The 120-mm mortar pits you attacked were, as far as I can judge, impregnable to anything except a very precise shell, bomb or rocket that would have had to hit the rock wall behind them. Ironically, by the time you attacked the 120s had moved to far less formidable sangars on Harriet – however, to attack them you would have had to approach directly from the south, over the sea, into the teeth of their AA guns and we would in all probability not now be corresponding!'

25. We were wasting our time – the Exocets were not there during the day. The launcher was mobile and, as we suspected at the time, like most high-value targets it was withdrawn and hidden in Stanley town during daylight hours.

26. Either option was valid in operational tasking, but while I was still on deck it was up to Flyco to make the decision.

27. There was some risk of frag damage as I flew through the bursts of rockets impacting short. Because of the shallow firing angle the impact pattern was very long.

28. From *Razor's Edge* I discovered that we had been scrambled to support an SAS team in trouble near Port Howard. Sadly, because we were unavoidably late and couldn't get any information on the radio, an SAS Captain was killed and his signaller captured. I wish we had been able to help.

29. Hugh Bicheno states that Jeff was caught by an Argy Special Forces Anti-Aircraft trap.

30. The pilot told me that he 'escaped' narrowly with his Wessex from two different warships, having been messed about continuously by non-aviation 'Fishhead' Senior Officers who had no idea how to make sensible use of a Wessex. Eventually, he arrived ashore where he was able to assist full-time with the essential helicopter re-supply effort – the job he had gone down south to do in the first place.

31. In 2002 this was still the case.

32. The rockets, travelling at Mach 2, would level off and cruise for some distance about 3 feet above ground on their own reflected Mach Wave.

33. This was Category 3A Forward Air Control. In Category 3C Forward Air Control all details were known to the pilot before take-off.

34. All-Altitude Interception: In the Falklands, Argy Canberras and Lear Jets could operate almost with impunity at high altitude (above 40,000 feet). The Sea Harrier was not a High Altitude Interceptor and there were severe limits on our SAM defences at this altitude. In the UK things were worse: in the Tornado F3 the RAF had purchased a fighter that could not operate effectively much above 30,000 feet. Even the Javelin could do better.

Index